W.A.P. Martin
Pioneer of Progress
in China

W.A.P. Martin
Pioneer of Progress in China

by
Ralph Covell

CHRISTIAN
UNIVERSITY
PRESS

A Subsidiary of Christian College Consortium
and Wm. B. Eerdmans Publishing Company

Copyright © 1978 by Christian College Consortium
11 Dupont Circle, N.W., Washington, D.C. 20036

Library of Congress Cataloging in Publication Data

Covell, Ralph R.
  W. A. P. Martin: pioneer of progress in China.

  Bibliography: p. 276.
  1. Martin, William Alexander Parsons, 1827-1916. 2. Missionaries—China—Biography. 3. Missionaries—United States—Biography. 4. Missions—China. I. Title.
BV3427.M295C68   266'.023'0924 [B]   77-13321
ISBN 0-8028-1715-7

*To my wife, Ruth, who bore patiently
with me the long hours I spent with W.A.P.M.*

Contents

Preface

INCREASING ATTENTION has recently been given to the work of missionary notables in China. Prominent among these have been Young J. Allen, Peter Parker, and Timothy Richard, whose contributions to journalism, medicine, reform, and famine relief were unique and significant. A relatively neglected figure has been William Alexander Parsons Martin.[1]

Few Americans have been as widely and deeply involved in Chinese life as W. A. P. Martin. Even among a generation of missionaries who had few furloughs and often left their bones in distant lands, there is no parallel to Martin's nearly continuous residence of sixty-six years (1850-1916) in China. During his early missionary career in Ningpo (1850-1860), he distinguished himself in pioneering new religious approaches to the Chinese, worked for the success of the Taiping Rebellion, and later, when this movement seemed doomed to fail, accepted a post as interpreter with two diplomatic missions to North China.

Martin's work as interpreter led him to permanent residence in Peking where, although continuing to think of himself as a missionary, he worked in several different roles, the most important being administrative head of the Peking T'ung Wen Kuan, the forerunner of Peking Imperial University. In this position he pioneered modern state education in China, developing programs in law, science, mathematics, and political economy. Martin either participated in or observed nearly every aspect of Sino-American contact between 1860 and 1900, traumatic years that brought

1

China from its exalted position as "center of the world" into the family of nations.

The special significance of Martin's career is that he interpreted his varied experiences to friends in both East and West. His book, *Evidences of Christianity,* and *The Peking Magazine,* the first journal devoted exclusively to reform in the Middle Republic, presented Western faith and culture to the Chinese mind. Innumerable articles and books in English, especially *A Cycle of Cathay* and *The Lore of Cathay,* attempted to explain the exotic enigma of China to his Western audience.

In a true sense Martin was a bridge between East and West, a pioneer in the difficult art of cross-cultural communication. No other American who lived in nineteenth-century China left so much material illustrating the source, nature, intensity, and development of his reaction to Chinese life and society, or the methods by which he translated his Western concepts into a Chinese milieu. He sought the "wholeness" of China, salvation in the broadest sense, embracing both material and spiritual progress. His every task, every book, every article was designed to accomplish this goal. Nineteenth-century China was a place for pioneers, and Martin found full scope for his interests and abilities in its virgin frontiers.

His long, useful life and prolific writing earned him the plaudits of many Chinese and American friends. The Chinese government granted him the rank of mandarin of the third class in 1885 and of the second class in 1898. He was personal friend to many high-ranking Chinese government officials, particularly those within the Department of Foreign Affairs (*Tsungli Yamen*). Three American universities awarded him honorary doctorates for his contribution to China. John W. Foster, Secretary of State under President Harrison, stated that either Martin or the Englishman Robert Hart deserved to be ranked "the most distinguished and useful foreigner in China" in the generation preceding the Boxer Rebellion.[2] Dr. Arthur H. Smith commented that "Dr. Martin is a 'pyramid' with the widest base and the highest peak that was ever seen in the ranks of at least American missionaries in China."[3] Charles Denby, United States Minister to China in the early 1900's, called him the "foremost American in China."[4]

Many "missionary biographies" are written as "house histories" or as encomiums to particular individuals. Few attempt to be critical, to give historical perspective, to examine cross-cultural problems, to compare their subject with his or her contemporaries, or to organize material according to intellectual concepts. In one sense, this book is a biography of Martin. He is worthy of our attention, for an examination of his life adds specific detail, rather than pious guesswork, to a general understanding of the American missionary enterprise in China in the nineteenth century. Every effort, however, will be made to guard against lauding him as a missionary, and to examine his career critically in light of the standards, values, attitudes, and beliefs dominant in the period when he lived. The result, hopefully, will be a type of "cross-cultural" intellectual history that will pinpoint both problems and possible solutions involved in this difficult type of human communication.

Notes

1. Bits and pieces have been written about some of his work, or a particular viewpoint, or an institution with which he was connected. Two master's and one bachelor's theses have explored certain dimensions of his life, but no investigation has been made of his total contribution.

2. John W. Foster, "An Appreciation of Dr. W. A. P. Martin," *Indiana University Alumni Quarterly* (1917), 134.

3. *Ibid.*

4. *Ibid.*, 134-35.

CHAPTER ONE

"The Missionary from Indiana"

THE AMERICAN missionary message in China was always a mixture of Biblical faith and American culture. New England was the initial cultural "holy land" to serve as a model for overseas religious expansion. Francis Wayland, later to be named president of the Triennial Convention of American Baptists, in his famous message, "The Moral Dignity of the Missionary Enterprise," declared that "our [missionary] object is to render that Caffrarian Kraal [where there is filthiness and brutality] as happy and as gladsome as that ... New England village."[1]

As pioneers moved west carving a new society from the wilderness, they consciously modeled it on the society left behind in the East. Names of towns, kinds of education, styles of housing, and cultural forms reflected familiar patterns. These, in turn, became models for further westward expansion, even to the distant land of China.

Both the work and thought of William Alexander Parsons Martin, often identified by his colleagues in China as "the missionary from Indiana," reflected his frontier experience. The American West was the "holy land" that molded him to be a pioneer of progress on the frontier of an ancient civilization.

Evangelistic concern for the "destitutions" of the frontier was a dominant theme in the Martin household. W. A. P. Martin's father, also named William, often spoke to his son about the religious devotion of his own parents, Jacob and Catherine Martin, who earnestly preserved in their Pennsylvania farm home the faith brought with them from Ireland. The elder William spoke particu-

5

larly of the impression made by a sermon on the last judgment which his father read to him before he was eight years old.[2] Regular family worship, the care and concern of his mother, and the warmth and fervor of the frontier religious experience eventually led W. A. P. Martin's father to enter Bourbon Academy at Paris, Kentucky.[3] The school's president, the noted revivalist John Lyle, embodied both the "enthusiasm" of the nearby Cane Ridge revivals, in which he had been an active participant, and the scholarship of an itinerant preacher who read his New Testament in the original Greek. Following five years of general training at Bourbon Academy, Martin studied theology for two years with Lyle, who had been specifically appointed to this task by the West Lexington Presbytery.[4]

In 1817, after several years of pastoral experience as an ordained minister in Kentucky, William Martin was sent to southern Indiana as a missionary working under the Kentucky West Lexington Presbytery.[5] He was not the first missionary to penetrate this wilderness area. From 1802 to 1815 the General Assembly of the Presbyterian Church, organized in 1789, had appointed eleven missionaries to go to Indiana for periods lasting from one to six months.[6] Presbyterian synods in New York, Philadelphia, Cincinnati, and New Brunswick, as well as state mission societies — the Domestic Missionary Society of New York and the Missionary Society of Connecticut in particular — sent Presbyterian, Methodist, and Baptist missionaries in an intensive crusade to make this virgin ecclesiastical territory a "Western Zion."[7]

Although William Martin had primary responsibility for specific congregations at Livonia, Salem, and Blue River, he found time to establish several other churches, to hold revival meetings, to give pastoral help to scattered believers, and to serve on the board of the Indiana Missionary Society. "Billy" Martin, as he was affectionately called, was widely known as the local expert on starting new churches.[8] His example of sacrificial labor to bring religious progress to Indiana's frontier was not lost on his son, who later integrated his many activities in education, science, and diplomacy with aggressive evangelism. After his death in Peking in 1916, a fellow-missionary commented,

> Dr. Martin never allowed the example and teachings of his father, a faithful and effective pioneer preacher, enduring hardness, but

laying up foundations for future greatness, to be forgotten. He held these up as the model for all young men, foreigners and Chinese alike, to emulate.[9]

William married Susan Depew in 1811, and he and his wife considered Christian missions to be the epitome of a life dedicated to God. When eventually, after the birth of five daughters, three sons were born into the home, each of them was named after a missionary. Claudius Buchanan Henry Martin was named after Claudius Buchanan, a Scotch Presbyterian, who served as Chaplain to the East India Company in India, and for Henry Martyn, tireless translator of the Bible into Persian and Urdu. Samuel Newell Martin was named for Samuel Newell, one of the early pioneers of the American Board of Commissioners for Foreign Missions (ABCFM), who sailed for India with Adoniram Judson on February 18, 1812. W. A. P. Martin's initials represented two missionary "heroes," William Alexander, his uncle, who went to the Sandwich Islands as a missionary with the ABCFM, and Levi Parsons, an ABCFM missionary to the Jews in Palestine.[10]

Martha Venable, W. A. P. Martin's oldest sister, went to South Africa with her husband under the ABCFM in 1834 when Martin was only seven years old, and her letters home to Livonia were always a source of inspiration. After the Venables returned to America in 1839, she often related to her younger brothers "stories of excitement and adventure" about the vicious wars between the Zulus and Boers. At her death in 1896 Martin wrote a loving tribute to her memory and confessed that "through her influence her two younger brothers had their faces turned to the foreign field."[11]

What missionary literature existed in the 1830's and 1840's undoubtedly found its way into the Martin home and contributed to the missionary atmosphere with which the parents surrounded their children. *The Missionary Herald,* the monthly publication of the ABCFM, may have furnished some of the data needed for the names given to the Martin boys. *The Foreign Missionary Chronicle,* founded in 1833 as the promotional organ of the Western Foreign Missionary Society, was circulated widely among the churches, as was *The Foreign Missionary*, created in 1838 shortly after the founding of the Presbyterian Board of Foreign Missions.[12] The Synod of Indiana, in which William Martin was an active participant, actually made a motion to introduce "the Missionary Chronicle . . . into every family in our connexion,"[13] with the result that its circulation jumped to 7,260 by 1847.[14]

The developing interest of local churches in foreign missions was another factor contributing directly to a mission atmosphere in the Martin home. The Synod urged in 1834 that a "sermon on missions be preached on Sunday evening at candlelight."[15] In 1841 a motion was passed requesting churches to set aside the first Sunday in November as a day of prayer "to send forth more laborers into the harvest" and to supplement this at a convenient time with a sermon on "a call to the ministry."[16] Churches were called in 1845 to a "strict and faithful observance of the Monthly Concert" of prayer for missions.[17]

William Martin's belief in education also influenced his son. Presbyterians in Indiana prided themselves on an ecclesiastical system that sought to develop well-educated pastors in the New England pattern. Baptist and Methodist preachers, on the other hand, were largely laymen who had only the "Divine ordination" and depended on "gifts of the Holy Spirit" and their own sense of identification with the common man to communicate their message to the multitudes of religious illiterates.[18]

Unfortunately, the Presbyterian tendency to perpetrate an Eastern academic mold on the frontier won fewer converts than did the poor sermons, rough speech, and crude lifestyle of the more informal Baptists and Methodists. One writer commented that

> They [the Presbyterians] kept answering questions the frontiersmen were not asking. Both the Old School and the New School held and preached a theological system which was complex and mature. They were fascinated by the intricacies of total depravity, election, limited atonement, irresistible grace, and perseverance of the saints. They liked to preach on predestination, regeneration and human ability. Even when the doctrine preached seemed inevitable and right, as much of it was, it continued to be graduate school material offered to kindergarten. There were not many Presbyterian preachers on the Indiana frontier, and few of those present were good communicators to the settlers.[19]

William Martin was too much an activist to fit entirely into this mold. On occasion, however, he paraded his hard-won learning for the edification of his hearers, laboring in a written sermon for some three pages over the Greek term for "propitiation."[20] He differed little from his colleagues in feeling that Greek, Hebrew, and Latin were among the timeless requirements for the ministry, whatever the minister's environment.

As would be expected of a man with these convictions, Martin committed himself with vigor to a variety of educational projects. Although educational opportunities on the frontier were much poorer than in the East, Indiana had hardly been abandoned to barbarism, nor was it an educational wasteland. The Land Ordinance of 1785 provided for the support of public schools. Specific Indiana constitutional provisions, and the educational acts of 1816 and 1818, had led to plans for a state educational system of county seminaries, "mixed schools of all grades, from the infant classes, through the higher elementary and secondary forms, fitting for professional schools or classical studies in the State University."[21] Although the seminaries were public schools, they were largely financed by student tuition and private funds. At both elementary and secondary levels the curriculum included geography, history, natural philosophy, chemistry, astronomy, geometry, algebra, mental and moral philosophy, Latin, Greek, and French. These courses, strong disciplinary methods, and broad humanistic goals aimed to recreate the New England educational experience on the frontier.[22] Between 1818 and 1844 over sixty county seminaries were organized in Indiana,[23] but a public educational system providing free "common schools" for most children would not come until 1852.[24]

Communities, church groups, secular "educational societies," and individuals were given "every legislative encouragement" to incorporate and organize schools to meet the frontier's increasing educational demands.[25] One of the first private schools was William Martin's Academy at Livonia. Martin intended the academy, opened first in his own home, to educate his children and those of his neighbors, but the efficiency and quality of the school soon attracted students from other counties and states, and new premises and facilities were obtained.[26]

A major portion of the curriculum was identical with that of the county seminaries, but the addition of the New Testament and religious studies reflected Martin's concern that "Christianity and education should go hand in hand in the development of society" as they had in New England.[27]

Martin's Academy pioneered in the common education of the sexes. His own daughters, and then all girls whose families allowed them to break with tradition, were educated in the same classes with boys. Mrs. Martin and Martha, the daughter who was later a missionary to Africa, assisted in the training program. Female education was talked about frequently in the early nineteenth century, but few people in Indiana went as far as Martin to actually educate young ladies.[28] This growing interest in the education of girls in the United States finally contributed to a similar emphasis by American missionaries in China.

The school continued until 1831 when internal church difficulties in Livonia forced Martin to leave there. During its existence the academy prepared men to be teachers, physicians, and lawyers, although its principal aim was considered to be ministerial training.[29] Many who preached the Presbyterian faith in southern Indiana were graduates of the school.

William A. P. Martin, born April 10, 1827, at the family home in Livonia, received none of his formal education at the "Log Cabin College," but he must have felt its impact. By the time he was four years of age, he had learned a few Latin phrases through his association with students at the academy.[30] Furthermore, it molded his perception of the ministerial task, and the school's success in training leaders for Indiana's frontiers undoubtedly contributed to his decision to make education a major part of his missionary work.

The elder William Martin's direct involvement in the academy at Livonia was only the most important of his several educational activities. In 1823 he and three others were appointed to a committee to lay plans for the formation of a Presbyterian college. They chose to locate it in Hanover, and in 1830 the Synod of Indiana voted them control of a private academy which had been founded in 1827 by a Presbyterian minister.[31]

At about the same time that the Synod planned to establish a liberal arts college, it also desired to organize a theological seminary. Informal theological education as a type of "on-the-job" training under the guidance of established pastors or college teachers had been the early pattern in Indiana, even as it had been previous to the founding of Andover and Princeton.[32] But in the East, as now in the West, formal institutions soon replaced informal education. Andover (1808), Princeton (1812), Auburn Seminary in New York (1818), and Union Theological Seminary in Virginia (1824) filled needs in the Eastern states. Western Theological Seminary (1825) near Pittsburgh[33] and Lane (1829) at Cincinnati helped meet the demand for ministers in the West, but Indiana Presbyterians were not satisfied. In 1830 the Synod of Indiana voted to establish a seminary as the theological department of Hanover Academy. They immediately sought students with ability, good character, and proper academic background "to provide . . . an adequate supply of . . . ministers . . . to defend the faith against infidels and . . . the doctrines against heretics."[34]

The crucial issue of these years when William A. P. Martin was growing up, an issue in which his father was deeply involved, was the controversy between the Old School and New School factions within Presbyterianism. According to Leonard Trinterud the divisions within the Presbyterian fold that appeared to polarize these "rationalist" and "evangelical" emphases were not merely circumstantial. Rather, they were rooted in divergent strains within Puritanism and, culturally, in the English and Scotch-Irish origins of the Presbyterian church.[35]

The particular circumstances that divided Indiana Presbyterians in 1838 can be traced in the Synod minutes. Doctrinal rumbles appeared in 1834, when a resolution was affirmed against a certain "Act and Testimony" circulated among the churches, denying original sin, imputation (either of Adam's sin or of Christ's righteousness), and the vicarious nature of the atonement, claiming that fallen man was able to obey God's commands and to regenerate himself.[36]

The organizational issues of the controversy surfaced in 1837 when the Synod voted, with Martin in the affirmative, to approve the General Assembly action that dissolved the Plan of Union of 1802,[37] and accused both the American Home Mission Society and the American Educational Association of being a threat to the "peace and purity" of the Presbyterian church.[38]

Motions on slavery, the third issue producing the split, had been made frequently through the years with no apparent discord. However, once the division had occurred, the nature of the problem was clear. The Livonia Presbyterian church was split during Martin's pastorate, and the New School faction, which formed a new church, strongly supported abolition. It refused to receive slaveholders or anyone who received wages derived from slave labor into the church. It sent delegates to the New School Presbytery at Salem and asked whether the church should tolerate "sentiments" which claimed that "part of the human family has no souls, that God has not made of one blood all nations of men and that the African race is not descended from Adam."[39]

The Old School church's comment on slavery was largely limited to vague statements of denunciation and support for the American Colonization Society, and this was apparently Martin's personal position. When he married Susan Depew, he inherited from her parents, whose original home was Virginia, a family of slaves who proved an embarrassment to him. Apparently it was to escape continuing entanglement in this compromising situation that he, like many contemporaries with a similar conscience, moved his family to Indiana.[40] In his will of May 25, 1849, he provided for the freedom of his wife's slave family in Kentucky — six people in all — only on the condition that they go to Liberia under the care of the American Colonization Society.[41]

Martin also participated directly in the organizational phase of the struggle between the Old School and New School churches. He went to the church at Redford for a three-day series of meetings without consulting either the session or the missionary pastor, a graduate of Andover Seminary who was serving under the American Home Missionary Society. He warned strongly of the errors of the New School heresy and won over six members of the congregation who wished to "remain Presbyterian with him."[42]

Despite the heated disagreements concerning organization, theology, and slavery, fraternal relations among the pastors were never completely severed, and the differences did not affect the content of sermons, the nature of church services, and the day-to-day life of the congregations.[43] Most of the pastors agreed to disagree with far less animus than did their Eastern colleagues. Rudolph noted that

> John Finley Crowe of Hanover was Old School but was aided by an American Home Missionary Society commission. Even W. W. Martin, solidly Old School, reported the revival at his Livonia church through the pages of the New School *Indiana Religious Intelligencer.* Further, he served with Isaac Reed and John Dickey

as an officer of the Indiana Missionary Society to locate missionaries of the American Home Missionary Society when they arrived in Indiana.[44]

Although the Martin home was filled with an atmosphere of evangelism, missions, education, and the clashes of ecclesiastical and theological wars, William and his brother Samuel, older than he by two years, led normal, active lives, swimming, hunting, and fishing together in the Indiana woods.[45] "Father" Martin was often dissatisfied with the training his boys received in local schools and supplemented it with personal tutoring in Greek and Hebrew.

The Martin children were surrounded by the teaching, example, and activities of pious parents deeply committed to the service of God. With this intense Christian environment and the personal instruction of their father, they all made natural and undramatic decisions to follow Christ. A later critic's superficial conclusion that Martin did not have "an intense religious experience" and that his "emotional commitment to Christianity was less strong than [his] emotional commitment to Western secular culture" is not warranted by the mere absence of an emotional conversion experience.[46]

When Samuel and William had finished their preparatory education and matriculated at Indiana University in Bloomington in 1843, the entire family went with them. No clear statements may be found to explain why William Martin felt the need to supervise his two sons at this stage of their education. He may have wanted to continue to supplement what he considered to be poor quality education, although young William already had a good reputation for his skill in Greek, demonstrated in the examination required of all entering the freshman class.[47] Was there some anxiety about either the theological climate or the moral tone of life at the university? Were there signs of rebellion against parental traditions or deviations from the truth of the Christian faith?

Bloomington, Indiana in 1843 would seem to have offered little enticement to moral looseness or even to reckless spending of money. The University's historian, James Woodburn, commented,

> The student's opportunities for spending money were very meager in those days. He was shut in beyond the reach of allurements and the temptations to spend money. There was no rail-

road leading in or out of the little village until 1853. There were no 'movies' or theaters to take the student's time or money. There were no fraternity houseparties, or annual dances or 'informals' or initiation fees or weekly dues to eat into the parental pocket-book. There was only one fraternity existent in 1850, and that *sub rosa*. A dance by the sanction of the University and within its walls would have been a scandalous thing. It may be difficult for us to remember that there were no girls in the University at that time nor for nearly twenty years to come. No 'Book Nook' with its attractions and convenient restaurant. There was not a soda foun-tain in town, and ice cream parlors were later enterprises, though at the Downs' bakery and Sidney Pullen's candy-store stick candy and gum drops might have been obtained.[48]

But if morality was at a high point, the same could not be said for religious life among the students. Martin related that there was no Young Men's Christian Association or Christian Endeavor on campus and that the prayers and teaching at the daily required chapel were of little value to him. Apart from Samuel, there was no other church member in the Beta Theta Pi fraternity to which they both belonged.[49]

In its early days, Indiana University, although a state institu-tion, was thought of as a Presbyterian school. The first four pro-fessors were Presbyterian, and the Board of Trustees, consisting of a majority of Presbyterian members, had a Presbyterian elder as its chairman until 1854. This Presbyterian dominance in the control of the institution was gradually relinquished, and by Martin's stu-dent days its essentially secular character was very evident.[50]

Martin's father, a staunch adherent to the Old School camp, probably felt ill at ease over the theological defection of the univer-sity's president, Andrew Wylie. For nearly fifteen years a Presbyte-rian minister, Wylie was greatly discouraged by the Old School-New School divisions and, feeling that he had been personally mistreated by the ecclesiastical courts, he withdrew from his church affiliation. This traumatic experience brought him to the point where he decried "all systems of theology, regret[ted] all creeds and confessions," and believed "orthodoxy has no place, orthopraxy all place. . . ." Following this period of serious doubt and questioning, Wylie joined the priesthood of the Episcopal Church at Vincennes, Indiana in May, 1842.[51]

Andrew Wylie, largely because of his broad and tolerant

spirit, was very influential in shaping the minds of W. A. P. and Samuel Martin. Wylie's book, *Sectarianism is Heresy,* written to reduce the impact of his leaving the Presbyterian church, is a good example of this. Confessing at the outset his inability "to work the infinite into a system," he urged his readers to simple faith in God that would "not depend on their ability to digest the systems of either Calvin, or Arminius, or Priestly, or any other philosophical teachers."[52]

Martin's own developing interest in China, first aroused by the beginning of hostilities with Great Britain in 1839,[53] may have been spurred by encountering the idea of "Manifest Destiny" in Wylie's lectures on Sacred History. According to Wylie

> Around this world is stretched a belt between 20° and 50° north latitude. In it (with few exceptions) has occurred all the great events that have transpired on the Globe. England is one of those exceptions. This belt may be called the historical belt. Civilization began in Central Asia and westward rolled the ball of Empire. When it struck America, it struck it at Plymouth rock and James River, within these bounds. And now it is hovering near the Pacific. *When it reaches there some great event will probably happen. As the moving influence moves on in this belt, some great events are constantly happening.*[54]

Wylie was not alone in these views. In a series of editorials written for the *St. Louis Enquirer*, 1818-19, Thomas Hart Benton, famed United States Senator from Missouri, spoke of America's westward path of empire as following "the course of the heavenly bodies," and of completing the circle back to Asia where "their first parents were originally planted." Following a predetermined path, America's mission was to bring "science, liberal principles in government, and the true religion to the peoples of Asia. . . ."[55]

The American frontiersmen, advancing across the trans-Mississippi region, were thought to be establishing the Republican Empire of North America, destined to become "permanent mistress of the world."[56] Reinforced with the vision of Anglo-Saxon superiority, focused in the 1840's on civilizing the Indians, absorbing German immigrants, and defeating Mexico, and with the hope to expand an Oriental trade that had already reaped rich dividends, the idea that "Westward lies the course of Empire" was not too difficult to believe. It undoubtedly furnished fuel to feed the flames of a brightly burning evangelical faith that wished to rid both the West and the Far East of irreligion, ignorance, and false beliefs. To be able to hitch one's own personal destiny to the inevitable progress of civilization as it spread across the continent, the Pacific, and into China was an exhilarating dream.[57]

Andrew Wylie's commitment to the Scottish school of philosophic realism, sometimes referred to as the "School of Common Sense," undergirded the total curriculum of Indiana University, was most directly articulated in the course of studies for the senior year, and influenced the thought of W. A. P. Martin.[58] This philosophical system was a reaction against what was considered "the germ of skepticism" in the work of Descartes, Hume, Locke, and Berkeley.[59] Its most notable proponents were Thomas Reid (1710-1796), who followed Adam Smith in the chair of moral philosophy at the University of Glasgow, and two professors at the University of Edinburgh, Dugald Stewart (1753-1828) and Thomas Brown (1778-1820). They contended that objects exist independently of the mind and can be perceived directly as they are. Knowledge is not gained through ideas or images of the real world, but from objects themselves. The truth of these assertions is self-evident through "common sense," in this system a synonym for reason.[60]

Although developed to meet particular philosophic problems in Europe, this system of thought appealed widely to American religious thinkers.

> It supported orthodoxy in theology, raised no dangerous questions, invited no intellectual adventures. It was a restatement of Locke [who for Americans was a political idol] against David Hume and contradicted Hume's skepticism by a blanket assertion that idea and object correspond so faithfully that Americans, intent upon their business, need never give a second thought to so unprofitable a worry.[61]

The doctrines of Scottish realism, taught to American youth through courses in mental philosophy, established several important concepts.[62] Belief in the objective reality of the external world and the doctrine of "cause and effect" led to an argument for God's existence. The basic premise was that "from certain signs or indications in the effect, we may infer that there must have been intelligence, wisdom, or other intellectual or moral qualities in the cause."[63]

Scottish philosophers and their disciples pointed out that man, in contrast to animals, has an intellectual faculty enabling him to perceive accurately, to organize his sensations, to remember, to imagine, and to make valid judgments. Therefore, man must not doubt the validity of what appears to him because of idealistic assumptions concerning the unreliability of either the external world or of his mind.[64]

Even as God is in His universe, so He has laws to run it. One of God's most important laws is morality. Grove observed, quoting Reid, that

> If we listen to 'the dictates of common sense, we must be convinced that there is a real excellence in some things, whatever our feelings or our constitution be,' and that a thing 'has its excellence from its own constitution and not from ours.' There are some things that 'ought to please, and others that ought to displease. If they do not, it is owing to some defect in the spectator.'[65]

Scottish realism advocated a spirit of scientific inquiry; the discovery of ancient fossils, theories of polygenesis, and arguments over hybridization had not yet shaken general confidence in the accepted views of the nature and time of man's appearance in the world.[66] Wylie confidently lectured in his classroom at Indiana University that

> According to the best authority, the world was created about 1656 before the flood. From the flood to the birth of Christ it was 2348 years. That the world had a beginning none can doubt. Everything must begin with something and at some time.[67]

The basic tenets of the "common sense" school were not unique to Presbyterians nor to the orthodox Christian Church. Deists espoused many of these concepts, as did Unitarians and infidels.[68] "Common sense" was essentially a philosophical and not a religious system. In the mid-nineteenth century most Americans believed in natural law, in "the free and responsible individual," and in America's mission to perpetrate its ideals at home and spread them among the nations of the world.[69] These were the "doctrines of the American democratic faith" and ran parallel to Protestant Christianity. Thus, what W. A. P. Martin received at Indiana University was not the distinctive factor in his intellectual background, and was supplemented by the nature of his theological education.

New Albany Theological Seminary, where Martin went for Biblical training in 1846, was the newly named and relocated successor of what had begun sixteen years earlier as the theological department of Hanover Academy. In 1833 the department was named Indiana Theological Seminary, and in 1841, encouraged by the promise of a sizeable grant of land and money from a wealthy benefactor, it moved to the prosperous little city of New Albany, on the Ohio River across from Louisville where Martin was later to teach for a short time in a Presbyterian school. Its faculty and administration fervently hoped that this move to a more central location would help it train more candidates for the ministry from both the North and South.[70]

At New Albany Martin was introduced to the formal study of the Sacred Scriptures and to the Calvinist theological system which supported the Scottish realism he had received from Andrew Wylie. He was particularly impressed with John Mathews, the president and first professor of theology, who arrived in 1831 and died while Martin was still at the seminary in May, 1848.[71]

Mathews' only textbook was the "Confession of Faith of the Presbyterian Church." Consisting of thirty-five articles embracing the whole gamut of the Christian faith starting from the Holy Scriptures, the Trinity, and the Fall of Man to the various doctrines of Salvation and the Last Judgment, this was a thorough, question-and-answer approach to didactic theology.[72] In one of his works, *The Divine Purpose Displayed in The Works of Providence and Grace,* Mathews argued persuasively for God's personal control over history and the universe. Martin had learned earlier that the laws of the universe supported his faith. Now he was taught that God Himself controlled the laws of the universe to accomplish His eternal purposes.[73]

During his seminary years he was probably introduced to William Paley's *Natural Theology,* which formed a portion of the book *Evidences of Christianity* that he prepared during his initial years at Ningpo.[74] Paley's books on moral philosophy and natural theology "were once as well known in American colleges as were the readers and spellers of William McGuffey or Noah Webster in the elementary schools."[75]

Problems which would later lead to the removal of the seminary to Chicago were already present during Martin's day.

Through the period from 1840 to 1848 its border location symbolized a readiness to train men from both the North and the
South. Unfortunately, as Rudolph put it,

> Indiana Theological Seminary tried to stay neutral on slavery
> when the students of her seven synods were choosing sides.
> Those who were anti-slavery went to Lane Seminary; those in
> sympathy with the South went to the Old School seminary at
> Danville after 1853. Few came to New Albany.[76]

The school moved to Chicago in 1859, and for a short while came
under the control of Cyrus McCormick, a strong disciple of the Old
School, who conditioned his support on strict adherence to traditional tenets and to "a policy of silence on slavery."[77]

Martin was probably not neutral on slavery. He had been
supported at school, at least in part, by money received through
his mother from the labor of her slaves. He resented the need for
this, and in 1845, at the conclusion of his junior year, he left school
to seek financial independence. Through the assistance of President Wylie he obtained a teaching position at a small school in
Leavenworth on the Ohio River. He continued his seminary studies
while teaching, and graduated with his class, which also included
his brother, Samuel, in 1846.[78] But he made no great declaration
of conscience concerning slavery.

During this time at Leavenworth Martin made a decision to
go to China as a missionary.[79] If this was indeed his first definite
decision to do so, the timing was significant. Between 1842 and
1844 the British, French, and American governments had signed
treaties with China permitting foreigners to live in five specific
Chinese ports. In December, 1844, and in February, 1846, the
Emperor Tao-kuang issued two edicts of religious toleration in
reply to a memorial from the Imperial Commissioner Ch'i-ying.[80]
The Opium War had first stirred Martin's interest in China, but the
treaties and edicts of toleration revealed an opening door.

When Martin went to New Albany to study theology, he was
greatly disappointed both by the teaching staff, consisting of only
three or four professors, and the caliber of his classmates. Temporarily abandoning plans to be a missionary, he left seminary and
taught in a Presbyterian parochial school across the Ohio River in
Louisville.[81]

An understanding of the Presbyterian parochial school movement during the period from 1846 to 1870 may shed light on Martin's later educational endeavors in China. A concern developed in the mid-1830's over the way in which the church was to be related to the education of the children of its members. A primary fear was that education was becoming increasingly secular, and that the public schools would not provide the desired religious training.[82]

Members of the Old School faction were fearful of doctrinal heresy to which their children might be exposed in schools sponsored by New School churches and in the public schools. In addition, they were disturbed by the steadily declining number of candidates for the ministry.

In order to deal with these problems, the Presbyterian General Assembly adopted on May 31, 1847, a report that advocated establishing a system of parochial schools,[83] an action which did not meet with universal approval either within or without the church. The Presbyterians were accused of being bigoted and sectarian. Charles Hodge urged further attempts to obtain public funds for private educational programs. Other Presbyterian leaders felt that, with or without religious education, the public educational system must be supported.[84] Some doubted whether it was the business of the church to educate children in secular subjects, while others urged that the Bible, and religion in general, could be taught in the public schools in a non-sectarian fashion.

Even though all the issues were not resolved and differences of opinion continued to exist, the parochial system was inaugurated, and between 1846 and 1870 246 schools were established in twenty-eight states.[85] The movement was most popular between 1846 and 1853. Schools regularly increased in number each year, and optimism was at full tide. However, lack of financial support, dissatisfaction with the overinvolvement of many ministers in this secular work, shortage of adequately trained Christian teachers, increasing public control over elementary education, general apathy over the need for the Bible in the educational process, and a continuing attack on the whole philosophy of the parochial movement from within the church brought a decline in interest and growth between 1853 and 1862. After 1862 emphasis shifted to using the parochial approach to train the children of French and German-speaking immigrants, and in 1870 the parochial plan of education was abandoned by the General Assembly.[86]

But this short period gave Martin a taste for teaching and the opportunity to exercise the abilities he later demonstrated so well. It also foreshadowed the struggle he would have in China, deciding whether to be an educator or an evangelist. The early success and later failure of the parochial school approach was mirrored in the successive stages of his own missionary career, which saw him first committed to Christian schools in Ningpo, but later to a secular school in Peking.

While Martin was teaching at Louisville, his mother came to visit a sister living near there. He went to see her one Sunday, taking along a French historical novel to read while traveling on the boat. Finding it morally repugnant, he threw it into the river in disgust. As he reflected on this incident, it led him one step further in his determination to make missionary work his life vocation. This was the turning point in a struggle which had taken place over two years; Martin soon resigned his position at Louisville and returned to theological studies at New Albany.[87]

W. A. P. Martin's call to missionary work was neither mystical nor intangible. In later life he remarked of the young Hudson Taylor, whom he had known during the Ningpo days, that "he was a mystic absorbed in religious dreams, waiting to have his work revealed—not idle but aimless."[88] Martin clearly believed that men everywhere needed the Gospel message and that Christ had commanded his disciples to go into all the world to win them. This was a clear call to duty which he must obey,[89] and this sense of responsibility never left him. In the mid-1850's he wrote home, "My heart is set on going to some place in the interior where the Gospel has not yet been preached."[90]

As China's doors seemed to open more widely in the mid-1850's Martin became restless to move on and wrote, "the same feeling which inclined me to seek a foreign in preference to a home field now impels me to look for a new sphere of labor."[91] During the turbulent early days of the American Civil War he recruited candidates for missions in Presbyterian seminaries at Princeton, Allegheny, Danville, and Chicago, arguing that

Amidst the unparalleled exertions now making for the preservation of our government, there is great danger lest the 'gentle charities' of the church be employed to feed the flame of war and the cause of Christ in far parts be suffered to languish. The Lord infuse into his people the spirit of that *higher patriotism* which they ought to cherish as citizens of Zion, so they will not permit their home troubles to deter them from prosecuting the *conquest of the world*.[92]

Even at this early stage of his life, he viewed the aim of missions as comprehensive. His graduation oration, delivered in New Albany in May, 1849, was entitled, "The Uses of Physical Science for a Missionary."[93] Shortly before sailing for China, he expressed the desire to have time in the field for "scientific studies" and inquired whether perhaps he should study medicine before leaving.[94] When he had been in China less than a year, he suggested that one of the best ways to present missions to young people would be to devise a geography text for use in the "common schools." The interrelationship between Christianity and civilization was first on the list of facts he wished to emphasize. It could be shown, he explained, that "the first impulse in civilization came from the introduction of the Gospel and that every stage of [civilization's] future progress may be taken as an index of its influence." He believed that such a text could teach that "under the best forms of paganism men would always be found more debased than under the worst phases of Christianity [Romanism] and always less degraded where paganism embodies most of the principles of the true religion."[95] This belief in the connection between Christianity and civilization was to dominate his thought throughout his long career.

Martin may have been influenced toward this idea by reading letters and magazine articles from Canton where missionaries had established a hospital, an educational association, and a Society for the Diffusion of Useful Knowledge. He was undoubtedly familiar with the printing work of S. Wells Williams and the medical ministry of Divie Bethune McCartee, later to be his colleague in Ningpo.[96]

But a more important source for Martin's comprehensive view of life and of missions was his own perception of the relationship between the Christian faith and culture in his own land and its projection upon the whole world. Enlightenment thought, the Great Awakening, and the American Revolution had destroyed the colonial establishment of religion, but the churches still aimed at fashioning a Christian society where morals and religion would be partners.[97] Scottish realism, natural theology, millennialism,[98] enlightenment ideas of progress, and nationalism[99] all contributed to this vision.

Territorial expansion to dislocate Indians, subdue Mexicans, and to take over British territory was justified in the name of civilization and both political and religious liberty.[100] Science, moral reform, and proclamation of the Gospel would be used to Christianize the nation. A type of Old Testament Biblical theocracy, although a rather secular theocracy in the minds of many, was to be voluntarily recreated in God's chosen America, which would then be a light to the entire world. It was an age of vibrant optimism in unlimited progress.[101]

Signs of this progress abounded everywhere. Territorial expansion had occurred in Florida, Canada, Texas, Mexico, and Oregon. The steamboat and locomotive were revolutionizing transportation. Prisons were being reformed, some progress was perceived in the struggle against slavery, a state prohibition law was passed in Maine in 1851, and women were more nearly equal to men than they ever had been. Significant educational innovations had been pioneered by Horace Mann in Massachusetts. A devastating depression (1837-43) had been overcome, and from 1844 to 1857 the economy was characterized by large-scale industrial growth.[102] On the world scene, the European revolutionary movements in 1848 were initially viewed as signs of the spread of democracy.[103] What Christian young man going to China would not have succumbed to the temptation to link the progress he saw and felt with Christianity?

The expansion of the Christian faith was equally significant. During the colonial period the Mayhew family, John Eliot, David Brainerd, Eleazar Wheelock, and others made notable efforts to evangelize Indians in New England and New York.[104] An active interest in foreign missions did not develop until after the Revolutionary War and was closely linked with early British missions, particularly the formation of the Baptist Missionary Society in 1792 and of the London Missionary Society in 1795.[105]

Cross-Atlantic exchanges of information and inspiration plus revivals among American students at Williams College and Andover Seminary led to the organization of the American Board of Commissioners for Foreign Missions (ABCFM) in 1810 and the Triennial Convention of American Baptists in 1814. Fires of revival, assurance that the imminent conversion of the Jews would bring in the "time of the Gentiles" around the world, early expectation of the millennium, and belief in the prevailing power of prayer—nurtured and stimulated by the popular concerts of prayer—gave impetus to sounding the Gospel out to all portions of the world.[106] W. A. P. Martin, preparing in 1849 to go to China where there were scarcely more than three hundred Protestant Christians,[107] was strengthened in the knowledge that he was one more soldier in an army that had been occupying and conquering heathen lands for Christ since the first decade of the century.

A few voices warned against the danger of confusing the faith with civilization. Rufus Anderson, foreign secretary of the ABCFM from 1832 to 1866, felt that social uplift was a by-product of the Gospel, but he doubted the value of "the creation among heathen tribes and nations of a highly improved state of society, such as we ourselves enjoy."[108] Martin had had little exposure to and no training in "mission theory" at this point in his life, and he said nothing that would indicate whether he perceived the "civilization" he linked with the Christian faith as the aim or the result of missionary work.

Many of W. A. P. Martin's arguments for missionary service were undoubtedly similar to those advanced by his sister-in-law Margaret, who used them to persuade her father, Andrew Wylie, to let her go to China with Samuel Martin.[109] Asserting that the desire to be a foreign missionary was "no new thing with either myself or Samuel," she presented numerous arguments to convince her parents: Americans had many churches with good preaching and the Bible, whereas the heathen did not; "the perishing millions cannot be saved without faith in Christ"; Christ ministered among the poor and needy and not only to the rich and opulent; the millennium would never come "if we all live at this poor dying rate"; she and Samuel did not live in the age of miracles and must exert themselves in this task; common sense suggested that a poor sick man at one's door needed alms more than a rich one; one had to choose between doing good or the most good; the devotion of believers should certainly be greater than that of those who went to the end of the earth "to gain a few paltry sums . . .";[110] the heathen had souls as well as believers did, and their perishing condition should move believers; she and Samuel shared a conviction of duty; women as well as men had to do all in their power "to extend the Kingdom of Christ upon the earth"; she believed the Bible, and sacrifice was needed to put it into "heathen languages." Margaret Martin concluded with a ringing affirmation that "God will overcome all difficulties" and then asked, "Are you not then willing that I should go? Write immediately."[111]

Neither the curriculum nor student life of New Albany Theological Seminary placed much emphasis on missions which could have contributed to Martin's missionary vision. A Society of Missionary Enquiry, organized by students on many campuses to discuss the missionary vocation, was not formed at McCormick until the late 1850's.[112] Nor was there a Chair of Missions, such as that developed at Princeton after 1836, at New Albany.[113] Candidates for missionary service with the Presbyterian Church came from several seminaries including New Albany, and each year an officer of the Board of Foreign Missions wrote to the theological schools to see who wished to go abroad as a missionary.[114] Often the Corresponding Secretary of the Board would visit a campus if interest warranted it.[115]

Although W. A. P. Martin indicated that his initial interest in China began when he was a boy of twelve and the "boom of British cannon [was] battering down her outer walls,"[116] this small flame fanned into a consuming fire as Presbyterian mission efforts commenced in China. The first news about China and her needs appeared in *The Foreign Missionary Chronicle* in May, 1838. After writing about open doors to reach Chinese in the Eastern Archipelago, the writer expressed his fear lest "the Presbyterian Church will continue to stand with her arms folded while the millions of China are perishing in her sight."[117] Responding to this type of concern, the first Presbyterian missionaries went to Singapore in 1838, and within the next six years stations were opened in Canton, Amoy, and Ningpo.[118]

John Lloyd, one of the Presbyterian missionaries at Amoy, the port to which Martin was first assigned, wrote extensively concerning the needs of that city, his own work of preaching and tract distribution, and the desperate need for more recruits. He expressed his doubt that the Presbyterian Church would be held "guiltless" in her hesitating response to the "degraded, ignorant, perishing population" of this "idolatrous race."[119]

Some missionaries utilized historical and Biblical arguments to press their claims for China's needs. They connected the prophecy in Isaiah 49:12 referring to the "land of Sinim" with "Sin Ch'in or Tsin," historical names for China, and confidently asserted this to be a "direct prediction of the conversion of the nation to God."[120]

Later in his life Martin confessed to some struggle between the call to domestic missions and the spiritual needs of China. To a pioneer in spirit the impressive progress of home missions, which had seen an increase of workers from 101 to 570 and the addition of 943 churches over a twenty-year period from 1830 to 1850, would tip the balance in favor of a mission to the Celestial Empire with its paltry three hundred believers.[121]

W. A. P. Martin applied to the Foreign Mission Board on January 10, 1849, "expressing a preference for China or Japan."[122] He had already been licensed, an initial step required by the Board, by the New Albany Presbytery on June 30, 1848.[123] One of his professors at New Albany, the Rev. Daniel Stewart, newly appointed in 1846 to the chair of Ecclesiastical History and Church Government, wrote the Foreign Mission Board a letter recommending Martin "as a suitable person to be a missionary," and he was duly appointed to Amoy, China on January 29, 1849.[124] Although the letter of application was required to state motives for foreign service, the Board left most matters to the care of local presbyteries. They could better determine within the context of ecclesiastical structures and service whether the candidate met their requirements of "piety, love to Christ and for the souls of men, amicable disposition, common sense and sound judgment."[125]

W. A. P. Martin's appointment to China excited the New Albany Presbytery. He was the first person "raised up in the bounds of this Presbytery" to enter foreign missionary service. Therefore, its members enthusiastically invited him, beginning with the close of the seminary year in the spring of 1849, "to visit as many of our churches as he shall find to be practicable previously to his embarkation and preach to them on the subject of foreign missions." They expressed the hope that the Presbytery would "become responsible for Mr. Martin's entire support."[126] In view of the possibility of his sailing in June with the Moses Coulter family,[127] he was ordained at Livonia on October 2, 1849.[128]

Samuel Martin had originally applied for appointment to the Foreign Board on November 28, 1848, shortly after his licensing. He delayed processing his application until the date of William's ordination when he again notified the Board of his desire. He was appointed on October 15, 1849. Since William's initial designation to Amoy, John Lloyd had died, and the station was abandoned by the Presbyterians. Therefore, on November 12, 1849, both he and Samuel were reassigned to Ningpo, with a vague hope that they could occupy Shanghai when it was opened up to Presbyterian work.[129]

Marriage, the "last preparatory measure," as the *Missionary Manual* put it, remained to be settled. His earlier courtship of Margaret Wylie Martin's sister was a thing of the past, but he did not wish to go to China unmarried. He had hoped to find a girl in Indiana before he went East to finalize his agreement with the Board,[130] but when these hopes did not materialize, he proceeded to New York.[131] Following the completion of his business in New York, he visited friends near Abington, Pennsylvania, where he met Jan VanSant.[132] A short courtship ended with marriage on November 13, 1849,[133] and ten days later, he and Jane, Samuel and Margaret, and Mr. and Mrs. Justus Doolittle of the ABCFM sailed from Philadelphia on the Lantao.[134]

As W. A. P. Martin commenced a life-time involvement of sixty-six years in China he was in a unique sense the product of a frontier "education." This included both the "deliberate and purposeful efforts" of direct education — the formal curriculum and concepts of the structured classroom — and the many other influences of family, pioneer life, social milieu, church community, and Midwestern American ethos that were less deliberate, but no less significant in their total educational impact. This unique configuration of school, family, church, local community, and nation was the way in which American culture had been transmitted to him and would profoundly influence how he interpreted American culture and Christianity, both in word and deed, in the Chinese context.[135]

Notes

1. Francis Wayland, "The Moral Dignity of The Missionary Enterprise" (Boston, 1827), 24. This message was first delivered October 26, 1823, at the First Baptist Church in Boston. Robert Torbet, *Venture of Faith* (Philadelphia, 1955), 94.

2. Hanford A. Edson, *Contributions to The Early History of the Presbyterian Church in Indiana* (Winona Lake, 1898), 102.

3. Robert Stuart Sanders, *Presbyterianism in Paris and Bourbon County, Kentucky 1786-1961* (Louisville, 1961), 41-42.

4. Sanders, *Presbyterianism*, 3; Robert Davidson, *History of the Presbyterian Church in the State of Kentucky* (New York, 1847), 118.

5. William W. Sweet, *Religion on the American Frontier, 1783-1840. A Collection of Source Materials* (4 vols.; Chicago, 1936), II, *The Presbyterians*, 778-79; Keith Kensinger, *Pilgrims Under God* (Salem, Indiana, 1966), 26-27.

6. L. C. Rudolph, *Hoosier Zion* (New Haven, 1963), 40-41.

7. Roy M. Robbins, "Crusade in the Wilderness, 1750-1830," *Indiana Magazine of History*, XLVI (June, 1950), 124; John Dickey, *A Brief History of the Presbyterian Churches in Indiana*, included in Chapter 10 of *Centennial Memorial of the First Presbyterian Church of Indianapolis* (Indianapolis, 1925), 389-92; James A. Woodburn, "Pioneer Presbyterianism," *Indiana Magazine of History*, XXII (December, 1926), 339-52; Edson, *Presbyterian Church in Indiana*, 56-57.

8. Edson, *Presbyterian Church in Indiana*, 104, n. 2; Warder W. Stevens, *Centennial History of Washington County, Indiana* (Indianapolis, 1916), 355.

9. "In Memoriam—The Rev. W. A. P. Martin, D.D., LL.D., of China," in North China Minutes, 1917. Appendix D.

10. Arthur Smith, "The Life and Work of the Late Dr. W. A. P. Martin," *The Chinese Recorder*, XLVIII (February, 1917), 117.

11. W. A. P. Martin, "An African Pioneer," *Missionary Review of the World*, New Series IX (June, 1896), 449-51.

12. Robert Speer, *Presbyterian Foreign Missions* (Philadelphia, 1901), 12-13; Arthur J. Brown, *One Hundred Years* (New York, 1936), 13-37.

13. Minutes of the Synod of Indiana (O.S.), 1845, 183-84.

14. *Tenth Annual Report* of the Board of Foreign Missions of the Presbyterian Church in the U.S.A., 1847, 7.

15. Minutes of the Synod of Indiana, I, 1834, 173.

16. *Ibid.* (O.S.), 1841, 97.

17. *Ibid.* (O.S.), 1845, 183-84.

18. Sweet, *Religion on the American Frontier, Presbyterians,* 60.

19. Rudolph, *Hoosier Zion,* 17.

20. *Ibid.,* 139-44.

21. Richard Boone, *A History of Education in Indiana* (New York, 1892), 48.

22. *Ibid.,* 51. Also see Louis B. Wright, *Culture on the Moving Frontier* (Bloomington, Indiana, 1955), 56-58.

23. Boone, *Education in Indiana,* 58.

24. Rudolph, *Hoosier Zion,* 169.

25. Boone, *Education in Indiana.* He listed seventy-three schools formed by these groups from 1816 to 1851.

26. Minnie Clark, "The Old Log College at Livonia," *Indiana Magazine of History,* XXIII (March, 1927), 75. Her statement of his aim as "elevating the lives of folk gathered there — a little community in an almost unbroken forest" is significant. 73.

27. A quotation about the academy by a Rev. Barr and quoted in Kensinger, *Pilgrims,* 34.

28. A Synod motion was made in 1832 to establish female schools in the belief that proper education for girls "will preserve our free institutions" and help all citizens be "enlightened and virtuous." Minutes of the Synod of Indiana, I, 1832, 136-37. Little progress was made in the education of girls, at least in southern Indiana, until the late 1840's, when the Salem Presbytery took steps to form a Female College. An impelling motive at this time was a growing fear that Romanism, "the danger of the West," would ensnare "our females in their many, well-endowed schools." "Female College," *Salem Presbytery Reporter,* I (April, 1850), 25-27.

29. Boone, *Education in Indiana,* 68.

30. Albert Porter, "An American Mandarin," *Outlook,* August 24, 1907, 885.

31. Minutes of the Synod of Indiana, I, 1830, 101-2.

32. Elwyn Smith, *The Presbyterian Ministry in American Culture* (Philadelphia, 1962), 72.

33. "Real" westerners in Indiana thought of this school as "entirely too far east to be considered even as a western school." Minutes of the Synod of Indiana, I, 1826, 13.

34. Edson, *Presbyterian Church in Indiana*, 241, and Minutes of Synod of Indiana, I, 1830, 73.

35. Leonard Trinterud, *The Forming of An American Tradition* (Philadelphia, 1949), 261-64; 169-95.

36. Minutes of the Synod of Indiana, I, 1834, 187.

37. By the Plan of Union of 1802 Presbyterian and Congregational churches pledged to work together in many phases of their work, including the evangelization of the West. In 1826 the American Home Missionary Society was formed and, although it became a missionary arm of both groups, it was utilized largely by Congregational missionaries from New England. Colin B. Goodykoontz, *Home Missions on the American Frontier* (Caldwell, Idaho, 1939), 63.

38. Minutes of the Synod of Indiana, I, 1834, 234-37. The problem of the AHMS was not merely organizational. It was feared as the Trojan horse which would bring New England's liberal theology into the Presbyterian Church. From the New England perspective, its own theology, honed in its conflict with Unitarianism, seemed to be perfectly orthodox. Outsiders, however, viewed it as "Hopkinsianism," a form of Calvinism emphasizing human responsibility more than the sovereignty of God. Sweet, *Religion on the American Frontier*, *Presbyterians*, 106.

39. Minutes of Session of New School Livonia Presbyterian Church, June 6, 1841, and March 27, 1845.

40. Kensinger, *Pilgrims*, 27-28. Arthur Smith in "Life and Work of Martin," 116, noted that Mrs. Martin brought three of these slaves with her to Indiana and that she did not send them back until her children were all educated. William's will, his desire to come to Indiana to escape the problem of slavery, and the general anti-slavery feeling in the state do not favor this statement. Some of the slaves may have come to Indiana for a short period of time and then returned while W. A. P. Martin was still quite young, possibly when the Martin family moved from Livonia in 1831.

41. Kensinger, *Pilgrims*, 27-28.

42. Rudolph, *Hoosier Zion*, 74, 131-32. The author suggested that this action was an expression of his " back country training" and his lack of understanding of New England.

43. *Ibid.*, 144-47.

44. *Ibid.*, 121. The final sentence of this quotation is not relevant since this type of cooperation occurred in the late 1820's.

45. W. A. P. Martin, "A Brother's Tribute," *The Chinese Recorder*, XXXV (March, 1904), 134.

46. Peter Duus, "Science and Salvation in China: The Life and Work of W. A. P. Martin (1827-1916)," in Kwang-ching Liu, ed., *American Missionaries in China* (Cambridge, 1966), 34.

47. Porter, "An American Mandarin," 886; *Catalogue of Indiana University, 1844-5,* 10. The subjects for examination were Arithmetic, English Grammar, the Grammars of the Latin and Greek Languages, Caesar's Commentaries, Cicero's Select Orations, six books of Virgil's Aeneid, and the first course of Jacob's Greek Reader.

48. James A. Woodburn, *History of Indiana University* (Bloomington, Indiana, 1940), 153-54.

49. *Catalogue: Indiana University, 1844-5,* 14, and Porter, "An American Mandarin," 886.

50. Edson, *Presbyterian Church in Indiana,* 229-30; Rudolph, *Hoosier Zion,* 178-80.

51. Theophilus Parvin, *Address on the Life and Character of Andrew Wylie, D.D.* (Indianapolis, 1858), 37.

52. Andrew Wylie, *Sectarianism is Heresy* (Bloomington, Indiana, 1841), vi-viii.

53. W. A. P. Martin, *A Cycle of Cathay* (3rd ed.; New York, 1900), 19.

54. John McCollough, Lecture Notebook giving some lectures by Wylie in May, 1851, on Sacred History. It is probable that Martin was exposed to the same material five years earlier.

55. Henry Nash Smith, *Virgin Land* (Cambridge, 1950), 25-26.

56. *Ibid.,* 40.

57. For discussions of this concept in American history see Frederick Merk, *Manifest Destiny and Mission in American History* (New York, 1963), and Albert Weinberg, *Manifest Destiny* (Baltimore, 1935).

58. *Catalogue of Indiana University, 1844-5,* 12.

59. "Thomas Reid," *The Encyclopedia Britannica,* 11th Edition, XXIII (Cambridge, 1911), 51.

60. *Ibid.* Reid and others did not intend that the term "common sense" be understood as "the unreasoned beliefs of common life" in opposition to "the reasoned conclusions of philosophers."

61. Perry Miller, *American Thought I. Civil War to World War I* (San Francisco, 1954), x.

62. Sydney E. Ahlstrom, "Scottish Philosophy," *Church History,* XXIV (September, 1955), 257-72.

63. S. A. Grove, *The Scottish Philosophy of Common Sense* (Oxford, 1960), 147.

64. Dugald Stewart, *Outlines of Moral Philosophy* (Edinburgh, 1793), 48-51, 70-71; Grove, *Scottish Philosophy,* 149.

65. Grove, *Scottish Philosophy,* 235; Stewart, *Moral Philosophy,* 143.

66. William Stanton, *The Leopard's Spots: Scientific Attitudes Toward Race in America, 1815-59* (Chicago, 1960); George Marsden, *The Evangelical Mind and the New School Presbyterian Experience* (New Haven, 1970), 142-51.

67. McCollough, Lecture Notebook, XIII.

68. William K. Wright, *A History of Modern Philosophy* (New York, 1941), 248.

69. Ralph Gabriel, *The Course of American Democratic Thought* (2nd ed.; New York, 1956), 12-39.

70. Daniel Fisher, *The Story of the Seminary* in *McCormick Theological Seminary — Historical Celebration* (Chicago, 1910), 13-17.

71. LeRoy Halsey, *A History of McCormick Theological Seminary of the Presbyterian Church* (Chicago, 1893), 33, 46.

72. *The Constitution of the Presbyterian Church in the United States of America.* Including the Confession of Faith, the Shorter Catechism and the Longer Catechism (Philadelphia, 1839); Halsey, *McCormick Seminary*, 45.

73. Halsey, *McCormick Seminary*, 45.

74. Wilson Smith, *Professors of Public Ethics. Studies of Northern Philosophers Before the Civil War* (Ithaca, 1956), 215-16. Paley is listed in Appendix B as a textbook used at Bowdoin, Brown, Columbia, Dartmouth, Princeton, Union, Western Reserve, Williams, and Yale at various times in the 1830's and 1840's. Such a small seminary as New Albany was not included in his survey.

75. *Ibid.*, 44.

76. Rudolph, *Hoosier Zion*, 186-87; Halsey, *McCormick Seminary*, 48.

77. Rudolph, *Hoosier Zion*, 187.

78. Porter, "An American Mandarin," 886; Arthur Smith, "Life and Work of Martin," 116. William W. Martin came to Bloomington in April, 1843, shortly after W. A. P. M. and Samuel had entered Indiana University. He returned to Livonia over a full year before their education there was completed. Was W. A. P. M.'s departure in 1845 a factor in this? What types of family tensions might have been created by this decision to leave school?

79. Porter, "An American Mandarin," 886.

80. "Toleration of Christianity," *The Chinese Repository*, XIV (April, 1845), 195-99. *Ninth Annual Report* of the Board of Foreign Missions of the Presbyterian Church in the U.S.A., 32-33.

81. Arthur Smith, "Life and Work of Martin," 117. An obituary notice indicated he had been "Professor of Ancient Languages at Anderson Institute." *North China Herald*, December 23, 1916, 304. Was this the

parochial school? A close friend stated, "He was offered a tempting educational position in his own state before he came to China, but he refused to consider it." "In Memoriam — the Rev. W. A. P. Martin of China." This offer may have been at "Anderson Institute" or one made subsequent to his graduation. At any rate, the characteristic tendency to emphasize academic titles and position is clearly seen.

82. Lewis Joseph Sherrill, *Presbyterian Parochial Schools* (New York, 1969), 11-13.

83. *Ibid.*, 27.

84. *Ibid.*, 39, 34.

85. *Ibid.*, 73-83, Table IV.

86. *Ibid.*, 46-69. The subject matter in these institutions was similar to that in the public schools — provision on differing levels for reading, writing, spelling, arithmetic, grammar, algebra, geography, and Latin. The religious subjects were distinctive and included several components: the Bible was used devotionally and as a textbook; there was prayer both in the classroom and in regular prayer meetings outside of school hours; a variety of catechisms were recited, most related in one way or another to the Longer or Shorter Catechism; and students engaged in singing and efforts at personal work, conversion, and revivals.

87. Arthur Smith, "Life and Work of Martin," 117.

88. Martin, *Cycle*, 214.

89. R. Pierce Beaver, ed., *To Advance the Gospel* (Grand Rapids, 1967), 17, noted that whereas the *gloria Dei* was "the major motive in American missions from the seventeenth century until the rise of overseas missions," it was replaced in the first half of the nineteenth century by motives of "obedience and pity for the perishing souls of the heathen."

90. China Letters of the Board of Foreign Missions of the Presbyterian Church in the United States of America, IV, Martin to Board, #45, n.d. China Letters are subsequently abbreviated "CL."

91. CL, IV, Ningpo, Martin to Board, #5, January 30, 1854.

92. CL, Martin to Board, #326, August 10, 1861.

93. Porter, "An American Mandarin," 886.

94. CL, III, Martin to Board, #108, April 2, 1849.

95. W. A. P. Martin, "A Missionary Geography Needed," *The Home and Foreign Record*, III (February, 1852), 51-52.

96. Kenneth Scott Latourette, *A History of Christian Missions in China* (London, 1919), 217-27.

97. Robert Handy, *A Christian America; Protestant Hopes and Historical Realities* (Oxford, 1971), Chapters 1 and 2.

98. For discussions of the impact of millennialism on foreign mis-

sions see Marsden, *Evangelical Mind,* 182-98; J. F. Maclear, "The Republic and the Millennium," in Elwin Smith, ed., *The Religion of the Republic* (New York, 1971), 183-216; R. Pierce Beaver, "Eschatology in American Missions," in Von Jan Hermelink and Hans J. Margull, eds., *Basileia. Walter Freytag zum 60 Geburtstag* (Stuttgart, 1959), 60-75.

99. See particularly R. Pierce Beaver, "Missionary Motivation Through Three Centuries," in Jerald C. Brauer, ed., *Reinterpretation of American Church History* (Chicago, 1968), 113-39, and Donald Lord, *Mo Bradley and Thailand* (Grand Rapids, 1969), 36-51.

100. Arthur Ekirch, *The Idea of Progress in America 1815-1860* (New York, 1951), Chapter 2.

101. Ekirch, *Progress in America*, Chapters 1, 4, 5, 7, and 9; John Bodo, *The Protestant Clergy and Public Issues, 1812-48* (Princeton, 1954); Ray Billington, *The Protestant Crusade, 1800-1860* (New York, 1938).

102. Donald B. Cole, *Handbook of American History* (New York, 1968), 89-106.

103. Ekirch, *Progress in America*, 54-58.

104. R. Pierce Beaver, ed., *Pioneers in Mission* (Grand Rapids, 1966), 11-16.

105. Passive interest in foreign missions existed through the friendship between Cotton Mather and A. H. Francke of the German pietist movement. Ernest Benz, "The Pietist and Puritan Sources of Early Protestant World Missions," *Church History,* XX (June, 1951), 28-55.

106. Oliver W. Ellsbree, *The Rise of the Missionary Spirit in America, 1790-1815* (Williamsport, Pa., 1928), 122-45.

107. Arthur Brown, "Memorial to W. A. P. Martin," Minutes of the Board of Foreign Missions of the Presbyterian Church in the U.S.A., XXXIV, January 15, 1917, 319.

108. Rufus Anderson, *The Theory of Missions to the Heathen* (Boston, 1845), 4-5.

109. Martin, *Cycle,* 212. He explained that he and Samuel "fell in love, not with the same girl, but with sisters." "I fell out," he explained without giving any reasons. John W. Foster, who graduated from Indiana University ten years later than Martin, wrote, "When I was a student at the University . . . there was a legend amongst us that young Martin had won the heart of one of the attractive daughters of our President, but that Dr. Wylie refused to allow him to take her to that barbarian country so far away from home." John W. Foster, "An Appreciation of Dr. W. A. P. Martin," *Indiana University Alumni Quarterly,* January, 1917, 129. Margaret (nee Wylie) Martin's letter to her parents dispels this legend, unless we assume that William's courtship was earlier or that Wylie allowed one daughter to go to China and not the other. The "falling out" was probably

due to other reasons and may help to explain why W. A. P. M. left school in 1845.

110. Martin once wrote about the Taiping Rebellion, "Some stupendous providence of this kind seems called for to quicken the zeal of the people of God to make them as eager to come and gather jewels for our Saviour's crown in the dark mines of China as people of the world are to go to California and Australia for gold." CL, III, Ningpo, Martin to Board, #251, June 28, 1853.

111. Letter, Margaret Wylie to her parents, n.d., Harris Collection, Indiana University Archives.

112. Olav Myklebust, *The Study of Missions and Theological Education* (2 vols.; Oslo, 1955), I, 141-42.

113. *Ibid.,* 149.

114. Minutes of the Executive Committee of the Board of Foreign Missions of the Presbyterian Church in the U.S.A., V, 1846-1855, November 12, 1849, 151.

115. Helen Nevius, *The Life of John Livingston Nevius* (New York, 1895), 95.

116. Martin, *Cycle,* 19.

117. *Fifth Annual Report* of the Western Foreign Missionary Society (Philadelphia, 1837), 20.

118. Speer, *Presbyterian Foreign Missions,* 108, 119.

119. John Lloyd, "China: Amoy Mission," *The Foreign Missionary Chronicle,* XVII (May, 1849), 129. See also *The Foreign Missionary Chronicle,* XIV (October, 1846), 300-1, and XVI (November, 1848), 324-26.

120. A Missionary in China, *The Land of Sinim or An Exposition of Isaiah 49:12, Together with a Brief Account of the Jews and Christians in China* (Philadelphia, 1845), 19, 28-29, 145-47.

121. *Annual Report* of the Board of Missions of the General Assembly of the Presbyterian Church in the U.S.A. (Philadelphia, 1851), 18.

122. Minutes of the Executive Committee of the Board of Foreign Missions, V, January 22, 1849, 109.

123. This, in the Presbyterian Church, was no simple procedure. First, Martin gave a Latin exegesis which was referred to the committee on languages for approval. He followed this with a "critical exercise" on Isaiah 52:14, 15, and two "Popular Lectures" on I Peter 1:3-5 and Ephesians 2:8. Each of these steps was considered a part of "trials for licensure." Later at that same meeting of the Presbytery, he was examined in Hebrew. Only with the successful conclusion of these several rigorous requirements was William, along with his brother Samuel and several other candidates, given final approval and issued a printed certificate of

licensure. Beyond the academic examinations good moral character, "experimental acquaintance with religion" and "being in the communion of the church" were also required. Minutes of New Albany Presbytery, June 29-30, 1848, 69, 73.

124. Minutes of the Executive Committee of the Board of Foreign Missions, V, January 29, 1849, 109.

125. *A Manual Prepared for the Use of Missionaries and Missionary Candidates in Connection with the Board of Foreign Missions of the Presbyterian Church* (New York, 1840), 13. No mention is made of a "call." The 1840 edition of the manual, apart from some slight changes with respect to the missionary outfit, is the same as that for 1862. We may, therefore, assume it was the one in use at the time of Martin's appointment.

126. Minutes of the New Albany Presbytery, April 6, 1849, 105-7. "Entire support" may have meant only travel to point of embarkation, passage to China, and the outfit expense, which was $600 for married missionaries, less the value of articles given to them by the churches. The annual salary of about $600 was probably not included. It was recommended that not more than $40 or $50 be expended on books, since the Board was forming libraries at different stations and planned to furnish these with periodicals and "other papers." *A Manual Prepared for the Use of Missionaries,* 15. Also see CL, II, Memo, September 30, 1846, #78.

127. CL, III, Martin to Board, #108, April 2, 1849.

128. At the Presbytery meeting in April, Mark 16:1, later changed to Matthew 28:20, was assigned to him as the text for his trial sermon. Following the delivery of this sermon at the meeting on October 2, it was voted that "Mr. Martin having recently gone through all the parts of the trials required by the Constitution of our church, and they having been severally sustained, it was resolved to dispense with any further examination." Dr. Wood, Professor of Biblical Criticism and Oriental Literature from New Albany Theological Seminary, preached the ordination sermon from John 12:13 on "Blessed is the King of Grace that cometh in the name of the Lord." The service concluded with the ordination prayer and a Mr. Heart, substituting for William W. Martin, who declined the privilege, delivering the charge to "the newly ordained evangelist." Minutes of the New Albany Presbytery, April 6, 1849, 107, and October 2, 1849, 13.

129. Minutes of the Executive Committee of the Board of Foreign Missions, V, October 15, 1849, 136, and November 12, 1849, 140. This was understood by the field. CL, III, Ningpo, Loomis to Board, #147, April 13, 1850.

130. CL, III, Martin to Board, #108, April 2, 1849.

131. Not an easy trip in 1849. He went from Louisville to Cincinnati by boat, from there to Sandusky by rail, to Niagara by boat, to Albany by

rail, and finally to New York City by boat. Porter, "An American Mandarin," 886.

132. No records have been found that give any details about her background.

133. *North China Herald,* December 23, 1916, 304.

134. Martin, *Cycle,* 17. The ship originated from Boston, but the two Martin families boarded at Philadelphia.

135. For a discussion of the theories of education implicit in the above paragraph see Lawrence A. Cremin, "Further Notes Toward a Theory of Education," *Notes on Education,* No. 4 (March, 1974), 1-6, and Theodore R. Crane, "The Dimensions of American Education," in Crane, ed., *The Dimensions of American Education* (Reading, Mass., 1974), 238-48.

CHAPTER TWO

The Beginning of Protestant Missions in Changing China

WHEN W. A. P. MARTIN and his colleagues reached Hong Kong on April 10, 1850, they entered a China on the eve of change — a change provoked by the West's advance into China and the consequent emergence of new relationships that would bring this ancient civilization into the "family of nations." Chinese contact with Europe was minimal before the thirteenth century and was less significant for China than for the West, which gained such items as the "wheelbarrow, the sailing carriage, the cross-bow, the iron-chain suspension bridge, the magnetic compass . . . , paper, printing, [and] moveable-type printing. . . ."[1] During the thirteenth and fourteenth centuries the Mongol empire in China provided bridges for the travel of religious personnel between Europe and the Chinese capital at Khanbalik.[2]

Modern commercial intercourse between China and the West began with the arrival of the Portuguese at Canton in 1517. After numerous mistakes in their relationships with the Chinese, the Portuguese were badly rebuffed and in 1557 were confined to a small settlement in Macao. During this period Spain and England competed with Portugal for the China-Europe trade.[3]

From 1644 to 1684, the Ch'ing dynasty was still busily engaged in establishing its control over the empire, and the attendant internal disorder, particularly as it affected Formosa and the southern China coast, greatly inhibited foreign trade.[4] From 1685 until 1759 the Western sea powers carried on trade with China in the ports of Canton, Amoy, Foochow, and Ningpo. It was purely a commercial venture and no diplomatic contacts existed. From the

Chinese viewpoint, even though the Western powers paid no tribute, they were really not "nations," as the West would view sovereign nations, but "barbarians."

From 1760 to 1842 Western trade with all Chinese ports except Canton was interdicted. From the Western viewpoint, living and trading conditions at Canton were intolerable and could only lead to eventual conflict. Foreign merchants were restricted to one portion of the city known as the "factory" area, their wives were not allowed to be with them, nor could they even use their considerable spare time for instruction in the Chinese language. Should any conflict resulting in injury or death arise with a Chinese, the Chinese courts afforded no guarantees of justice as usually understood in the West. Matters of duties, warehouse arrangements, prices, and the actual export-import arrangements were often unsatisfactory.

In the late eighteenth and early nineteenth century, in order to find markets for the many goods being produced by her industrial revolution, Great Britain tried twice to develop better trade arrangements with China. The Macartney mission in 1793 and the Amherst mission in 1816 both failed badly to reach their goals of establishing permanent British representation in Peking, opening more ports, fixing a tariff rate, and establishing a trading station for British use parallel to that used by the Portuguese in Macao.[5]

When the East India Company relinquished its trade monopoly with China in 1834, Great Britain sent an official government representative to Canton to care for both trade and political matters. China did not recognize his official position, since to the Chinese his only status was that of a "barbarian," and though, to them, this seemed a normal and expected attitude, it created a difficult climate for amicable settlement of the ever-increasing problems between the two nations.

The occasion, if not the cause, of the impending conflict was the opium trade. Portugal had been the main importer of opium to China since early in the eighteenth century, but Britain overtook Portugal in 1773 as the East India Company gained a monopoly over the planting and sale of opium in India. Despite prohibitions by Chinese emperors against the use, sale, growth, or importation of opium in the eighteenth century, the trade flourished and had disastrous moral and economic implications for the Chinese. It did, however, furnish Western traders — American as well as British — with a product greatly demanded by the Chinese, a product for which they were prepared to connive.

In a famous memo to Queen Victoria, Lin Tse-hsü, appointed Commissioner at Canton in 1837, chided Great Britain for seducing the Chinese people and condemned the traders at Canton, arguing for principles of natural law.[6] Misestimating the might of Western arms, he challenged Great Britain to armed warfare, confining traders at Canton and destroying 21,306 chests of opium.[7]

This aggressive policy led to the ignominious defeat of the Chinese. Their humiliation was specified in several stipulations of the Treaty of Nanking: the cession of Hong Kong; opening of the five ports of Canton, Amoy, Foochow, Ningpo, and Shanghai to consuls, merchants, and missionaries; a most-favored-nation clause; extraterritoriality; a fixed tariff; and the right of Britain's warships to protect her commerce. Americans, by the Treaty of Wanghia, July 3, 1844, arranged to prohibit the opium trade and received the privilege of establishing hospitals and churches in the five open ports. The French Treaty of Whampoa, signed October 24, 1844, provided for the toleration of the Catholic faith.[8]

Concerning this critical turning point in the relations between China and the West, John Fairbank has observed that

> Until that time [1842] relations with the West had been based upon the ancient Chinese tribute system; after that time they were based upon the 'unequal' foreign treaties. Under the tribute system foreign trade had been restricted to the picturesque 'factories' of old Canton. But 1842 began a new era — the opening of China to Western commercial exploitation.[9]

This new era brought changes which dwarfed those that had come before. To once more quote Professor Fairbank,

> Seen from the Chinese side, no political collapse in history has been more cataclysmic — a decline from an age-old supremacy over the known world to an abject partitioning into spheres of foreign domination, all in the space of one lifetime between 1842 and 1898.[10]

Other historians have reached the same conclusion. Professors Wittfogel and Feng have observed that

The growing inner crisis did not lead, as in former times, to the collapse of a disintegrating dynasty only. It ushered in the collapse of imperial Chinese society itself, a society which in one form or another had existed for more than 2000 years.[11]

Although the impact of the West was obviously related to these changes, it was not their sole cause. Western arms, commercial enterprise, and missionary evangelism served to strengthen, rather than shatter, Japanese society. In some very elusive way, the varied expressions of Western imperialism triggered certain responses within Chinese society; these responses in turn served as catalysts to produce disequilibrium and eventual disintegration.

For example, the Treaty of Nanking in 1842 brought prosperity to the silk-raising and tea-producing areas of China, but caused great hardship in others where native industries, not adequately protected by the tariff, were dealt a severe blow.[12]

Furthermore a rapid increase in population, unjust distribution of land resources and a virtual doubling of the farmers' tax burden due to the rise in the price of silver, triggered by the import of opium, increased the sense of financial unrest.[13]

A variety of natural calamities in the 1840's and 1850's — floods, drought, insects — contributed to economic hardship and, along with a national sense of humiliation, produced the climate for peasant revolts.

The most important of these — the great Taiping Rebellion — originated with two Hakka peasants, Hung Hsiu-ch'uan and Li Ching-fang, disillusioned by their failure in the examinations, whose exposure to Christian theology[14] and Confucian utopian writings stirred them to visions of a Chinese society free from idol-worship, opium smoking, gambling, drinking, unequal distribution of land, and other social evils. They organized an association for the worship of God (*shang-ti*) which embodied many Christian ideals, notably a system of ten commandments, regular church attendance, hope for an ideal society on earth, and vigorous opposition to all idolatry. This organization regarded itself as God's people in China, and Hung referred to himself as the Younger Brother of Jesus Christ. The movement was idealistic enough to appeal to rich and poor alike, and with revolutionary fervor, under the new name of the "Heavenly Kingdom of Great

Peace" (*T'ai-p'ing t'ien-kuo*), it broke out from its base in Kwangsi in April, 1852, took the Wuhan complex of cities on the Yangtze River, and then proceeded eastward to subdue Nanking by March, 1853.[15]

The Heavenly Kingdom was far different from most earthly ones. It initiated a system of communal ownership of land and property, developed a unified civil and military administration, promoted a Christian culture, including among other things examinations based on the Bible and Christian tracts, created a type of egalitarian society, and, above all, sought to overturn the Manchu dynasty.

The Taiping political goal of replacing the Manchus was fundamental to accomplishing the rest of their aims. They failed to obtain a working alliance with numerous anti-Manchu societies because they vigorously opposed idol-worship and were determined to create a new kingdom rather than restore the Ming dynasty.[16] Even more critical was the fact that the Taipings were not able to obtain support from the Western powers. The latter, particularly England and America, adopted a neutral stance at first, realizing that their treaty privileges were contingent upon the continued existence of the dynasty. In the late 1850's Western neutrality changed to opposition to the Taiping movement as earlier high hopes for a Christian China and extended trade were dashed by indications of Taiping inability to govern, the movement's reckless disregard for life and property, and by internal dissension among the Taiping leadership.[17] Their judgment appeared vindicated when the rebels met their final defeat at Nanking in 1864.[18]

The Taiping Rebellion did not interrupt the normal relations of the Occidental powers with the Chinese government. The first Western treaties with China specified that their provisions would be reviewed and revised after twelve years. Great Britain particularly was anxious to obtain several new concessions: residence of foreign ministers in Peking, new treaty ports on the Yangtze River, and indemnity payments.[19] Initial negotiations early in 1856 were fruitless, but late that year Chinese authorities seized the lorcha *Arrow,* a small Chinese ship registered with the British in Hong Kong and flying the Union Jack, and another war broke out. The ensuing confrontation between the British consul, Harry Parkes, and the Chinese viceroy, Yeh Ming-ch'en, brought progressive misunderstanding and led to the capture of Canton by combined British and French forces in December, 1856.[20]

As a result of this conflict, Great Britain, France, the United States, and Russia demanded that the Imperial government in Peking grant the desired concessions. After the British and French marched on Tientsin in 1858, the Emperor yielded and agreed upon separate treaties for each of the four Western nations.

The Chinese, however, were still reluctant to give in, and insisted upon special conditions for the ratification of the treaties. This led to a renewal of hostilities in 1859-60 and the tragic destruction of the Summer Palace in Peking. When the treaties were finally ratified, the new agreements, logical extensions of the initial agreements signed in 1842-44, made possible a widespread penetration of the Empire by Westerners.

A major outside force stimulating China's response to the West was the missionary enterprise of which W. A. P. Martin was a representative. He joined in an effort that had commenced in China over a thousand years earlier, and which was well-established at Ningpo, the site of his first missionary labors.

The Christian faith first entered the Chinese empire in the seventh century at the beginning of the T'ang dynasty. The Nestorian creed had spread extensively in Syria and Persia in the centuries following the apostolic age, and a missionary from one of these outposts apparently came to China's capital in 635 A.D. Within a short time the new religion was officially endorsed by the reigning Emperor T'ai-tsung and, under the direction of a metropolitan, spread to several of the leading cities of the empire.[21]

Following a severe persecution of the Nestorian faith in the middle of the ninth century, Christianity disappeared in China, not appearing again until the time of the Mongol Emperor, Khubilai Khan, who sent with the two Polo brothers, Nicolo and Maffeo, a request to the Pope asking that one hundred religion and science teachers be sent to him at the capital in Khanbalik. A papal interregnum resulted in a delay, and eventually only two Dominicans accepted the challenge, and they turned back without reaching their goal.

During the twelfth and thirteenth centuries the travels of the Polos and of two Franciscan friars, serving as diplomatic envoys, revealed to Europeans previously unsuspected religious freedom in the Mongol Empire. In 1294 the Pope responded by sending John of Montecorvino, who, with the Emperor's favor, erected a church and baptized nearly six thousand converts by 1305. The work was solidified under an Archbishop of Khanbalik, and within the next twenty or thirty years Roman Catholic churches had been established in what are today Ch'uanchow, Hangchow, and Yangchow.

Nestorianism had entrenched itself as the faith of a number of tribes — Kerait, Ongut, Uighurs — linked with the Mongols and entered China proper again at this time. However, with the collapse of the Mongol empire in 1368, the Franciscans, Nestorians, and a small group of Armenian Christians disappeared as an effective force in Chinese life. Christianity, basically no more foreign in principle than Buddhism, was proving far less resistant to the vicissitudes of life in China than was the Lotus faith.[22]

This interruption of the Christian movement in China lasted for two centuries until the world-wide expansion of European Roman Catholic countries in the sixteenth and seventeenth centuries. Francis Xavier, the great Jesuit missionary, first used Shangch'uan, a South China Portuguese trading center, as the base for his unsuccessful efforts to enter China in 1552. Macao soon became the center for the Roman Catholic missionary efforts. The Italian Jesuit, Matteo Ricci, was the true pioneer of the new era. After eighteen years of constant movement from one South China city to another, in 1601 he was finally allowed to settle in Peking. During the next nine years he was not only instrumental in establishing the church in Peking, but also pioneered the missionary strategy for which the Jesuits were to become famous. Ricci identified himself with the gentry and then used all the scientific and philosophical knowledge he possessed to gain the respect of leading officials. He studied and used the ancient Confucian classics, adopting Chinese rules of behavior, seeking to remove all cultural barriers to the Gospel. He was so careful in cultural accommodation that his close Chinese friends often professed uncertainty as to why he had come to China.[23] Yet he made converts among high officials and scholars in Peking.[24]

During the remainder of the Ming dynasty the Jesuit fathers made themselves indispensable to the Emperor with their scientific and mathematical expertise. Through skillful political maneuvering they survived the dynastic change in 1644 and enjoyed a period of growing influence on the Imperial household that lasted until 1722. The Jesuit Adam Schall von Bell was put in charge of the Department of Astronomy in 1645 and used this position to great advantage. The power and prestige he obtained through direct audience, discussing the stars, sun, eclipses, calendars — matters of cosmic significance to the Chinese — with the Emperor, won him great respect within the Court. In 1661 a change in rulers brought about his fall, but he was soon succeeded under K'ang-hsi by a Belgian Jesuit, Ferdinand Verbiest. Along with other learned Jesuits, Verbiest taught the Emperor, served as his advisor concerning a wide variety of matters, and acted as his interpreter during the diplomacy leading to the signing of the Treaty of Nerchinsk between China and Russia in 1689.

Thus, through Jesuit influence at the capital, which besides winning adherents to the faith provided protection for its propagation throughout the empire, the Catholic church grew to a community of two hundred thousand in the early years of the eighteenth century.[25] This was a period of relatively rapid growth, even though it resulted in a membership comprising only one-tenth of one percent of the population of China. It was not without serious problems, the most difficult of which has been called the "Rites Controversy." The innovative Jesuits, who arrived in China during the sixteenth century, were more flexible toward Chinese culture than were the Franciscans and Dominicans, who came later. With good conscience the Jesuits viewed ancestral rites as civil deference, not religious worship, accepted certain cultural traditions of Chinese funeral services, described Confucius in semi-sacred terms ("holy"), and used indigenous titles for God — *shang-ti* or *t'ien* — rather than the newly introduced *t'ien-chu* (Heavenly Lord).

Differences between the Jesuits and other orders who felt that such accommodation was non-Christian eventually led to conflict between the Pope and the Emperor K'ang-hsi. Viewpoints hardened progressively. In edicts issued in 1704, 1720, and 1742, the Roman church disapproved, ameliorated, and finally obdurately opposed the various Jesuit-approved innovations. K'ang-hsi was greatly aggravated by missionary dissension and Rome's implacable opposition, but he never withdrew his support from at least a few leading Jesuits.

His successor, Yung-cheng (1723-36), banned the Christian

faith in 1724 and Yung's son, Ch'ien-lung (1736-96), enforced this edict with fervor, but Catholic churches continued to exist throughout the Empire, and missionaries carried on as best they were able. Unequal enforcement of the Emperor's edict and various combinations of local circumstances resulted in cycles of forbearance and vicious persecution. Religious oppression was particularly strong in 1784, 1805, and 1811. Since the days of Ricci, few Catholic converts had come from the official class, and in local areas there was little sympathy for Christians whenever an official on-the-make wished to enforce Imperial edicts proscribing Christianity according to the letter of the law.[26] Despite some areas of encouragement, "the tale was of diminishing congregations, of ruined churches, and of steadily deepening shadows."[27] This somber picture was relieved a bit after 1815 as new missionaries entered China and as fresh impetus was given by the revival of the Society of Jesus, which had been banned by the Vatican in the mid-eighteenth century.[28]

Beginning in 1600 Protestant powers had begun to develop a colonial empire and soon established mission outposts in India, what is now Indonesia, and in Formosa, thus challenging the Roman Catholic monopoly on Christian missions in the East. In 1807 the London Missionary Society sent Robert Morrison to China as the first Protestant missionary there, but he soon accepted a position as translator under the British East India Company. This job afforded financial security and helped protect his clandestine efforts to produce and distribute Christian literature, most notably a translation of the entire Bible, a grammar of Chinese, a Chinese-English dictionary, and many Christian tracts. Morrison's recruiting brought William Milne and William Medhurst to the Far East. Unwilling to be restricted to the normal pattern of confined activity at Canton and Macao, Protestant missionaries settled in areas like Malacca, Batavia, Penang, Singapore, and Bangkok, where there were large overseas Chinese colonies. In the 1830's, Karl Gutzlaff, associated with the Netherlands Missionary Society, made trips along the China coast as far as Tientsin to distribute Christian literature. Gutzlaff's ministry stirred great American interest and proved an incentive to the aggressive promotion of American missions.[29]

In the period before the first treaties were signed in 1840 a few American missionaries sponsored by the American Board of Commissioners for Foreign Missions, the American Baptists, the Protestant Episcopal church, and the American Presbyterians, came to China. Like those before them, they preached, distributed literature, and did educational work. Their achievements were modest and restricted largely to the merchants who had little social prestige or political power within the Chinese empire.[30]

When the "unequal treaties" were signed in the early 1840's, Ningpo was one of the five ports opened to missionary penetration. Although Dr. Daniel MacGowan of the American Baptists carried on a medical work in Ningpo for several months in 1843,[31] the first permanent missionary work there was commenced in June, 1844, by Dr. Divie Bethune McCartee of the American Presbyterians.[32]

Ningpo appealed to missionaries because it was less anti-foreign than Canton,[33] had extremely pleasant surroundings, was thought to be healthful,[34] and was inhabited by people disposed to listen to the Gospel.[35] Located in Chekiang province, south of Shanghai, at the juncture of the Funglu and Yuyaou Rivers, which combined to form the Ningpo River just twelve miles from the sea, the walled city had a population of about two hundred thousand. Set on a large plain, it was semi-surrounded about fifteen miles away by a small range of forested hills that rose to two and three thousand feet.[36] The climate varied from a hot, humid one hundred degrees in the summer to a winter low of ten to fifteen degrees,[37] and did not prove to be nearly as healthful as had been anticipated.[38]

The first missionaries lived in temples and Chinese mud homes. Later, the Presbyterians erected several homes outside the city across the Yuyaou River, homes "as good as those which ministers in America have."[39] Well-constructed of brick and timber and equipped with stoves, carpets, and numerous windows, they protected their occupants more effectively than had the native homes from the heat, cold, dampness, and insects. The cost of construction was not cheap, for the timber came from Fukien, the glass from Canton, and locks, bolts, and hinges from Hong Kong or Shanghai.[40]

Dr. McCartee and the Richard Ways lived first on the nearby island of Chusan, which the presence of British troops made a safe initial haven.[41] After they moved to Ningpo, a dispensary and a street chapel were opened, plans were laid for a boys' boarding school, and when Mr. Cole brought the mission press from Macao, preparation was made to produce literature.[42] A Presbyterian church, comprised of six missionaries and one Chinese convert who had come with Mr. Way from Singapore, was organized in 1844. William Culbertson was elected to be pastor, and Way, Lowrie, and McCartee to be the ruling elders.[43] Evangelistic itineration created three very weak churches in nearby areas. This led to the organization of a Presbytery by 1846 and completed a structure for full ecclesiastical life.

This was not a strange procedure from the perspective of those who had come from Christian America. Even though there was no strong Chinese church — in fact, no church at all — Christianity had to be made visible.

> The utter ignorance of a Christian Sabbath, the universal idolatry of the people and the supposition on the part of the Chinese that the foreign barbarian had *no* religion, vexed their souls continually. So a church building was called for, not so much because of the immediate needs of the native church, as for a witness to the heathen.[44]

A formal ecclesiastical establishment also made possible the regular exercise of church discipline over the missionaries.[45]

Many issues arose to stimulate vigorous debate, particularly concerning the Boys' Boarding School, which had been established to convert young men and then prepare them for religious work. Should English be used or not? McCartee appealed to Alexander Duff's experience in India to argue that "the only way to wean them [the Chinese] from their strong prejudice in favor of their own books and their incorrect notions of church" was to give them Western scientific literature in English.[46]

The missionaries usually gave several reasons for starting schools in China: to communicate religious truth to the young; to diffuse general knowledge among the Chinese; to set standards for native schools; to send out men who would influence the public mind; to increase the rate of literacy in China and to train native authors to produce religious and learned literature.[47]

For men convinced that "oral preaching" was the *summum bonum* of their work, these missionaries were prolific in their literary work.[48] During the five years previous to Martin's arrival, they wrote twenty-nine separate works, ranging from tracts of several leaves to books over one hundred pages long. Eighteen works, 75,850 copies in all, were published in 1848. Most were tracts, brief doctrinal studies, and biblical portions.[49] They were all printed in the classical Chinese character which could only be read by a limited number of the population, even in Ningpo, where it was estimated that one-fifth of the city was engaged in some type of literary work.[50]

Missionary attitudes toward Chinese life and society were rapidly becoming stereotyped. The missionaries identified idolatry as the major antagonist. They spoke disparagingly to the Chinese, as well as to their supporters at home, concerning the pagan idols and "silly ceremonies" which made up a large part of Chinese daily life.[51] Homage to Confucius was "undoubtedly idolatry."[52] Walter Lowrie concluded early that the "whole system is radically wrong. They begin at the top and build downwards just as in their houses they first set up a skeleton frame, while the foundation is sand."[53]

The Roman Catholics in Ningpo offered the Protestants stiff competition. Catholic roots, of course, had been planted in China long before the treaty ports were opened. After 1844 the Catholic church assigned priests of different nationalities to supervise each port: Italians to Shanghai, Portuguese to Canton, Spanish to Amoy, and French to Ningpo and Peking.[54] The two French priests in Ningpo supervised two or three Chinese priests, educated at Macao, in a work including a chapel with a hundred converts, two schools, and a "foundling hospital" for fifty children.[55]

Most of the Presbyterian missionaries refrained from harsh criticism of the Roman Catholic work but members of some of the other mission groups were less temperate. An American Baptist missionary, Daniel MacGowan, referred to popery as "the mystery of iniquity" and commented sadly on the way Catholic missionaries had converted pagan temples in Chusan to "mass houses."[56] He described Good Friday festivities at Ningpo when Portuguese sailors performed a traditional attack on the effigy of Judas Iscariot, and, as an aftermath, nearly precipitated a bloody fight by assaulting a Cantonese junk.[57]

A fine spirit of cooperation existed, however, among all the

Protestant missions in Ningpo, and this made an impact upon the Chinese community. Missionaries frequently exchanged pulpits and, once a month, they tried to get together for a worship service.[58] These monthly "concerts of prayer" included a time of fasting and prayer in the morning and a sermon in the afternoon.[59] Discussion of work problems of common interest was also often part of the day's agenda.

In the view of the Ningpo missionaries, the problem with opium was much worse than that with "ardent spirits" in the United States, although they believed that some of those engaged in the opium traffic were "upright, honorable and gentlemanly men."[60] The Opium War, they felt, had not solved the problem. In the 1842 treaty arrangements Great Britain did not agree to prohibit the opium trade but she did wish to regulate it through some type of Western extra-legal arrangement, such as a duty or tax. When this failed, British officials hoped that the trade "should be carried on by parties of respectability" rather than by "desperados and pirates,"[61] and in the view of many this was accomplished. In 1845 about one-tenth of the total Chinese opium import was shipped through Chusan, near which five receiving ships were located. When Chusan was evacuated by the British troops in 1846, much of this activity was transferred to Ningpo, where it was encouraged both by the paucity of other trade and by the corruption of local officials.[62]

During these early years following the initial treaties with foreign nations, the Chinese government informally yielded more concessions to the outsiders. Legally, the missionaries were restricted to the five treaty ports and their immediate environs. In practice, they often spent several weeks away from their base of operation and traveled two or three hundred miles.[63] Walter Lowrie and David Abeel went to Ch'angchow, thirty miles inland from Amoy. The Chinese chose to be silent, but Sir Henry Pottinger, the British plenipotentiary to China, vigorously protested this kind of illegal activity.[64]

In general, American missionaries, with fewer American consuls to supervise their activities, traveled about more freely. Even where there were American consular officials, they tended not to enforce the letter of the law. In discussions held in Shanghai and Amoy from 1845 to 1848, British and Chinese officials informally agreed to limit inland travel to one day or thirty miles. By the end of 1848, even this limitation was not being enforced.[65]

Article Seventeen of the Treaty of Wanghia, made between China and the United States in 1844, provided that for the purchase of property "it will be necessary for the Chinese local officers, in company with the consuls and other officers, to consider and inquire into the feelings of the people. . . ."[66] After 1847, however, it was common practice for a missionary to deal directly with a Chinese property owner and to buy property if the protest by neighbors was not too violent.[67]

Even though the small band of Presbyterian missionaries had only been in Ningpo for a few years when W. A. P. Martin arrived, they were already experienced in the work, well-versed in the Chinese language and accommodated to established policies and attitudes. When the Martin brothers came to the field in 1850, they joined a community of "senior missionaries" who sought to teach them what they ought to do, think, and feel in their work with the Chinese people. This mold was as significant as W. A. P. Martin's frontier experience for setting the course of his future contribution to the Kingdom of God in China.

Notes

1. Wolfgang Franke, *China and the West* (New York, 1967), 2.

2. *Ibid.*, 5.

3. John Fairbank, *Trade and Diplomacy on the China Coast: The Opening of the Treaty Ports, 1842-54* (Cambridge, 1953), 48.

4. *Ibid.*

5. Henry McAleavy, *The Modern History of China* (New York, 1967), 43.

6. Ssu-yü Teng and John K. Fairbank, eds., *China's Response to the West: A Documentary Survey, 1839-1923* (New York, 1966). Document 1, "Lin Tse-hsü's Moral Advice to Queen Victoria," 26. "Suppose there were people from another country who carried opium for sale to England and seduced your people into buying and smoking it; certainly your honorable ruler would deeply hate it and be bitterly aroused."

7. W. A. P. Martin, *The Awakening of China* (New York, 1907), 155.

8. Immanuel C. Y. Hsü, *The Rise of Modern China* (New York, 1970), 237-38.

9. Fairbank, *Trade and Diplomacy*, 3.

10. *Ibid.*, 4.

11. Karl A. Wittfogel and Feng Chia-sheng, *History of Chinese Society: Liao, 907-1125* (New York, 1949), 24.

12. McAleavy, *History of China*, 58.

13. Hsü, *Modern China*, 270-75.

14. See Eugene Boardman, *Christian Influence Upon the Ideology of the Taiping Rebellion, 1851-1864* (Madison, 1952).

15. Hsü, *Modern China*, 275-82.

16. *Ibid.*, 283-87, 281.

17. *Ibid.*, 298.

18. Kenneth S. Latourette, *A History of Christian Missions in China* (London, 1929), 294-95.

19. Hsü, *Modern China*, 258.

20. *Ibid.*, 253-56.

21. A. C. Moule, *Christians in China Before the Year 1550* (New York, 1930), 65; P. Y. Saeki, *The Nestorian Documents and Relics in China* (Tokyo, 1951), 86.

22. Latourette, *Missions in China*, 61-77.

23. See Franke's translation of a description of Ricci by Li Cho-wu: "But I do not know how it is that he came here. It would be more than foolish if it were perhaps his wish to alter our doctrine of the Duke of Chou and of Confucius on the basis of his doctrine. I believe that this is not [the reason why he is there]." *China and the West*, 39.

24. Latourette, *Missions in China*, 96.

25. *Ibid.*, 102-30.

26. *Ibid.*, 131-84.

27. Stephen Neill, *Christian Missions* (New York, 1964), 205.

28. Kenneth S. Latourette, *A History of the Expansion of Christianity* (7 vols.; New York, 1941), VI, *The Great Century in North Africa and Asia, 1800-1914*, 263.

29. China Letters of the Board of Foreign Missions of the Presbyterian Church in the United States of America, II, Mr. Robert Orr of Clarion, Pennsylvania to Board, #86, 1842. China letters are subsequently abbreviated "CL."

30. Latourette, *Missions in China*, 209-27; Latourette, *Expansion of Christianity*, VI, 295-307.

31. Lida Scott Ashmore, *The South China Mission of the American Baptist Foreign Mission Society* (Shanghai, 1920), 5-6. Pre-treaty religious contacts, of longer or shorter duration, were made by Gutzlaff, Medhurst, Stephens, Lockhart, and Milne from 1832 to 1842 with no lasting results. A. W. Loomis, "A Brief History of Protestant Missions in Ningpo," Unpublished paper in CL, III, Ningpo, #147, April 13, 1850.

32. The dates of the other American Presbyterian missionaries who arrived before Samuel and William Martin were Richard Way and Walter Lowrie (1844), Richard Cole and William Culbertson (1845), A. W. Loomis and John Quarterman (1846), and Joseph Wight, Moses Coulter, and Henry Rankin (1849). N. C. Garrett, ed., *Jubilee Papers of the Central China Presbyterian Mission, 1844-94* (Shanghai, 1894), 2-3. American Baptist missionaries were Daniel MacGowan (1843), E. C. Lord (1847), and Josiah Goddard (1848). Church Missionary Society missionaries were Robert Cubbold and William Russel (1848) and F. F. Gough (1850). See William Dean, *The China Mission* (New York, 1859), 134-41; Alexander Wylie, *Memorials of Protestant Missionaries to the Chinese* (Shanghai, 1867), 285-87.

33. CL, II, Canton, Happer to Board, #73, July 22, 1846, and #75, September 25, 1845, told of potential danger in occupying Canton and of threats encountered by Chinese who would dare rent their homes to foreigners.

34. Dean, *China Mission*, 134.

35. D. P. Kidder, *Notices of Fu-chau and the Other Open Ports of China* (New York, 1848), 17.

36. Helen Nevius, *Our Life in China* (New York, 1869), 26.

37. Archdeacon Moule, *Personal Recollections of the Taiping Rebellion, 1861-63* (Shanghai, 1898), 15.

38. Dean, *China Mission*, 165-66, 169. Malaria, ague, and a variety of fevers forced the missionaries to retreat frequently to the cooler breezes of Chusan. Missionary wives and their small children in China were particularly susceptible to fatal diseases. From 1819 to 1859 fifty-one wives, twenty-five percent of the total personnel in China, died on their fields of labor. The average work-expectancy of each of the missionaries during this forty-year time span was only seven years.

39. Margaret Wylie Martin to her brother, John Wylie, #8, November 21, 1851. Harris Collection, Archives, Indiana University.

40. Margaret Wylie Martin to her sister, Elizabeth, #7, 1851. Harris Collection. Also see *The Missionary Magazine*, XXXI (January, 1851), 23-25.

41. Great Britain blockaded Ningpo in 1840 during the Opium War and captured it in 1841. After the Treaty of Nanking was signed in 1842, troops remained on Chusan Island and were only removed in 1845 after

China had finished her indemnity payments. See Eldon Griffin, *Clippers and Consuls* (Ann Arbor, 1938), 298; CL, II, Ningpo, Loomis to Board, #115, November 20, 1845.

42. CL, II, Ningpo, McCartee to Board, #97, July 12, 1845.

43. Garrett, *Jubilee Papers*, 4.

44. *Ibid.,* II, 22. Even in 1864 the Ningpo mission still had only four churches. 25.

45. Minutes of the Ningpo Presbytery carefully recorded, for example, that "the two Martins presented dismissal from the Presbytery of New Albany and were received into the Ningpo Presbytery." *The Home and Foreign Record*, V (April, 1854), 118.

46. CL, III, Ningpo, McCartee to Board, #144, February 7, 1850.

47. CL, II, Ningpo, Report of Special Committee, #127, 1845.

48. Men like Francis Wayland believed that oral preaching was "the *only* allowable kind of missionary labor." CL, VIII, Outgoing to Ningpo, #89, August 3, 1854.

49. CL, III, Publication Committee Report 1847-48, #135, 1848. See also Wylie, *Protestant Memorials*, 129, 134, 135, 139, 146, 148, 158, 194.

50. Kidder, *Notices of Fu-chau*, 17.

51. CL, III, Sixth Annual Report, Ningpo, #134, October 1, 1849; CL, Lowrie to Board, Ningpo, II, #114, October 14, 1845.

52. CL, II, Third Annual Report Ningpo, #167, October 1, 1846.

53. CL, II, First Annual Report Ningpo, #110, October 1, 1845.

54. H. V. Rankin, "Journal," *The Home and Foreign Record*, III (May, 1852), 152.

55. D. B. McCartee, Letter, *The Home and Foreign Record*, III (January, 1852), 21.

56. Daniel MacGowan, Letters, *The Missionary Magazine*, XXXIV (April, 1853), 106, and (February, 1853), 33.

57. Letter from Dr. MacGowan reprinted in *The Foreign Missionary*, XIII (December, 1854), 213-14.

58. W. A. Russel, Letter to *Church Missionary Record*, XXIV (December, 1853), 285.

59. H. V. Rankin, "Journal," *The Home and Foreign Record*, III (June, 1852), 177.

60. *Ibid.*

61. Fairbank, *Trade and Diplomacy*, 146-51.

62. *Ibid.,* 333. Ningpo engaged in silk and tea trade, but it was not on the main routes of international trade, 329. Griffin described Ningpo as "an unsightly backyard to Shanghai." Griffin, *Clippers and Consuls*, 301.

63. Fairbank, *Trade and Diplomacy,* 294-95. The author reported a trip of seven weeks through the silk and tea districts inland from Shanghai made in 1845 by Walter Medhurst of the LMS. CL, Lowrie to Board, #14, March 17, 1845, spoke of this itineration as the possibility now open that "we are unprepared to take advantage of."

64. Carl Cranston, "The American Missionary's Outlook on China, 1830-60" (unpublished Ph.D. dissertation, Harvard University, 1930), 126.

65. *Ibid.,* 126-28.

66. *Chinese Repository,* XIV (January, 1845), 35.

67. Cranston, "American Missionary Outlook," 129.

CHAPTER THREE

Pioneering New Paths of Mission Outreach in Ningpo

AFTER AN UNEVENTFUL trip to Ningpo the first order of business for W. A. P. Martin was the onerous task of language study. Morning, afternoon, and evening he immersed himself studying the difficult spoken Chinese language used at Ningpo. "In a few days," he reported, "the mist began to rise," and his study changed from an "irksome task [to a] . . . fascinating pastime."[1] In his limited spare time he went to the mission library, which usually rotated from one missionary home to another,[2] where a wide variety of books for research and study were available.[3]

Martin was not happy living in the somewhat isolated Presbyterian compound and so, within weeks, "insisted, although in a kindly way," on moving to the Chinese city. This "experiment" was cautiously approved by the mission body, and a small structure connected with the church building was modified for living purposes.[4] This move cut the Martins off somewhat from their Presbyterian colleagues, but they had companions in William Russel and Robert Cubbold of the Church Missionary Society who also had homes in the middle of Ningpo.[5]

What began as an unemotional experiment bristled with problems after a few years. By 1854 Martin had suggested that the Presbyterian property on the north bank of the river be sold and the press, homes, and schools be moved into the city.[6] Typically, his reasons were mustered carefully. To live in the city, he argued, was not injurious to health; he had lived there for four years, even during the summers, without a single day of recreation, and had suffered no ill effects.

Martin believed strongly that a city residence would promote more friendly relations with the Chinese, would expose the missionaries more thoroughly to the people, would break down prejudice, and lead many more visitors to their homes. With biting sarcasm, he asked, "If we complain of being confined to the five ports, is it not absurd to restrict ourselves to the *suburbs* of these ports?" Furthermore, he added, living in the city would enable missionaries to hold night meetings,[7] would allow their wives to contact Chinese women, and would also attract a better class of students to their schools.[8] Samuel Martin, for one, believed that the experiment was worthwhile, boasting that his brother "exerts more influence on more people than all of us together. He has daily calls from other provinces and distant parts of this province, while we have one in a month or maybe only in six months."[9]

Martin later described these years as "the most fruitful" of his life. He gained intimate rapport with many Ningpo residents. More important for the breadth of his later ministry, he was introduced to the official level of Chinese society and began to study Mandarin, which was indispensable for his later duties as interpreter in North China, and also a key to the educated court life of Peking.[10]

Despite Martin's arguments to the contrary, life in the city took its toll. The health of his family was badly impaired and eventually led to furlough after what was then thought to be a short span of ten years. Furthermore, a city residence exposed foreigners to dangers not faced by missionaries in fortress-like mission compounds. Piracy was so rife about Ningpo that the city was known as a "home for pirates and a battleground for cut throats."[11]

In this atmosphere of violence the only way to protect ships against pirate attacks was to convoy them to their destinations. Portuguese and Cantonese merchantmen used bribes, extortion, threats, and outright murder, contending so viciously for this privilege that the whole city was threatened with violence. On at least three occasions errant cannon balls narrowly missed Martin's house in the city,[12] and it was not uncommon for refugees from these frays — usually Portuguese — to seek safety in the Martins' home. For recreation, Martin frequently walked on the city wall, always courting the danger that Cantonese ruffians might mistake him for one of their Portuguese enemies.[13]

City life was, of course, far less a ghetto existence than living in the self-contained mission compounds and enabled William and Jane to escape the caustic criticism which one of their fellow-missionaries leveled against his colleagues on the north bank of the river.

> They preach very nicely but when the Chinese call on them they must stand outside. Some do not give them even a seat to sit upon and as to getting their noses into the fine sitting room, it is out of the question. To eat at the same table would be to lose cast [sic]. To keep them at a distance appears to be their idea of Christianity. . . .[14]

W. A. P. Martin's missionary labors — preaching, teaching in the church educational institutions, and writing or translating a variety of books and pamphlets — were not unique. What distinguished him from most of his colleagues was his commitment to a romanized orthography, a flexibility in his use of terms for "God," and an open attitude toward missionary methods. His attitudes in these areas reflected his passionate concern to take the Christian message to the common man; he was a pioneer as well as the spokesman for the progressive missionaries whose policies were constantly opposed by the more traditional faction led by Dr. McCartee.

Martin gave first priority to oral communication of the Gospel. With the help of a Romanized alphabet to record what he wished to learn, he made his first feeble attempt at preaching late in 1850, but it took another six months before he had "acquired a free command of a pretty large vocabulary."[15] Living in the city required him to assume the responsibility, in 1851, when still a language student, of helping to oversee the construction of a large church building in the center of Ningpo. Conspicuous from all portions of the city, a building of this grandeur, Martin believed, was a veritable house of Zion, from which the "Gospel would be diffused more widely . . . than by a humbler edifice."[16]

Undeterred by fear of mistakes, Martin seized every opportunity to proclaim his faith. His favorite forums were the city chapel and the larger downtown church to which his home was attached. Two hundred people would often crowd into the chapel to hear him expound one of the New Testament parables, probably the most interesting Biblical material that could be presented to a popular Chinese audience. In the church, where he usually had a more educated clientele, he lectured on Christian apologetics; these lectures, honed by question and answer discussions and further revision, he published in 1854 as *T'ien-tao su-yüan (Evidences of Christianity)*, a volume later judged to be the most popular Christian book ever published in China.[17]

Martin's evangelism was rewarded with several conversions, largely from the household of his teacher, Mr. Lee, who first believed and was then followed by his wife, sister, and mother.[18] Contrary to later charges by Dr. McCartee, Martin claimed that he did not accept just anyone as a convert. He quickly eliminated those with pecuniary motives, while he gave the benefit of the doubt to any whose motives seemed pure but who were deficient in comprehension, knowledge, and maturity.[19]

During this early period of his first term in China, Martin carefully avoided any task that would dim his vision for evangelizing the many Chinese towns and villages in the Ningpo plain.[20] Itineration, whether only a few hours' trip to "north-of-the-hills" (Shanpo)[21] or a longer journey to distant Hangchow, accomplished several purposes. First, of course, it disseminated the Gospel message. It also broke down prejudice against the missionary, enabled him to spend enough time with the people to understand them, broke him from the rut of a settled pastorate, and extended sufficiently beyond the institutional church in Ningpo to create a more truly indigenous Christian community.[22] John Nevius, one of William's closest friends, noted, for example, that converts at Ningpo were pupils at the schools, teachers, assistants, servants — all supported by church funds — while those at Shanpo accrued no financial gain, but were rather "only losers by being connected with us."[23]

Martin's two longest trips took him to Funghua with a Chinese preacher in 1854 and to Hangchow with Henry Rankin in late 1859. He often traveled at night in an *u-bong jin,* a dark covered boat about thirty feet long and six feet wide that carried several passengers and their luggage and afforded sleeping space as well.[24] As the rivers narrowed, he used smaller boats, or proceeded overland either by foot or carried in a palanquin.[25] He usually slept in monasteries even though they were "seats of idolatry." He occupied his daylight hours on these treks preaching in temples, sometimes to crowds of thousands, in pagodas, or in public halls made available to him; in distributing tracts and booklets; and in discussing the faith with the brave few who invited him into their homes. He shunned street preaching as "derogatory to the dignity of the Gospel."[26] Although Martin did not carry firearms to protect himself, he was careful to avoid confrontation with both the ever-present robbers and with antagonistic officials.[27]

The schools established by the missionaries in Ningpo were basically evangelistic in intent. Most of the educational strategies used in the 1850's were well established before Martin arrived on the field. In February, 1851, less than a year after he reached Ningpo, he established a day school not far from his home outside the South Gate, and in May of the same year, opened another day school inside the South Gate.[28] These schools, each with an attendance of about twenty, utilized various religious materials and some books on secular subjects, written by Karl Gutzlaff and other missionaries. In time, Martin would add to them himself.[29]

Nearly all missionaries not tied down with other responsibilities opened day schools,[30] and the school buildings were used for religious services in the evenings and on Sundays. Attendance at these services and the constant assimilation of Bible doctrine in the classroom made converts of a few students, who then disseminated the Gospel message to their neighborhoods.[31] Teachers in Martin's schools, and in the other day schools, were usually graduates of the Boys' Boarding School. It was the seedbed for teachers, preachers, and Chinese Christian citizens who had learned a trade on the school premises or through the school's system of apprenticing students to the local shops.[32]

Christian schools, more than most aspects of missionary work, threatened the structure of Chinese society by offering an alternate sort of education. Unofficial pressure forced one of Martin's schools to close in September, 1851. Persons claiming to represent city officials made minute inquiry concerning Chinese people working for foreigners or attending their schools. A wave of fear came over teachers, servants, and particularly the pupils and their families. After the school recessed for its annual vacation in

August, it was never able to get its students back.[33]

Although not directly involved in either, Martin felt that the Female Boarding School and the Boys' Boarding School were essential to the work of spreading the Gospel. He noted that women converts, freed from "the dupes of a crafty [Buddhist] priesthood who knew well how to take advantage of their ignorance," could save male converts from going astray and become "mothers of Christian families which God can use mightily for the conversion of the Empire."[34]

The Boys' Boarding School, in Martin's view, compared "favorably with the catalogue of studies in our American academies of medium rank," a statement he substantiated by frequently pointing to the academic attainment of some of its better students.[35] He admitted that "the scientific department is still deficient, owing to the scant supply of textbooks." He then added, and this is a significant clue to his early thinking, that

> It may fairly be doubted whether the style of education imparted is not better calculated to fit the pupils for usefulness among their semi-barbarious country men, than if it were Europeanized by a larger invasion of Western science.[36]

At this stage of his life, Martin viewed science as valuable for presenting the Gospel, but science took second place to evangelism among the masses, and to a system of general apologetics for the intellectuals. His colleague, Dr. Daniel MacGowan of the American Baptist Mission, who taught astronomy at Ningpo's Moon Lake College, an institution sponsored by the local mandarins, was even more reserved about the use of science,[37] refusing to use it in his lectures or magic lantern presentations in the Baptist chapel, since using it might make the Chinese believe that Christianity and science were the same and that to have one was to have the other. A similar attitude was expressed by the pioneer American Baptist missionary, Adoniram Judson, who had little patience with those who sought to prepare the Burmese mind to accept Christianity by using astronomical and geological concepts which broke down the cosmology of the Buddhist religion.[38]

Although Martin wrote a number of booklets during his Ningpo years,[39] one of his most significant literary ministries was his participation in the translation of the New Testament into the colloquial Ningpo language. This was a cooperative venture to translate the Scriptures, supervised by a local committee formed by the Ningpo mission groups.[40] Most of the work was done by Henry Rankin of the Presbyterians with the help of Dr. McCartee and Martin. With William Russel's help, Martin translated the first editions of John and Matthew in 1853,[41] but he apparently made little contribution to the remainder of the New Testament, which was completed in 1854. He translated large portions of the Psalms for use in public worship, and these selections were published in 1858.[42]

Even before his arrival in Ningpo, Martin was deeply interested in the question of opium.[43] During 1856 he spent several months preparing a book on the subject. The first two parts included a fictitious narrative describing the evil of opium use and traffic, and revealed something of the injury that the opium trade brought to China, to India, and to Great Britain. The final section was a chronicle of the pertinent facts concerning trade and legislation involving opium.[44]

One of his missionary colleagues, probably McCartee, complained to the Board about Martin wasting so much time on a useless project, to which Martin replied that "the missionaries are the only ones to speak out — the merchants are involved and the officials are fearful."[45] He further observed that "if the early missionaries had done more in pointing out the enormity of the opium evil, a curse might have been averted from China and a mountainous obstacle out of the way of Christian missions."[46]

This question was obviously embarrassing to the missionaries, who were frequently asked if they smoked or traded in opium.[47] Several hundred chests of opium were sold each month in Ningpo, and since many Americans were involved, there was some basis to Chinese suspicions of the missionaries.[48] Martin compared the whole business to the problem of liquor in the United States, and bluntly accused moneyed interests in England and America of kindling the horrid fires beneath the altar of an "insatiable Moloch" which annually consumed half a million Chinese.[49] He entertained the hope, very forlorn he confessed, that the increasing influence of the Gospel in China might "become effective far beyond the pale of the churches."[50]

In learning the spoken Chinese language at Ningpo without

the help of grammars or vocabulary lists, Martin found it helpful to devise a Romanized alphabet system, and did so in January, 1851. Otherwise, he would have had to immediately learn the complicated Chinese written system, thus further prolonging his period of study.[51]

This system was so convenient for his purposes that he taught it to his teacher and was greatly surprised to receive from him a nicely written invitation to dinner a few days later. When he shared this glad news with his fellow-Presbyterians, Dr. McCartee reacted negatively, but after several of the Church Missionary Society missionaries had shown interest, even he was willing to join in the experimental use of this tool.[52]

After the new alphabet had passed through the initial, experimental stage, it was introduced into several missionary schools, both those run by the Presbyterians and by other groups in Ningpo. Early in July, 1851, Martin petitioned the Publication Committee of the Presbyterians in Ningpo to allow its use in the female school and the Boys' Boarding School. The request was referred to the Executive Committee, who took it up with the Board at home. Martin, vacationing at Chusan, supported his plea with numerous arguments.

His principal rationale for Romanization was that it provided a speedy method for the ninety-five percent of the Chinese population that was illiterate in the complex character system to learn how to read. He argued that Chinese schools could make it their aim to teach the character, but that Presbyterian schools must have a higher purpose, namely training the mind and giving it useful information in the sciences and Western literature. For this, he reasoned, only the colloquial was sufficient, and the greater amount of knowledge obtained by the students would continue to enhance the reputation of the schools and attract more students. He also argued that Romanization would be a useful classroom tool for the missionary teachers, that it would increase the literacy of women, and that it would promote true Bible understanding which could become the basis for the deepened meaning of public worship.[53]

McCartee's objections, whether real or designed to hide more basic personal differences with Martin and his clique within the mission circle, were summed up in his conviction that with diligence the Chinese could learn the classical system and that the colloquial could be best taught, as demonstrated by missionaries such as William Boone, an American Episcopalian, and Walter Medhurst of the LMS, through the character. He pointed out that an experiment in Romanization had failed in Singapore and that in one of the Ningpo Presbyterian day schools over half of the pupils had been frightened away by it. Furthermore, he added, even should the system overcome its present defects and succeed perfectly, two suppositions he was not ready to concede, it could not work for all dialects, would be used only by people taught in mission schools, and would not displace the character.[54]

By the spring of 1852 Rankin reported that the mission was more ready to receive the Romanized script. It was being used to print a few booklets, and a Bible translation project, involving even McCartee, had been commenced in conjunction with the London Missionary Society.[55] At the annual meeting opposition to the Roman character had lessened to the extent that a motion was passed authorizing its use up to two hours each day as one of the regular studies in all the mission schools.[56]

The experiment continued during the next two years, both in the schools and in literature production. At the 1854 annual meeting the proponents of Romanization, encouraged by their success, overstepped themselves and boldly rammed through a resolution that the new script be made central in their educational system and that the character be used only with the more intelligent students.[57] McCartee protested angrily to the Board, claiming that results did not justify its wholesale use, and that the mission could not afford to let three men, who viewed the character as a "curse," push the standard Chinese written system out of the schools.[58] Martin and his friends were hardly deficient in their mastery of the written language,[59] but at least one of them saw Romanization as a "Christianized alphabet so to speak."[60] At a later time Martin himself expressed the view that Romanization was a "medium better adapted to the purposes of a Christian civilization."[61]

McCartee branded W. A. P. Martin

> . . . the originator of most of the new measures proposed . . . he is disposed to make remarks calculated to wound the feelings of those who can't think as he does, and hence we sometimes yield rather than provoke discussion. . . . It is time the truth was known. . . .[62]

The Board listened to McCartee, and reversed the decision of the mission conference at Ningpo. When Rankin learned of this setback, he was "deeply grieved . . . and felt I should resign, but there is no one to take my place and so I won't for a while."[63] Martin did not record his reactions, but he apparently accepted this reversal — a conservative decision which would thwart outreach in favor of teaching a classical system — with some grace and continued along the many avenues of service open to him. Books in the Romanized alphabet proliferated and met a need in the churches.

In later years Martin admitted that his early hopes for the use of the Romanized script with non-Christian Chinese, in either the colloquial or Mandarin, had not been realized.[64] He continued to sense the need, however, for a written medium of communication that would provide the masses a "way of escape from China's intellectual thraldom" and expressed the hope that the Imperial University might experiment with a new system.[65] An even more optimistic dream, expressed in 1907 when an international committee had prepared a standard orthography, was that a good alphabet system would abolish local dialects and make China a "people of one speech."[66]

These various missionary efforts to produce a simplified script stimulated reform activities by many capable Chinese educators in the early 1900's and led, ultimately, in the Republican period, to the National Phonetic Alphabet, the National Language Romanization, and other systems seeking linguistic unification of the Chinese empire.[67]

With all of the missionaries, including William Martin, producing tracts, booklets, and books, both in classical Chinese and in the Ningpo colloquial, a point of sore contention was the term to be used for the name of God. The problem was not new, and it refused to go away. Roman Catholics had wrangled over this for over a century in the celebrated "Rites Controversy" of the 1600's and 1700's and they ultimately settled on the newly developed term *t'ien-chu,* translated literally, "Heavenly Lord."

In general, the Protestants argued over two indigenous terms, *shen* and *shang-ti,* which, according to one's viewpoint, had no, little, or a great deal of idolatrous connotation. The first Protestant translations of the Scriptures by Robert Morrison in 1819, and by Joshua Marshman, English Baptist missionary, in

1822, used the term *shen* for God. When Morrison's version was revised in the mid-1830's, principally by Walter Medhurst and Karl Gutzlaff, they adopted *shang-ti* as the word for the true God and *shen* for lesser gods.[68] This revision was not fully acceptable to many, and in 1843 plans were laid for a new translation, to be called the Delegates' Version. The entire body of Protestant missionaries in China, no more than seventy or eighty persons, constituted the General Committee. The work was subdivided among local committees in each of the five treaty ports, cross-checked carefully with each center, and then referred to a final committee of elected delegates who met in Shanghai. Unable to agree on the term to be used for God, the New Testament committee left a blank space wherever the Divine name appeared, and allowed whichever Bible Society or agency might publish this version to fill in the term it preferred.[69] The American Bible Society edition used *shen* and the British and Foreign Bible Society adopted *shang-ti*.[70]

Presbyterian missionaries in Ningpo had been involved in this controversy before Martin's arrival. Walter Lowrie, before his tragic death at the hands of pirates in 1847, was the Ningpo representative working on the Delegates' Version of the Bible in Shanghai. He stood resolutely for *shen,* as did McCartee and most of the other Presbyterian missionaries.[71]

Further disputes, involving general principles of translation, embroiled the Old Testament Committee of the Delegates' Version, and resulted in the London Missionary Society's representatives separating to prepare their own version in 1851. Elijah Bridgman, ABCFM delegate, and William Culbertson, loaned to the project by the Ningpo American Presbyterian Mission, continued on their own and eventually completed the New Testament in 1862. Bridgman and others later produced a translation of the Old Testament. The Bridgman and Culbertson Version, as it came to be known, used *shen,* while the LMS Version continued the general British preference for *shang-ti*.[72]

The "term" controversy at Ningpo, which had probably brewed for several months, was thrown vigorously at the Foreign Mission Board of the Presbyterian Church by the protagonists in the fall of 1854. The occasion was a request, ultimately rejected by the Executive Committee of the Board, to allow the use of both *shang-ti* and *shen* in Martin's *Evidences of Christianity.* Martin used several arguments to defend his unusual request. First, he noted that even though *shen* might be the best word for God in the Sacred Scriptures, this preference need not extend to every piece of literature. Second, he argued the word *shang-ti* was a "title admirably suited to express the majesty of the Divine character." His third contention raised the question as to how the term *shang-ti* could be thought "idolatrous" when such a large number of heterogeneous missionaries — English and American, churchmen and dissenters, men from varied denominational affiliations — used it. He reported a recent revival in Amoy where God was called *shang-ti* and asked how this could happen where idolatry was taught. In the fourth place, he appealed to the example of the Taiping rebels, whose use of both terms presented the missionaries with the opportunity to accommodate to their phraseology and help to "reclaim them from error." Martin was not prepared to admit that the use of *shang-ti* in China's ancient books was idolatrous. Following the lead of James Legge, renowned LMS missionary scholar, he believed that the Chinese classics, unencumbered by the emendations of later converts of the Sung scholar, Chu Hsi, presented the picture of a deity without "form or body . . . and having justice, wisdom, power and goodness." If this were true the current manifestation of Chinese religion could be perceived as a devolution from its high beginning.[73]

Dr. McCartee contested the propriety of using both terms interchangeably, arguing that it would mistakenly teach that "the *shang-ti* of the Chinese classics *is* the Creator of all things." This, in his view, would break the First Commandment by exalting to the state of deity what Chinese everywhere clearly regarded to be an idol. He vowed to "protest printing this on our press as long as God gives me breath to speak."[74]

John Quarterman, in charge of the Presbyterian press, was equally adamant, and refused to proof, print, or circulate anything asking "a Chinese to worship the greatest of six idols." He accused Martin of using his book as a wedge to get *shang-ti* into the Scriptures themselves, and recommended that Martin publish *Evidences of Christianity* with his own money.[75]

Martin's supporters, largely the younger missionaries, outnumbered their opponents. His brother and John Nevius, although not too vocal, could always be counted on.[76] Rankin, strongly echoing Martin's views, stressed that Protestants did not have a Pope to solve the problem for them, but that God was working through the Taipings, like Martin advocates of both terms, to bring a solution.[77]

The Executive Committee of the Board objected strongly to Martin's avowed position that "the Chinese classics teach the worship of the true God" and expressed the view that "if these ideas are in the book [*Evidences of Christianity*] prepared to be printed, the Committee will object to it being printed at the Mission Press."[78]

Related to the question of "Christianity in Chinese" was the issue of which Bible version the missionaries ought to use in their work. In 1854 Martin and Rankin had started a theological class for the instruction of catechists. Although church history, natural theology, didactic theology, reading of religious allegories like *Pilgrim's Progress,* and homiletics were part of the curriculum, Scripture exegesis and exposition dominated. Martin and Rankin believed that a lucid version of the Scripture was necessary for this class.[79]

The version which the mission conference approved provisionally, while waiting for Bridgman and Culbertson to finish their work, was a translation made by Josiah Goddard, an American Baptist in Ningpo. Although it contained several "Baptistisms," as Rankin called them, it was judged to be better than the Delegates' Version or the London Missionary Society translation.[80] McCartee, already angry at Martin over the issue of a proper term for God, accused him of introducing the LMS Bible both to the theological class and to the Boys' Boarding School. This really did not surprise him, McCartee confessed, for "verbal accuracy and strict fidelity to the original are of little importance in the eyes of this brother compared with classic elegance of style providing the general idea is retained."[81]

Martin, responding to an Executive Committee request that he cease using the LMS Bible in his classes, claimed that he always had the Greek before him as he taught and that he used all of the versions available. He pleaded for the Foreign Board to show more toleration, reasoning that "missionaries will work better when allowed some liberty. Conscientious men who are acquainted with Greek, Hebrew, and Chinese should be presumed capable of deciding these matters and allowed to do so."[82]

Disputes over where missionaries should live, whether to use Romanization or not, the term for God, the proper version of the Bible, and a multitude of other issues, large and small, made mission meetings very tense. McCartee compared them to "a college debating society" with "loud declamations, satirical remarks, dictatorial decisions . . . and disparaging of personalities."[83] In his angrier moments he saw Martin as the culprit.

> The brother who always takes the lead on these occasions is an estimable man in many respects but is fickle, impetuous, hasty, and impatient of control or opposition. He has read a great deal, but not systematized what he has acquired and often advocates the most contrary doctrine or opinions. He is apparently predisposed to advocate the opposite of the usual or ordinary view of things, to show his independence of mind or to startle us by his originality.[84]

At another time he described him as a

> . . . good man and I trust a devotedly pious man and a useful man — very quick and brilliant but very sudden and hasty in his fancies. He is impatient of delay or opposition and often unscrupulous and harsh by the means and language by which he seeks to carry his point.[85]

When the heat of the discussion was past, McCartee's more objective evaluation was that

> We are composed of very heterogeneous materials. Some were brought up as Congregationalists and never entered the Presbyterian church till seminary and would like to follow the way they were brought up. Some of us were brought up among the strictest kind of old school and anti-new measure Presbyterians. Some, though Presbyterian, think sessions are out of place on the mission field. Some ladies prefer not to be connected with the Presbyterian church on the field but have 'all things in common' with those of other missions.[86]

Hardly the "strikingly homogeneous" group analyzed by Sidney Forsythe, this Ningpo community was a microcosm of its fragmented home constituency.[87]

Here, then, was the nub of the problem — different backgrounds, different perspectives, and very different personalities. What McCartee feared more than anything else about

Martin was what he took to be Martin's defective theological outlook. As a layman with a rather narrow training in medicine, McCartee did not have the educational background to fully understand some of Martin's beliefs. McCartee accused him of holding an heretical view on the Triune Godhead more akin to tritheism than to monotheism. Martin, he claimed, did not deny this but candidly admitted his inability to accept the orthodox formulas. He accused him of indoctrinating some candidates for baptism with these views, creating a difficult situation for the session which examined them.[88] McCartee speculated that his colleague's deviant beliefs were not discovered in America since he was "ordained before he was asked to subscribe to the Confession of Faith. Later when asked [if he did subscribe] he said, 'So far as he believed it to agree with the Bible.'"[89]

The cutting edge of the dispute was seen in terms of the admission of candidates to baptism. McCartee specifically postulated an elderly Confucian scholar who had no "sorrow for sin" and saw Christianity only as a completion of the Confucian doctrine. Martin, McCartee claimed, would baptize him right away and instruct him later.[90]

This type of disagreement over who could or could not be baptized touched at the very heart of still another issue. There was but one organized Presbyterian church in Ningpo, and the pastor — earlier Culbertson and later Way — controlled the session, and the procedures and qualifications for baptism. When the session made a questionable decision about a rotation plan for communion between the English and Chinese branches of the church, the Presbytery reversed it. Way resigned his position, and Nevius was elected to take his place. Before he could accept, William and Samuel Martin used their influence with the Chinese to persuade them not to have a pastor but to continue with Rankin as a stated supply.[91] Later, according to Way, Martin asserted that his intention was to "break up the church session so that everyone could have an equal voice [and thus baptize whom they desire] in church matters."[92]

Martin, though a Presbyterian by conviction, was not in favor of tight ecclesiastical control. The same majority that had precipitated near-dissolution of the session wished to give free rein to the work of Chinese catechists. Way complained that

> Native assistants are allowed to go into the surrounding territory without mission members to give out literature, to speak, and to do everything except dispense the ordinances. They are not really prepared and may be wrong in what they say. This makes them feel independent of us and violates Presbyterian order.[93]

Way was ready to grant wider freedom to Chinese workers only after they had served with a missionary in a one-year internship involving itineration.

These differences were a "matter of grief" to the Executive Committee at home, but there was no solution in sight. The Executive Committee reminded mission members that "the Providence of God has brought each individual of us into a certain relationship with all the others."[94] Way thought that the Ningpo personnel ought to be divided with the "brothers Martin" separated from the rest.[95] McCartee feared that the only method might be to pacify them, for "we couldn't force them for they would quit to start another church." He noted, for example, that Martin gave potential converts over to the

> . . . English Episcopal Mission who are not so strict in requiring actual proof of conversion and intelligent faith before baptism. . . . These men are not Presbyterian and for those of us who are it is difficult to work with them.[96]

All of the missionaries insisted that their differences concerned policy matters only, and that "in our social relations, no mission could get on more smoothly or harmoniously than ours."[97] This was not apparent to outsiders, and in the *North China Herald* Dr. MacGowan of the American Baptists commented sarcastically on the internal conflicts within the Presbyterian mission, suggesting that these, as well as the Presbyterians' vacillation when confronted with danger in a couple of instances, "had done irreparable damage to the missionary cause at Ningpo. . . ."[98]

After fifteen years of work, what types of results could Martin and his Presbyterian colleagues at Ningpo report? The church, including the congregation in the city and the three in the outstations, had received a total of one hundred fifty-one members. Sixteen of these were engaged as colporteurs, teachers, or catechists, including three preparing for the ministry. Only one day school remained in Ningpo proper, but the Boys' Boarding School and Girls' Boarding School continued. Thirty-two books, pamphlets, and tracts, representing a total published volume of 9,000,000 pages, were in print in 1860.[99]

These statistics were neither spectacular nor contemptible — about average in comparison to the other treaty ports. This was a period of exposure and experimentation. Cautious probes to spread the Gospel were made inland, but fears were expressed that unless God moved in His providence to open doors in a more dramatic way, no really great harvest would be reaped. W. A. P. Martin, already a pioneer in innovative missionary methods, was anxious to be God's agent in developing supplementary means of attack. He strongly believed that God moved in "mysterious ways his wonders to perform," and he hoped that these wonders might either come through the advent of a new "Christian" dynasty or through forcing the old one to throw its doors more widely open.

Notes

1. W. A. P. Martin, *A Cycle of Cathay* (3rd ed.; New York, 1900), 53.

2. Margaret Wylie Martin to her mother, #2, December 25, 1854. Harris Collection, Indiana University Archives. China Letters of the Board of Foreign Missions of the Presbyterian Church in the United States of America, III, Ningpo, Coulter to Board, #159, October 4, 1850. China Letters are subsequently abbreviated "CL." $50 was budgeted annually for purchasing books.

3. Among the 525 volumes were Nichelson's *Encyclopedia*, various Bible Commentaries, Calvin's *Institutes*, Alexander's *Evidences of Christianity*, Paley's *Natural Theology*, Williams' *Middle Kingdom*, thirty volumes of *The Missionary Herald*, twenty volumes of *The Chinese Repository*, ten volumes of *The Missionary Chronicle*, and many single volumes on geography, ancient history, and grammar. *Catalogue of the Presbyterian Mission Library* (Ningpo, 1851).

4. CL, III, Ningpo, McCartee to Board, #160, October 5, 1850.

5. CL, III, Ningpo, McCartee to Board, #214, March 10, 1852.

6. CL, IV, Ningpo, Way to Board, #32, November 14, 1854.

7. City gates closed at dusk and there were no boats to cross the river. Missionaries living on the north bank were not able then to work in the city at night and return home.

8. The material of this paragraph comes from CL, IV, Ningpo, Martin to Board, #45, 1854, n.d. This is an Annual Letter to accompany the Annual Report of early October.

9. CL, IV, Ningpo, Samuel Martin to Board, #34, December 5, 1854.

10. Martin, *Cycle,* 67.

11. E. B. Inslee, Letter, *The Home and Foreign Record,* VIII (December, 1857), 373.

12. W. A. P. Martin, "Journal Extracts," *The Home and Foreign Record,* VI (August, 1855), 244.

13. Martin, *Cycle,* 66; William Russel, Letter to *Church Missionary Gleaner,* V (March, 1855), 35-36.

14. CL, IV, Ningpo, Inslee to Board, #248, 1859.

15. Martin, *Cycle,* 58.

16. CL, III, Ningpo, Martin to Board, #184, May 31, 1851.

17. Martin, *Cycle,* 69-70.

18. *Ibid.,* 67-68.

19. CL, IV, Ningpo, Martin to Board, #52, March 31, 1855.

20. CL, IV, Ningpo, Martin to Board, #5, January 30, 1854. "Since my arrival here I have studiously avoided everything which would tend to fix me permanently. I twice declined taking charge of the boys' school. . . ."

21. See book with this title by John L. Nevius (Philadelphia, 1869).

22. CL, III, Ningpo, McCartee to Board, #214, March 10, 1852.

23. John Nevius, "The Work of Grace at San-peh," *The Foreign Missionary,* XVI (November, 1857), 187.

24. Nevius, "San-peh," 6-9. The Romanized name of the boat is in the Ningpo Chinese language.

25. W. A. P. Martin, "Narrative of a Visit to the District of Funghua," *The Home and Foreign Record,* V (February, 1854), 48.

26. Martin, *Cycle,* 110-11.

27. His good Presbyterian friend, Calvin Mateer, carried a revolver with him for self-defense when itinerating in Shantung, North China, as also did Timothy Richard, the noted Baptist missionary, on at least one occasion. Daniel W. Fisher, *Calvin Wilson Mateer: Forty-Five Years a Missionary in Shantung, China* (Philadelphia, 1911), 124; Timothy Richard, *Forty-Five Years in China: Reminiscences* (London, 1916), 40.

28. CL, II, Loomis and Culbertson to Board, #194, October 1, 1851. Martin's first school was started with his own money and then turned over to the mission. Eighth Annual Report. CL, III, Ningpo, #194, October, 1851.

29. *Ibid.*, and CL, II, Ningpo, Rankin to Board, #188, July 14, 1851. He mentioned Martin's "excellent" geography to be used in Martin's school and in the boarding schools.

30. Jane Martin established a girls' day school with the actual instructing done by Chinese teachers. "Thirteenth Annual Report: Ningpo Mission," *The Foreign Missionary*, XV (March, 1857), 311.

31. *Ibid.*, and W. A. P. Martin, "Journal Extracts," *The Home and Foreign Record*, IV (July, 1853), 209.

32. W. A. P. Martin, "Interesting Examination of Two Young Men With Reference to Licensure to Teach," *The Home and Foreign Record*, XI (May, 1860), 149; CL, III, #194; CL, III, Committee to Board, #244, February 15, 1853.

33. CL, III, Ningpo, Coulter to Board, #197, September 30, 1851.

34. CL, III, Ningpo, Martin to Board, #205, November 2, 1851.

35. Martin, "Interesting Examination," 148-49. Two graduates, seeking licensure to teach in the day schools, successfully passed an examination which comprised long memoriter recitations from the Chinese classics, the Westminster Catechism and the Bible, translation and exposition of textbooks, drilling on theology and apologetics, and a composition on the theme "We Know But In Part" in classical Chinese as well as in the local vernacular.

36. *Ibid.*

37. Daniel MacGowan, Letter, *The Missionary Magazine*, XXXI (December, 1851), 441-42.

38. Robert Torbet, *Venture of Faith* (Philadelphia, 1955), 59.

39. These include *Evidences of Christianity*, 1854; *The Three Principles; Religious Allegories; Paul's Discourse at Athens; Form of Church Government; The Assembly's Shorter Catechism*. He also wrote two short texts on geography and one on arithmetic.

40. CL, III, Ningpo, Rankin to Board, #213, March 3, 1852.

41. Note appended to cover of these Ningpo portions kept in library of American Bible Society, New York, New York.

42. Alexander Wylie, *Memorials of Protestant Missionaries to the Chinese* (Shanghai, 1867), 205. These included Psalms 1-34, 42, 46, 50, 51, 63, 65, 72, 84, 90, 91, 95, 96, 100, 103, 104, 110, 115-18, 121, 130, 139, and 145.

43. Letter, Rankin to Martin, January 26, 1850, found in Appendix of Mary Boggs, "William Alexander Parsons Martin: Missionary to China, 1850-1916" (unpublished M. A. thesis, McCormick Theological Seminary, 1948), 4. This letter appears to be in answer to Martin's inquiries, but it did not reach him before his embarkation.

44. CL, IV, Ningpo, Letter to Board, #83, February 25, 1856, and

Martin to Board, #86, May 22. 1856. Although many missionaries recognized the value of what he was doing, even offering to help facilitate its publication either in England or America, it apparently was never published. Unfortunately, the section of the "Two American Embassies," dealing with opium, possibly this manuscript, is missing.

45. CL, IV, Ningpo, Martin to Board, #86, May 22, 1856.

46. CL, IV, Ningpo, Martin to Board, #233, November 16, 1859.

47. M. J. Knowlton, Letter, *The Missionary Magazine*, XXXVII (April, 1857), 105.

48. Eldon Griffin, *Clippers and Consuls* (Ann Arbor, 1938), 301.

49. Martin, "Journal Extracts," *The Home and Foreign Record*, VI (August, 1855), 244.

50. Martin, *Cycle*, 88.

51. A later assessment that the Ningpo project was "the first attempt to introduce Romanization to the Chinese" overlooked earlier Catholic efforts under Matteo Ricci and many earlier Protestant activities, all among overseas Chinese in Penang, Singapore, and Amoy. J. A. Silsby, "Ningpo Romanization," *The Chinese Recorder*, XXXIV (September, 1903), 457; John De Francis, *Nationalism and Language Reform in China* (Princeton, 1950), 15. John De Francis observed that "in the fifteen year period between 1851 and 1866 some thirty-seven missionaries, more than one-tenth of all the Protestant missionaries who had ever worked in China, published Chinese materials in some form of phonetic script." 22.

52. Martin, *Cycle*, 54-55. Apparently he and others were miffed that Martin had worked out the details of the system with the CMS and then, supported by only a few of his own mission, had made *formal* application to the Presbyterian Press to print Romanized materials. CL, V, Shanghai, Culbertson to Board, #29, October 16, 1851.

53. CL, III, Ningpo, Martin to Board, #189, August 4, 1851.

54. *Ibid.*

55. CL, III, Ningpo, McCartee to Board, #204, October 17, 1851; CL, III, Ningpo, Rankin to Board, #213, March 3, 1852.

56. CL, III, Rankin to Board, #227, October 2, 1852.

57. CL, IV, Ningpo, McCartee to Board, #24, October 5, 1854; CL, IV, Ningpo, #39, October 1, 1854. Eleventh Annual Meeting.

58. CL, IV, Ningpo, McCartee to Board, #24, October 5, 1854. The three apparently were the two Martins (women did not vote) and Rankin. McCartee claimed that nine out of ten women servants could not use it, that only two Chinese adults had mastered it and that "our scholars can't read anything else."

59. Martin, *Cycle*, 58-64, defended his own proficiency against this objection.

60. CL, II, Ningpo, Rankin to Board, #188, July 14, 1851.

61. W. A. P. Martin, *The Lore of Cathay* (New York, 1901), 229.

62. CL, IV, Ningpo, McCartee to Board, #39, October 1, 1854.

63. CL, IV, Ningpo, Rankin to Board, #59, June 1, 1855.

64. CL, IV, Ningpo, Martin to Board, #17, July 7, 1854. He began to doubt even at this time that the colloquial script would spread among the people, although it "still is the only way the unlettered will ever have access to the Word of Life." As for its use with the "Court or Common dialect," this will only come when China has "Christian rulers who desire to put the Bible into the hands of all classes of their subjects." See also Martin, *Cycle,* 56.

65. W. A. P. Martin, "A Plea for the Romanizing of Local Dialects," *The Chinese Recorder,* XXXIII (January, 1902), 19.

66. W. A. P. Martin, "A Plea for Romanization," *The Chinese Recorder,* XXXVIII (September, 1907), 502.

67. De Francis, *Nationalism and Language Reform*, 52-57.

68. Douglas G. Spelman, "Christianity in Chinese: The Protestant Term Question," *Papers on China,* XXIIA (Cambridge, Mass., 1969), 28. *Shen* is a generic term for "god," while *shang-ti* means "heaven" or "Supreme Emperor."

69. Marshall Broomhall, *The Bible in China* (London, 1934), 63.

70. Kenneth S. Latourette, *A History of Christian Missions in China* (London, 1929), 262.

71. CL, III, E. C. Bridgman to Board, #64, November 22, 1847; McCartee to Board, #11, February 16, 1845.

72. James Dennis, *Centennial Survey of Foreign Missions* (New York, 1902), 134-37; Latourette, *Missions in China,* 262-63.

73. CL, IV, Ningpo, Martin to Board, #26, October 12, 1854.

74. CL, IV, Ningpo, Martin to Board, #24, October 5, 1854.

75. CL, IV, Ningpo, Quarterman to Board, #29, October 10, 1854.

76. Mrs. Nevius wrote that her husband adhered to the Old School but that he was "by no means extreme in his devotion to that branch of the church." Helen Nevius, *The Life of John L. Nevius* (New York, 1895), 266. This would imply a flexible attitude which, in China at this time, might reveal itself in a preference for the term *shang-ti*.

77. CL, IV, Ningpo, Rankin to Board, October, 1854.

78. CL, IX, Outgoing to Ningpo, #94, February 12, 1855.

79. CL, IV, Ningpo, Report on Theological Class, #37, October 1, 1854, and #72, October 1, 1855.

80. CL, IV, Ningpo, Rankin to Board, #59, June 1, 1855.

81. CL, IV, Ningpo, McCartee to Board, #24, October 5, 1854. Several missionaries objected to the LMS translation. It was a free rendering, eliminated alleged redundancies (such as condensing Genesis 2:2,3 to one verse), seemed not to be based on a doctrine of verbal inspiration, and took liberties with the text, e.g., "wool" in Rev. 1:14 was translated "silk floss." CL, III, Ningpo, McCartee to Board, #180, March 29, 1851; CL, V, Shanghai, Culbertson to Board, #34, December 11, 1851.

82. CL, IV, Ningpo, Martin to Board, #56, March 31, 1855.

83. CL, IV, Ningpo, McCartee to Board, #24, October 5, 1854.

84. *Ibid.*

85. CL, IV, Ningpo, McCartee to Board, #52, March 31, 1855.

86. CL, III, Ningpo, McCartee to Board, #252, July 5, 1853.

87. Sidney Forsythe, *An American Missionary Community in China, 1895-1905* (Cambridge, Mass., 1971), 11.

88. CL, III, Ningpo, McCartee to Board, #252, July 5, 1853, and IV, Ningpo, #52, March 31, 1855. Many years later Martin half-jestingly wrote that "their answers touching the mystery of the hypostatic union of persons in the Trinity came very near getting their instructor in trouble. Their statements were objected to as smacking of Sabellianism, which in them was imputed as ignorance but in me was denounced as heresy." He noted that he and Culbertson had a pleasant exchange of correspondence on the matter. Martin, *Cycle*, 69.

89. CL, III, Ningpo, McCartee to Board, #252, July 5, 1853.

90. CL, IV, Ningpo, McCartee to Board, #52, March 31, 1855.

91. Samuel Martin's side was that "the church members did not want an election and drew up a petition to the effect." CL, IV, Ningpo, Samuel Martin to Board, #82, February 22, 1856.

92. CL, IV, Ningpo, Way to Board, #32, November 14, 1854; Samuel Martin to Board, #82, February 22, 1856.

93. CL, IV, Ningpo, Way to Board, #55, April 28, 1855.

94. CL, VIII, Outgoing to Ningpo, #55, January 20, 1852.

95. CL, IV, Ningpo, Way to Board, #32, November 14, 1854. The problem was not just with them, according to their opponents, but with their ability to influence others more orthodox than they, such as Nevius who "has a disposition naturally inclined to yield even important questions rather than strive or argue for them." CL, IV, Ningpo, McCartee to Board, #170, Nov. 22, 1858.

96. CL, IV, Ningpo, McCartee to Board, #57, May 31, 1855.

97. CL, III, Ningpo, McCartee to Board, #252, July 5, 1853.

98. CL, IV, Ningpo, Inslee to Board, #104, March 27, 1857.

99. *Twenty-fourth Annual Report,* Board of Foreign Missions of the Presbyterian Church, 1861, 72-75.

CHAPTER FOUR

Agent of God's Providence in Opening China's Doors to the Gospel?

MISSIONARY INTERPRETATION of how God's sovereignty opened China's doors to the Gospel differed very little from the Chinese concept of the "Mandate of Heaven." The rise and fall of Chinese dynasties, usually after decades of destructive struggle, was explained in terms of the supernatural in order to make it acceptable to the masses.

> The people accepted the winner as part of an overwhelming fate ... thus the awe and respect for the supernatural was a vital factor in putting the coat of morality and honor on a dynastic founder, who was basically a master at the manipulation of force and violence.[1]

No moral guidelines helped to determine the Mandate of Heaven; it was a fatalistic explanation for what had already occurred. Heaven had given its verdict — man must accept the decision unquestioningly.

Ironically, this was often the philosophy of Christian missions in China. Note, for example, the evaluation given in a recent book,

> In the 1840's the Christian church, like a mighty army, moved into China with its banners flying. On these banners were inscribed the words of Scripture: 'I am He that openeth and no man shutteth.' One hundred years later the church was on the march again, but this time it was coming out of China. Its banners, tattered and torn, were dragging in the dust. But on those banners were inscribed the words of Scripture: 'I am He that shutteth and no man openeth.' By purely human definition the first event was a victory.

The second was a tragedy. But both were engineered by God. It was He who opened the door in the 1840's. It was He who closed the door in the 1940's.[2]

Foreigners were free to occupy treaty ports, and there was limited opportunity to preach. Therefore, *ex post facto,* this must be a door that God had opened. No other criteria were utilized to determine whether this was, in fact, God's open door. And when the missionaries left — partially because of uncontrollable forces set in motion by circumstances surrounding their own entry into China — it was also God's will, albeit a tragedy. God's providence, in both instances, became a convenient means to gloss over human error and to excuse the need for ethical judgment. And to the degree that some of God's servants were involved in the actual process of forcing the door open, the Christian movement espoused the doctrine that the end justified the means.

Early American missionaries in China were always closely linked with their own government in political and diplomatic activities. Dr. Peter Parker and Elijah Bridgman, for example, acted as joint secretaries to the American Legation, under Caleb Cushing, that was responsible for negotiating the Treaty of Wanghia with China in July, 1844. Parker later served in a variety of government posts culminating with his appointment as United States Commissioner to China in 1855.[3] Samuel Wells Williams, a missionary with the ABCFM, also assisted in drafting this treaty and later occupied a number of positions with the United States government in Peking.

Of the Presbyterian missionaries in Ningpo, D. B. McCartee, Richard Way, and John Quarterman took up duties with the American consular service, which, far more deficient in men, money, and organization than the British service, was anxious to find any agents who could speak and write Chinese.[4] On one occasion, William Bradley, the American consul in Ningpo, officially asked Martin and Richard Way to assist as assessors in the Consular Court in which one Charles Jackson, an American seaman who had been convicted once previously for attacking a Chinese, was indicted for assault and battery on a British sailor from the *Commorait.*[5] On at least one occasion Martin successfully interceded before the *tao-tai,* the leading local Chinese official in Ningpo, for the life of a tailor — not a Christian convert or inquirer — who was falsely accused of being a soldier with the Triads, a secret society.[6]

Emotionally, W. A. P. Martin was deeply committed to the task of evangelism. Intellectually, he was perplexed by the relatively slow progress of Christianity in China. His reading of history — particularly the story of thousands of conversions to Christ in the South Sea Islands — and his conviction that the true faith must overcome all obstacles, led him to expect that God would certainly do something unexpected to establish His kingdom in China. One possibility was that He was using the new indigenous movement — the Taiping Rebels — to establish a Christian dynasty. Another was that He was unifying the "Christian" nations to force the old dynasty to "give in" and allow Christian missionaries to travel and evangelize throughout China. Martin himself was deeply involved in both of these matters. His concern — as in all of his innovative early activities in Ningpo — was the masses. In these two instances the means were more political than religious, although for one who saw Jehovah as the God of history, such a distinction was ultimately meaningless.

Poor communication within China prevented many missionaries from learning much about the Taiping Rebellion until after it had left its southern base. In Canton some had the "very general impression" that the rebels were "somehow connected with foreigners and Christianity."[7] Not until the summer of 1853 was information concerning the relationship between Hung Hsiu-ch'uan, the Taiping leader, and Issachar Roberts, a Southern Baptist missionary who had instructed him in the Christian faith at Canton, made public to the general missionary body.[8]

The Presbyterian missionaries at Ningpo took notice of the Taiping movement early in 1853. Samuel Martin expressed the hope that it would be "one method by which God will work a revolution in favor of the Gospel," as the old dynasty was demolished.[9] John Quarterman already saw the missionary dilemma: should the rebels win they might "lead instead of following like disciples ... if they are beaten ... the imperialists may suspect us of having originated the whole affair."[10]

W. A. P. Martin's initial recorded reaction interpreted the Taiping movement as beneficial to Christian missions. He suggested that this "stupendous providence" would open the empire to preachers and thus stimulate missionary interest and recruiting in the American churches. His optimism was not shared by A. H.

Happer, a fellow-Presbyterian at Canton, who wrote in *The Presbyterian,*

> The advocates are expecting that a universal gush of sympathy will carry away the Christians of Great Brittain [sic] and the United States in favour of the rebellion owing to their religious creed. This is the reason why I feel more solicitude than might otherwise appear meet to have the religious community set right on this point.[11]

There were many mediating Presbyterian opinions between these two opposite viewpoints.[12] William Culbertson, initially optimistic, found his enthusiasm dimmed by first-hand contact with the rebels when he went to Nanking on the U. S. *Susquehanna* as interpreter for Robert McLane, the United States High Commissioner to China.[13] Joseph Wight felt that the Taipings might ultimately be no better than "Mormons or Mohammedans," but that the church ought to be prepared for a great harvest.[14] Dr. McCartee, possibly as an automatic reaction against Martin's enthusiasm, doubted the success of the rebel cause.[15] Nevius and Rankin were mildly optimistic. The former observed that "God is making them [the rebels] an instrument of punishing this nation for its long continued and gross idolatry" and that their destruction of superstition would open the hearts of the Chinese to the Gospel.[16]

Martin, not content to watch the rebellion at a distance, determined "to exert some influence on the course of events."[17] He felt that the rebels needed instruction to purge their obvious Christian commitment from its gross error. He was less concerned with their heresy than surprised by the truth they evidenced, and with some difficulty he persuaded his Ningpo colleagues to give their blessing to a trip he proposed to make to Nanking in the summer of 1853.[18] McCartee, as would be expected, opposed such a venture. Noting that the British interpreter, Meadows, unlike Martin well-versed in Mandarin, had failed to get through the government lines, he challenged Martin's claims that he could learn enough Mandarin in ten days to make the trip. McCartee pointed out that there were no reliable guides to take anyone into the rebel camp and that, should Martin be stopped by either group, he would be treated as an enemy. He also argued that since the insurgents were given to a policy of indiscriminate slaughter quite opposite to the spirit of Christ, it would be unwise for a missionary to implicate himself in a rebellion against the sovereign of the country. Why not wait, he argued, until missionaries could help them without risking their own cause?[19]

Notwithstanding the opposition, Martin had the necessary conference votes and proceeded to Shanghai. He was not the first missionary to attempt such a hazardous journey. A Methodist missionary, Dr. Charles Taylor, had reached the rebel camp at Chin-kiang in June, 1853, after failing in an earlier attempt in May. In July he made a third attempt with Issachar Roberts and was subsequently turned back from Chin-kiang by the Imperial fleet.[20]

All of these attempts were made over the opposition of Humphrey Marshall, the American High Commissioner to China, who repeatedly warned Taylor and Roberts of the Congressional Act of August 11, 1848, which stated "that murder and insurrection or rebellion against the Chinese government [by Americans resident in China], with interest to subvert the same, shall be capital offenses, punishable with death."[21] Missionaries attempting such journeys also faced obvious danger from Chinese authorities who might deal with them without regard to their rights of extraterritoriality.

Aware of Marshall's prohibition, Martin "put to sea from Woosung in a thunder storm . . . to elude the vigilance of the United States Marshal."[22] He managed to get near Chin-kiang, but after close brushes with the Imperialists and river pirates, he returned to Shanghai. Forty years later he confessed that this venture was "foolhardy," commenting that "there are few men who have not reason if they but know it, to thank God for failure as well as for success."[23]

Marshall was aware of his venture, for in writing about Taylor, he also commented.

> On the return of this missionary, another immediately departed for the same destination; but, not equally adventurous, did not reach Chin-Kiang. These men go out '*to preach the Gospel*,' but their hearts are enlisted in the cause of the rebels.[24]

He was even more blunt in replying to Issachar Roberts' request for permission to visit Hung Hsiu-ch'uan.

Friendship for the Emperor of China is inconsistent with familiarity . . . at the camp fires of his foes. . . . Would not one be worse than the heathen, who, residing under the protection and these treaty guarantees, should assist and encourage . . . the overthrow of the government? . . . The intemperate zeal, or the improper interference with politics of Christian missionaries, in past cultures, closed the eastern empires of China and Japan against intercourse with Western nations. Just emerging from their protected seclusion, it would be most unfortunate for themselves and the world that the first display before the eyes of China and Japan should be the torch of civil war, lighted on the altars of their country by Christian teachers of religion![25]

The Presbyterian Board of Foreign Missions was less than happy with Martin's trip up the Yangtze. They agreed with McCartee that

It is premature in the present state of the contest, for missionaries to visit the camp of the insurgents . . . this cannot be done without the appearance of taking sides with them . . . strict neutrality on the part of the missionaries both in appearance and reality is the wisest course at present.[26]

When the members of the Board learned that the trip had been made, they commented "we would have voted against his going, if we had been there, because of the risk in the present state of the contest."[27]

Missionary enthusiasm for the Taiping insurgents waned in 1854 after military failures; among other things the missionaries became disillusioned with the rebels' Christian profession.[28] Martin's support for the rebellion, based on principle and his understanding of God's providence rather than on Taiping military victories or their pure Christianity, wavered only slightly. He commented that, although he was interested in this great conflict,

We do not fold our hands and await its issue . . . the weapons of our warfare are not carnal, and whatever be the success of those who trust in chariots and horses, it is ours to be instant in the preaching of the Word, watching thereunto with all prayer.[29]

To watching and prayer Martin added study. His own reading of the Taiping literature produced considerable empathy, even for the leaders' many blasphemous claims. Noting, for example, their proclivity to personify natural forces like rain, clouds, thunder, and lightning in their various leaders, he observed that since they had little understanding of total Scriptural truth and since the term used for Holy Ghost in Gutzlaff's Bible was "wind,"[30] it was only natural that their second-in-command would be called "Holy Ghost."[31]

Unfortunately, whatever potential the rebel movement had to either change China or to prepare the way for a more orthodox Christianity, Issachar Roberts, who had the most intimate contact with Hung Hsiu-ch'uan, was not a man of Martin's flexibility. Roberts' limited educational background, violent temper, and inability to distinguish between the important and less important tenets of his faith, led to his departure from the rebel camp and to his downgrading the rebels before his fellow-missionaries.[32]

Fearful that threatened foreign intervention against the rebels would lead to a Manchu victory and reprisals against those who had supported the rebellion,[33] Martin took the case of the Taiping rebels to Caleb Cushing, United States Attorney General and formerly the American High Commissioner to China.[34] In a series of letters to Cushing which were printed in the *North China Herald,* Martin set forth the most systematic public plea on behalf of the Taipings that had yet been made by any American.

In his first letter, Martin clearly stated his religious presupposition: the Taiping rebellion was the "instrument of a superhuman Power." He then pointed out, appealing to past Chinese history, that any war of dynastic succession would be long and bloody but that America should not help prolong the life of the expiring Manchus. He listed several reasons for adopting a policy of neutrality: the Manchus, in effect, had lost the "Mandate of Heaven"; to help them would make the Emperor feel that America was his "tribute state"; Nanking, the rebels' capital, was a far better place from which to rule the Empire than Peking; and to assist the Manchus was to abet them in their racial struggle against the Chinese.[35]

Martin's second letter, a verbose nine thousand words in length, continued to press for a neutral policy that would deny support to "an illiberal, effete, pagan and foreign dynasty." He also felt the burden of trying to defend the rebels against accusations of savagery, and compared this period with the blood-letting at other times of dynastic change, further claiming that the insurgents were no different from Cromwell and his "abstemious, devout and image-breaking fighters."[36]

Martin argued that neutrality was also demanded by virtue of the fact that "Christian" America must not commit fratricide by aiding the Manchus against an indigenous Christian party. To maintain this point, Martin defended the Taiping brand of Christianity against charges that it was heretical.

> When has Christianity in its incipient stages not presented the appearance of being spurious? The process both with nations and individuals is purgative . . . was not the religion of the Middle Ages exceedingly crude and imperfect? And yet light was made to shine out of darkness.

He suggested, going back even further into history, that the New Testament itself revealed ignorance and irregularities that could easily be labeled false by a critical outside observer.[37]

From this perspective, he asked if Hung's visions and trances differed in kind from Constantine's vision of the "cross-emblazoned banner?" He contended that Hung's pretension to be the "son of God" was not a claim of natural identity with God but only a title of dignity to maintain status before his followers.

Granting, however, for the sake of argument, that the Taiping profession of the Christian faith might indeed be false,[38] Martin asked if this false religion would not still be a more fruitful soil in which to plant the true seed than that afforded by Taoism and Confucianism, "equally devoid of any religious principle, [and] at deadly antagonism with the Gospel." Chiding the Roman Catholics, whom he accused of seeking to profit from Protestant embarrassment at being identified with the iconoclastic rebels, Martin inquired,

> Are not Protestants easier to convert than pagans? And would not a ruler who styled himself the 'younger brother of Jesus Christ' be more likely to submit to the Holy See than one who calls himself the 'Son of Heaven'?[39]

To appeal to commercial interests, which were fearful that along with their prohibition of opium the Taipings might end all foreign trade, Martin argued that "having imported a foreign religion, they would soon appreciate the value of other imports; and having imbibed the spirit of Christianity, they would fraternize with foreigners. . . ." In effect, he was arguing that China would not only be open to the Gospel but to all of the beneficial forces of Western civilization. "One [dynasty] shuts against it [the brightness of Western civilization] the decayed sight of age; the other opens to it, the weak eye of infancy."[40]

From the beginning, the American government's policy toward the Taiping rebellion had been cautiously neutral.[41] Humphrey Marshall's own sympathies vacillated between the Manchu imperialists and the rebels. Above all, however, he did not wish to allow either Great Britain or Russia to use civil strife to violate Chinese territory and dismember the Empire. In late 1853 Marshall was replaced by Robert McLane who was able to work more cooperatively with the British, and the two powers, while largely pro-Imperial in sentiment, took a "watch and wait" attitude that even acknowledged the possibility of negotiating with two governments.[42]

W. A. P. Martin's advocacy of a passive neutrality — support neither government — changed to advocating active neutrality — support both — by the summer of 1857.[43] He spelled out this position in two more long letters to Cushing.

Martin's reasons for recommending this "two-China policy" were basically the same as his earlier reasons for passive neutrality: Nanking had established a viable government which should be recognized, and the Taiping government would promote more trade with the West. He felt that the existence of two governments — one in Nanking for central China and the other in Peking for northern China — would create a better situation for progress. The spread of the Christian faith and social gains in central China would be an incentive, he believed, for the Manchus to improve the conditions of their subjects. A two-government policy would also promote America's interests in China. Martin recommended that to "divide and conquer is the stratagem to be employed in storming the citadels of oriental exclusiveness. The rival dynasties may readily be played against each other." Equal commercial privileges, he asserted, could thus be obtained both along the coast and up the Yangtze River. The progress of Western civilization in the Empire was not to be promoted by the gradual penetration of Christian principles, but by adroit political maneuvering — a process designed to promote America's interests over those of China. Among "Christian brothers" in an international family, what was good for one would be good for the other.

In 1856, caught up in the enthusiasm of the moment, Martin wrote to John Lowrie, Corresponding Secretary of the Board of Foreign Missions, that "I have been assured in the most flattering terms that these letters have had an important influence on the sentiments of the foreign public and particularly on foreign officials resident in China."[44] He substantiated this claim only by further asserting that "these letters delayed the day of intervention."[45] Teng Ssu-yü, noted Sinologist, reasonably concluded that "the influence of Martin's letters, if not negligible, was not as great as he thought."[46] More than any other private American citizen, however, Martin actively tried to influence the direction of his country's policy. In many ways, this was more important than his success or his failure. He saw his duty — participation in one more phase of making China a Christian nation — and he acted upon it.[47]

From 1857 to 1860 the missionaries were thinking about treaty revision, which they hoped would extract more privileges from the Manchus. However,

> The great victory of the Taipings over the imperial forces near Nanking and its neighboring districts in 1860, the attempted religious, political and social reforms under the premiership of the famous Hung Jen-kan, and the Taiping eastward expansion recaptured the attention of missionaries.[48]

Hung Jen-kan, the Shield King, belatedly realizing the need for foreign support, invited missionary leaders to visit the rebels at Nanking and Soochow. Several groups of British and American missionaries accepted this invitation in 1860-61 and were generally impressed with the Taiping leaders' Christian faith, their friendliness and desire for trade, and the fact that the cruelty and destruction, so widely reported in the foreign press, were nowhere evident.[49]

In a journey to Hankow late in 1860, Griffith John of the London Missionary Society obtained from rebel leaders an Edict of Religious Toleration which granted missionaries the right to live and preach the Gospel in the insurgents' territory.[50] John also transmitted to his colleagues the following memo from Chung-wang, the Loyal King, at Nanking,

> You have had the Gospel for upward of 1800 years, we only as it were eight days. Your knowledge of it ought to be correct and extensive. Ours must necessarily be limited and imperfect. You must, therefore, bear with us for the present, and we will gradually improve. As for the Gospel, it is one, and must be propagated throughout the land. Let the foreign brethren all know that we are determined to uproot idolatry and plant Christianity in its place.[51]

Shortly after this, however, influenced by a number of factors, missionary sentiment changed sharply. The Taiping attack on Shanghai in August, 1860, posed a threat to foreign trade.[52] An apparent change of heart by Hung Jen-kan and other leaders seemed to indicate that, rather than depend on missionaries, they preferred to use "native means" to evangelize China.[53] The missionaries possibly drew some hasty conclusions from reports indicating a deepening defection in the rebels' religious views.[54]

One scholar has suggested that the Taiping inability to take Shanghai contributed to the disillusionment of the pragmatic missionaries, whose views waxed and waned with military success and failure. The missionaries were seemingly given to "blind approval of all military moves on the part of the supposedly Christian forces as manifestation of the providential working of their God of battles."[55] But this interpretation of missionary attitude does not apply to W. A. P. Martin, whose approach and evaluation were related to deeper issues and principles.

In 1860 a foreign mercenary force, "The Ever Victorious Army," was organized under Frederick Ward, later expanded to include Chinese recruits, and reorganized under General Gordon; in 1863 it captured Soochow. When Tseng Kuo-fan and his Hunan Army subdued Nanking in 1864, the Taiping Rebellion, which had continued over fourteen years (1850-64), ravaged portions of sixteen provinces, and destroyed over six hundred cities, was finally ended.[56]

In later years Martin did not appear to be embarrassed by his consistent support of the rebel government at Nanking.[57] Nor did he ever agree with others who felt that missionary support for the Taipings had hurt the Christian cause in China.[58] Further reflection only increased his conviction that "the suppression of a revolution by force *ab extra* always reverses the wheels of progress; and in this instance who can tell by how many centuries it has postponed the adoption of Christianity by the Chinese people."[59] By the mid-1890's he wondered if active American support for the rebels in 1856, at the time of the Arrow War, might not have prevented the "loss of fifty millions of human lives and opened the country much more quickly to the 'assimilation of new ideas.' "[60] He observed that "following the early church, in the absence of any modern model, his [Hung Hsiu-ch'uan] converts expected and received spiritual gifts. Shall we describe such manifestations as hysteria, hypnotism or hypocrisy?"[61]

While still in the passive neutrality stage of his thinking, Martin sought further supplementary means to establish God's Kingdom in China. The opportunity was afforded by the outbreak of hostilities over Chinese seizure of the *Arrow,* a small Chinese ship with British registration, in Canton. This open conflict, the culmination of many years of smoldering resentment between the British and the Chinese in the Canton area, signaled the impending breakdown of the early treaty system, by then in urgent need of revision.

In Martin's view, these incidents at Canton were a

> . . . step in the chain of providence,[62] by which God is preparing China for the reception of the Gospel . . . none but the sceptic can for a moment doubt. . . . I am disposed to regard it as a providential interference on behalf of the semi-Christian insurgents.[63]

Martin conceded that the quarrel between England and China was over very trivial matters, but

> To the man of reflection it presents a striking instance of what is so often noticed in the course of history — God accomplishing his great and wise purposes by allowing man to pursue his petty, private and unjustifiable ends.[64]

He contended that through this war China was "being humbled at the feet of Christian powers,"[65] and although he stated that he did not wish to force his religion on the Chinese, he felt that force could give the Gospel "free course in the Empire."

For several years Martin had served off and on as an unpaid interpreter for Dr. William Bradley, the United States Consul at

Ningpo. When he learned that William Reed, the United States Minister, was going to North China to negotiate a treaty with China, he applied for, and was given, a position on the American delegation.[66]

How did Martin justify leaving his missionary work for this venture in diplomacy? One of his stated reasons for taking the position was that he might "promote the missionary cause in the treaty renewal and have some weight in securing the desired provisions for liberty of conscience. . . ."[67] What specific proposals he had in mind to promote the cause of missions are not known. His interviews with Reed convinced him that the United States Minister would not "neglect the interests of missions and the safety of native Christians," and he was equally sure that the "Lord has brought [this] about and He will care for the issues."[68]

The American delegation arrived off Taku in northern China in mid-April, 1858. Martin's task was to serve as interpreter for Reed and Samuel Wells Williams, formerly of the ABCFM and now secretary to Reed. Martin apparently had no part in major policy decisions, although his advice was constantly sought on matters of translation and protocol. The American and Russian delegations negotiated immediately with the Chinese diplomatic representatives. Great Britain and France, incensed that the Imperial government did not accord them more status by sending a negotiator with "plenipotentiary powers," attacked the Chinese positions and captured Tientsin.[69]

Although grieved at the carnage, Martin took almost childish glee in viewing the conflict from the decks of the U. S. *Antelope.* "My long cherished wish to see a battle was realized . . . there was sublimity in the scene."[70] The battle lasted only two hours, but Martin attached cosmic significance to it — by possibly inciting a revolution that would overturn the dynasty it could be "a step in the world's progress."

At this stage in his life and ministry, Martin wavered between advocating force and the pricks of his Christian conscience. He regretted the British and French action and felt that Reed's neutral stance was correct. Yet "in the dispensation of Providence it seems to be necessary that these conceited Asiatics should be humbled by the Sword, before they are exalted by the Gospel."[71]

Foreign lives and property, he observed, were the most secure in Amoy, Ningpo, and Shanghai where "the fist of John Bull has dealt the hardest blow ... the natives are humbly obsequious in their bearing toward a race they no longer despise."[72] Force, in lieu of a common religious faith or "the acknowledged principles of international law," was the only way to deal with a people who are "proverbially proud and perfidious."[73]

On the other hand,

> I cannot but think (without quarrelling with Providence, and laying all the blame on the perverseness of men) that all this might have been effected in a much better way; for had Christian nations displayed, through their centuries of intercourse with this empire, the beneficence of the religion which they profess, they would long ago have dispelled fear, disarmed suspicion, opened the whole country to their commerce, and the hearts of its inhabitants to the Gospel. Longfellow only clothes a Christian's faith in a poet's language, when he says,
>
>> 'Were half the power that keeps the world in terror,
>> Were half the wealth bestowed on camps and courts,
>> Given to redeem the human mind from error,
>> There were no need of arsenals and forts.'[74]

Both Martin and Williams gave tracts and Christian Almanacs to their Chinese counterparts. The recipients suggested that the moral maxims, particularly the Ten Commandments, contained in this Christian literature were more applicable to the British and the French — they urged Martin to use the material to enjoin them not to kill and covet. The British and French could hardly be Christian, the Chinese commented, "for they killed the Chinese with opium merely to gain."[75] Their advice was particularly appropriate coming as it did only hours before the sneak British-French attack on the Taku garrison.

Residence of foreign ministers in Peking, new treaty ports on the Yangtze River, indemnity payments, and the "inland transit dues" were among the major issues discussed in Tientsin.[76] To Martin and Williams, however, nothing was more important than to obtain an article guaranteeing religious toleration. Reed's directives instructed him to work for a clause on religious freedom,[77] but he did not give this high priority. A sense of history impelled him to wish to sign the American treaty on June 18, 1858, the anniversary of Wellington's victory at Waterloo, and he would tolerate no delay to continue negotiating the terminology of a toleration article.[78]

The first attempt to draft a toleration clause was too specific, even though the Chinese did not challenge it immediately. It read in part,

> Hereafter it shall be lawful for any citizen of the United States, preaching the doctrines of Jesus Christ . . . to pass freely . . . through all parts of the . . . Empire . . . being also allowed the privilege of residence and safe treatment and hereafter no Chinese who professes the said doctrines shall be punished or interfered with . . . on account of his faith.[79]

After this was rejected, the Americans did nothing more until June 14, when the Russian Treaty which contained in its eighth article the provision for Christian (*t'ien-chu*)[80] missionaries to travel and preach in the interior if they possessed special passports, was signed.[81] Williams modified the phraseology to include both Protestant and Catholic missionaries, eliminated a reference to passports, and submitted it to the Chinese for their consideration.

After making Williams and Martin wait all day for their reply, the Chinese negotiators finally granted, early in the evening of the seventeenth, all that was included in the Russian Treaty. Within several hours, however, they submitted a counter-proposal restricting American missionaries to the open ports under their consular jurisdiction. Their note made clear that they feared American missionaries would carry on trade and, much more important, have their wives and families with them. "The novelty of foreign women travelling about the country had presented itself to their minds as an objection to allowing Americans to preach Christianity."[82] Reed, whether with Williams' and Martin's advice or not, rejected this outright, and it appeared that the American Treaty would say nothing about religious liberty.

Early on the morning of June 18 the two missionary diplomats tried again with equally bad results. This Chinese counter-proposal would, in effect, make it "illegal for a native to profess Christianity anywhere else than at the treaty ports."[83] With time for the signing of the treaty rapidly approaching, both Martin and Williams took sedan chairs and visited their Chinese counterparts personally, determined "to beseige [sic] them into the concession of something more liberal."[84] After some bickering, a final form, drafted by Williams and amended slightly by Reed, was accepted without change. This form, containing no specific reference to missionary travel rights, was also acceptable to Reed, who did not wish there to be any statements in the treaty that would recognize a "distinction as to rights between missionaries and merchants."[85]

Incorporated as Article 29 of the American Treaty of Tientsin, it read as follows:

> The principles of the Christian religion, as professed by the Protestant and Roman Catholic churches, are recognized as teaching men to do good, and to do to others as they would have others do to them. Hereafter those who quietly profess and teach these doctrines shall not be harassed or persecuted on account of their faith. Any person, whether citizen of the United States or Chinese convert, who, according to these tenets, shall peaceably teach and practice the principles of Christianity shall in no case be interfered with or molested.[86]

Although criticized by some missionaries as too vague and therefore subject to many violations, this clause suited Oriental sensibilities more satisfactorily than anything previously submitted. Williams clearly saw this. Whether Christianity would or would not be tolerated in China did not depend, in his view, on treaties or on further application of force, but rather on "the power of a consistent earnest exhibition of such teaching and living in winning the ignorant heathen to an inquiry into the precepts of our faith."[87] "The people," he urged, "need to be educated up to them [the treaties]." To him this meant that many more missionaries must come to China and face the risks of preaching the Gospel even though they would be largely "unprotected."[88] He recognized that the Chinese had yielded to the Tientsin treaties as "the least of two evils" and that anyone who worked and lived under their privileges and demands had best face this fact realistically. He believed that "more force may be necessary and yet gradual contact and the advance of knowledge is best . . . ignorance is powerful and we need to be careful not to trigger a reaction by stimulating the worse side."[89] A later critic has observed that "Christianity was, in a measure, like opium, being imposed upon China without the consent of the people. The Chinese were free to abstain from either, but they were not free to prohibit them."[90]

Martin, younger than Williams and by temperament more optimistic, tended to be more idealistic and naive, although developing circumstances did not allow him to be completely unrealistic. To some degree he thought that "the Government had become persuaded to the advantages of a new system of policy."[91] While never denying that military victories at Canton and Taku were God's means of paving the way for these unexpected results, he thought that an even greater manifestation of God's sovereignty was the disposition of the Christian powers to propose, and the Chinese to accept, the proposals for religious liberty.[92]

In the fall of 1858 he wrote to the American public that the treaty showed that,

> Christian missionaries are already felt as a power in the world. Politicians are convinced that missionaries are the medium through which the mind of the West must act on that of China. Their deeds of benevolence cherish a kindly feeling in the hearts of the Chinese. . . .[93]

The negotiators on the scene, he believed, were agents of a higher cause than they knew, not merely obtaining a few diplomatic and commercial privileges, but "opening this mass of ignorance, pride, superstition and pollution to the entrance of Christian truth and knowledge," which would then assure "the peace and perpetuity of all that is worth having among Chinese policy and institutions."[94]

To his own Board he wrote even more effusively that,

> All barriers are withdrawn and four hundred millions of pagans invite the evangelical enterprise . . . that the chief nations of the earth should thus conspire to advance the cause of Christ is a glorious harbinger of his universal sway. It shows . . . that the conversion of the Chinese is now so far from being regarded as an unclear enterprise that cool, calculating politicians stipulate for the propagation of the Gospel and the protection of converts.[95]

After his initial euphoria, further reflection on what had actually transpired helped Martin find other reasons for China's new liberality. First, "it is no longer within their power [not] to do so."[96] The Chinese could really do nothing else. As he explained many years later to a group of mission supporters in a tabernacle in Clifton Springs, New York, "they [the gates of China] did not . . . roll back to the sound of celestial music, but to the roar of Western cannon."[97]

In the second place, Martin admitted that the Chinese were guided by pure political expediency. "China found it in her interest not to reject their demands."[98] Within eighteen months after the Tientsin agreement, several instances of local persecution convinced him not only that Chinese agreement had been granted merely to gain some immediate advantages, but that government officials never intended to comply with it.[99] Confessing that his opinions had "undergone considerable change," he concluded that "no stipulation of the Chinese government is to be relied on further than foreign power can be brought to enforce its fulfillment."[100] He further suggested that the Emperor granted toleration for fear that the foreigners might support the Taiping rebels.[101]

Shocked out of naiveté by a feeling that he had been duped, Martin wondered if the Chinese could be trusted. Fortunately for his future career in China, new opportunities and new friends helped him reach a more positive attitude, even though he retained some very deep suspicions. Williams' problem was different — "a subtle question in equity and ethics." "How far," he asked, "is a nation bound to observe a stipulation, whose import it had no means of ascertaining, and how far ought it to be forced to carry out a promise in a treaty obtained from it by fear and intimidation?"[102] Martin and his missionary colleagues never really answered this question, choosing instead to put it out of mind and palliate their conscience by taking refuge in God's "Providence" and the conviction that ends justify means. Martin had once raised the question of the relationship between "God's providence and the perverseness of man," but he never returned to it.

The advantages of each of the four treaties were granted to all of the powers by "the most-favored-nation clause." The Chinese text of the French treaty, by some strange maneuvering, contained the right, extended to all, of "buying land and building houses in the interior." The British treaty provided for opening many more ports than did the other treaties, and also provided for foreign ministers to reside in Peking. These "derivative rights," as Martin called them, opened the entire Empire to missionary penetration, even though actual residence in the interior was neither clearly permitted nor refused.[103]

Martin's chief criticism of each of the four treaties was that Tientsin itself was not made an open port. This, he argued forcefully, only laid the foundation for resumption of hostilities.[104] Furthermore, the onward "march of Providence" would be thwarted if the "four Christian nations," having occupied Tientsin for several weeks, should surrender it again to the "unmitigated sway of Pagan delusion."[105]

After this three-month interruption Martin returned to Ningpo early in July, 1858, "his head crowned with earthly honors."[106] He resumed preaching, itineration, and writing, and also served on five of the six standing mission committees.[107] Only two converts had been added to the church that year, but he said he was not discouraged. The great result that he reported to the Board was that China was now "open from Canton to the Great Wall and the Yellow Sea to the Himalayas."

Even before his journey north with Reed, Martin had written to the Board about returning to America. Mrs. Martin and his four boys, who ranged in age from two to eight years, were in poor health, and he was in a quandary about what to do.[108] He suggested that he might send his family home alone, go back to America with them, stay in China for another year, or transfer to the north where the climate was cooler. A year later, after the Tientsin trip, he was more inclined to go to northern China and specifically suggested Yang-chou, one of the new open ports in Shantung, as a possibility. He believed that this city would be a *point d'appui* for advance into the mountainous province — "the birthplace of Confucius and Mencius, and the home of the best blood in China."[109]

Later, in May, 1859, Martin's overtures to John Ward, new American Minister to China, to serve as his and Williams' interpreter for another American delegation to the north, where the Tientsin treaties were to be ratified, were accepted, and he proceeded to Shanghai. Writing to the Board about this new opportunity, Martin expressed his desire to find a location for work in Peking while he was on this diplomatic mission, and to take his family there by autumn. He expressed readiness, however, to come home with his family if the Board did not accept his plan.[110]

The American delegation met twice with the Chinese ministers at Shanghai and then went north in mid-June to join the British and French who had refused to talk with the Chinese representatives at any other site than Peking. The Chinese prohibited the allied powers from going to Peking via Tientsin, suggesting rather that they use the land route, proceeding inland from Pei-t'ang, north of Taku.[111] Frederick Bruce, the British minister, viewed this as an insult and tried to force his way up the Peiho. The Chinese opened fire from their forts overlooking the harbor and inflicted such losses that the British forces retreated to Shanghai. Williams called their defeat the worst they had experienced in Asia "since the march out of Cabul."

Martin did not often argue with Providence, but he confessed at this juncture that he had little sympathy with British policy.

> The war was rekindled, and the Chinese were accused of bringing it about by treachery. But were they wrong in barring the way to a city that was not opened by treaty? Had the allied ministers a right to expect to reach Tientsin in their steamers when they had neglected to secure it by stipulation? Not only were they aggressors in firing the first shot, they were clearly wrong in the whole issue . . . it is a thousand pities that the occasion for unchaining England's thunder should be in one instance to exact payment for the destruction of a prohibited drug, in another to procure satisfaction for the insult implied in the Chinese exercising summary justice on their own people, in a third a mere quibble of words, in the last the assertion of a privilege which the negotiators had forgotten to secure . . . it grieves one to see the most enlightened party so continually in the wrong. What estimate will a Chinese statesman on such a retrospect form of the morality of England?[113]

Martin was not the only American who felt this way. Williams was always offended by "the overbearing conduct" of the British,[114] and William Culbertson, a Presbyterian missionary in Shanghai, compared their Peiho action to Russia trying to sail her fleet up the Thames.[115]

The British military reverse at Taku in 1859, along with the pervasive rumor that missionaries were engaged in the coolie trade, dimmed the optimism that had spread through the missionary community during the previous year.[116] In anticipation that there would be no difficulties with treaty ratification, John and Helen Nevius had gone to Hangchow in 1858, only to be forced to leave after meeting increasing rigidity from local officials.[117] Griffith John, encouraged earlier by meeting nothing but "smiles and goodwill" among the Chinese, complained that the Peiho defeat had dramatically changed their attitudes.

> They imagine now that our future stay hangs upon their goodwill and pleasure . . . people, who but three months ago were as harmless as doves and very respectful, are now as bold as lions and often intolerably impudent.[118]

Within a short time after the 1858-1860 treaties were signed, anti-missionary riots began to occur with disturbing regularity wherever the Gospel was preached. Poor communication, his unwillingness to face facts, and his defensive attitude concerning the missionary movement led Martin to state that from 1860 to 1890 there were only about twenty major incidents.[119] Recent studies by Professor Lü Shih-ch'iang of the Department of History at the Academia Sinica, now located in Taipei, Taiwan, indicate that from 1860 to 1874 alone there were over four hundred separate conflicts between missionaries and local officials which involved some destruction of property and serious misunderstanding.[120] These riots culminated in the Boxer Rebellion of 1900, and, in a more dramatic way, in the "standing up of the Chinese people" in 1949, when every element of Western imperialism, including the missionaries, was expelled from China.

To what extent was this a result of missionary use of a noble end to justify a sordid means — aligning with military force, allegedly God's tool in opening China, to make the Gospel available to Chinese people? Professor Lü, a Buddhist, makes this observation,

> Investigations . . . tend to show that Christianity and the Confucian tradition are not necessarily incompatible; that Christian evangelism in China, without political and military support, could have had a chance to survive and spread, through peaceful means and gradual and mutual understanding, granting at the same time that certain forms of conflict were to be expected before total harmony might be achieved between the two heritages.

> That so many unfortunate or tragic incidents [riots] had erupted
> was not due so much to a difference in dogmas as to such human
> weakness as selfishness and greed.[121]

Following the completion of his official duties at Peit'ang,
Martin took a brief three-week trip to Japan accompanied by his
oldest son, Pascal, whom he hoped would find relief from severe
paralysis as a result of this sea voyage.[122] After returning from this
delightful interlude, Martin had high hopes that the Executive
Committee of the Board would approve his plans to go to North
China.[123] His request, however, was refused,[124] and in early
November the mission conference in Ningpo recommended that
he return to the United States on furlough.[125] The conference listed
four considerations affecting this decision: Martin's ten years of
service in China, the health of his family, the inadvisability of
moving to North China at that time, and the education of Martin's
children.

Martin accepted their recommendation with reluctance,[126]
admitting that "the *highest* type of service is to wait on the Lord
without binding oneself to only a term of years or one certain place
by an irrevocable vow, and go where He calls and labor where He
commands."[127]

On January 31, 1860, the Martin family left Ningpo for
Shanghai to take passage for America on the *Golden Rule*.[128]
Aboard ship, ready for his first furlough and reflecting on his
many varied activities of the past ten years, Martin wondered if it
were not better for missionaries to go to the field unmarried, adapt
to it, learn the language well, and "then, if need be, go home after
eight or ten years and choose a wife."[129] He agonized over the
difficulties of rearing a family in a foreign country, complaining
that although "daughters can well be taken care of in China, it is
the ruin of boys to keep them over the age of twelve, or longer than
they can be kept indoors."[130]

As he returned home for his furlough Martin could already
envisage, if dimly, the path of his future ministry. His diplomatic
journeys to North China had awakened his concern for the needs
of Peking. Such a move into a cooler climate would solve some
health problems, remove him from his unfortunate conflict with
Dr. McCartee, and satisfy his compulsive desire to pioneer. Even

more important, it would turn his attention from the multitudes of South China to the leadership elite of the north. His concern would shift from the base of the pyramid to what he liked to call the "shining summit."[131] Evangelism would continue to be a major thrust of his work, but to an increasing degree he would pioneer bringing to China the total "Christian" culture of law, science, and education. As he left China, then, in 1860 he was entering a transitional period in his work which, by 1869, would take him completely out of the institutional missionary structure.

Notes

1. C. K. Yang, *Religion in Chinese Society* (Berkeley, 1967), 132.

2. Herbert Kane, *Understanding Christian Missions* (Grand Rapids, 1974), 93.

3. Alexander Wylie, *Memorials of Protestant Missionaries to the Chinese* (Shanghai, 1867), 82-83.

4. Despatches from U. S. Consuls in Ningpo, 1853-1896, I, Mr. Bradley to William March, July 19, 1856, and R. G. Humphrey to John Appleton, July 16, 1857.

5. Despatches from U. S. Consuls in Ningpo, 1853-1896, I, #11, Bradley to Reed, February 15, 1858. No American jails existed in Ningpo (or in all of China), and the usual course was to send a man like Jackson to Shanghai where he was detained in a jail on any U. S. ship in port, or under the care of a U. S. Marshal.

6. Margaret Wylie Martin to her mother, #2, December 25, 1854. Harris Collection, Indiana University Archives.

7. *The Chinese Repository*, XX (July, 1851), 497-98.

8. S. Y. Teng, *The Taiping Rebellion and the Western Powers* (Oxford, 1971), 184.

9. China Letters of the Board of Foreign Missions of the Presbyterian Church in the United States of America, III, Ningpo, S. Martin to Board, #247, n.d. China Letters are subsequently abbreviated "CL."

10. CL, III, Ningpo, Quarterman to Board, #249, May 14, 1853.

11. *The Presbyterian*, XXIII (July 16, 1853), No. 29, and quoted in John B. Littell, "Missionaries and Politics in China — The Taiping Rebellion," *Political Science Quarterly*, XLIII (December, 1928), 576.

12. Littell in "Missionaries and Politics," observed that all mis-

sionaries, British and American, of all denominations, whether conservative or liberal, as well as foreigners involved in secular work in China could be divided into three basic categories: enthusiastic proponents, moderate sympathizers, and ardent opponents. 571.

13. CL, V, Shanghai, Culbertson to Board, #69, April 12, 1853.

14. CL, V, Shanghai, Wight to Board, #72, June 1, 1853.

15. CL, III, Ningpo, McCartee to Board, #260, June 7, 1853.

16. John Nevius, Letter, *The Home and Foreign Record,* XI (October, 1860), 308.

17. W. A. P. Martin, *A Cycle of Cathay* (3rd ed.; New York, 1900), 127.

18. CL, III, Ningpo, McCartee to Board, #260, June 7, 1853.

19. *Ibid.*

20. Teng, *The Taiping Rebellion,* 186-87; Littell, "Missionaries and Politics," 581-87.

21. *United States Statutes at Large*, IX (1845-50), 278, quoted from Littell, "Missionaries and Politics," 581. McLane, successor to Marshall as High Commissioner, changed this crime in late 1854 to a "high misdemeanor" carrying a fine of up to $10,000 and a jail sentence of up to three years.

22. Martin, *Cycle,* 129.

23. *Ibid.,* 130-31. Very foolishly, he had in his possession a letter "tendering my services to the rebel chief."

24. *House Executive Documents,* 33rd Congress, Session 1, Document #123, 184. Marshall to W. L. Marcy, Secretary of State, June 21, 1853.

25. *Ibid.,* 185-88, Marshall to Roberts, June 20, 1853.

26. CL, Outgoing, IX, Ningpo, #80, September 27, 1853.

27. CL, Outgoing, III, Ningpo, #83, January 2, 1854.

28. Teng, *The Taiping Rebellion,* 193. Some of this disillusionment was also the result of the poor treatment accorded McLane at Nanking in 1854. CL, IV, Ningpo, Martin to Board, #17, July 7, 1854.

29. CL, IV, Ningpo, Martin to Board, #5, January 30, 1854.

30. The Greek term *pneuma* may mean spirit, Spirit, breath, air, wind, etc.

31. CL, IV, Ningpo, Martin to Board, #17, July 7, 1854.

32. Teng, *Taiping Rebellion,* 197, 201. Roberts, at Hung's personal invitation, was at Nanking from October 13, 1860, until January 20, 1862. Martin wondered about Roberts' "tact and breadth" and speculated that he may have rebuked the rebels for their plundering or that he may have

insisted on immersion as the proper form of baptism rather than their usage of washing their breast with a towel. Martin, *Cycle,* 131-32. Yet, he admitted that "no foreigner could have exerted any beneficial influence . . . [how do you] mould the theology of a people who received revelations from heaven?"

33. CL, IV, Ningpo, Martin to Board, #90, July 16, 1856; Martin, *Cycle,* 133.

34. Teng, *Taiping Rebellion,* 190-91, suggested that Martin did not go to Peter Parker, then United States High Commissioner, or to the Secretary of State, because he feared they would have the same attitude toward him as Marshall had had toward Roberts.

35. This letter, totaling about 6500 words and written on April 17, 1856, appeared in the *North China Herald,* May 3, 1856, 158-59.

36. He also compared the rebels' rapid conquests with "Sherman's march toward the sea . . . combined with Garibaldi's successful assault on the Kingdom of Naples." This, however, was written many years after his early letters. Martin, *Cycle,* 128.

37. He referred specifically to the Corinthian church and to the sons of Zebedee asking Jesus to give them favored seats in the Kingdom of God.

38. He believed that although there was some adverse missionary reaction against the Taipings, that most of the opposition came from opium merchants. "And it is they who criticize their religion and cause Christians in America not to like it. Sapient judges! They discern the truth and violate it themselves." CL, IV, Ningpo, Martin to Board, #90, July 16, 1856. He never appeared to have thought through the possibility that the "Taiping Rebellion had no popular support" and depended largely on force and the Chinese ability to "bend with the wind." Teng, *Taiping Rebellion,* 409.

39. Martin, *Cycle,* 141.

40. All of the material in Martin's second letter may be found in the *North China Herald,* June 7, 1856, 179-80.

41. Tyler Dennett, *Americans in Eastern Asia* (New York, 1922), 223; John Foster, *American Diplomacy in the Orient* (Boston, 1903), 211.

42. Te-kung Tung, *United States Diplomacy in China, 1844-1860* (Seattle, 1964), 121-50.

43. *North China Herald,* June 13, 1857, 183-84, and June 20, 1857, 186-87.

44. CL, IV, Ningpo, Martin to Board, #90, July 16, 1856. Robert Cobbold's approval of this statement would indicate that he felt some of these officials were Britishers.

45. Martin, *Cycle,* 133. By this he meant that the letters had delayed until 1860 the formation of a foreign mercenary army under the leadership first of Frederick Ward and later of Charles Gordon.

46. Teng, *The Taiping Rebellion*, 191.

47. Martin's activities on behalf of the Taiping Rebellion were not restricted to these letters exerting public pressure on American government officials. He wrote both news articles and interpretive essays to inform the readers of the *North China Herald*, most of the ex-patriate community in China, about current activities and historical perspectives of the Nanking insurgents. See *North China Herald*, VII, October 4, 1856, 38-39; VII, April 14, 1857, 151; VII, December 27, 1856, 87.

48. Teng, *Taiping Rebellion*, 193.

49. *Ibid.*, 178-79.

50. R. W. Thompson, *Griffith John* (London, 1908), 147.

51. *Ibid.*, 148.

52. Teng, *Taiping Rebellion*, 182.

53. Letter of William Muirhead of the London Missionary Society and quoted in Robert Speer, *Missions and Modern History* (New York, 1904), II, 52-54. Within the closely knit Taiping organization the master sergeants were responsible for the evangelization of units of twenty-five families in conquered territories. Immanuel Hsü, *The Rise of Modern China* (New York, 1970), 285.

54. Teng, *Taiping Rebellion*, 195-96, suggested that this kind of a reaction by a J. L. Holmes was "perhaps hasty and over-subjective."

55. Earl Cranston, "The American Missionary's Outlook on China, 1830-1860" (unpublished Ph.D. dissertation. Harvard University, 1930), 232.

56. Kenneth S. Latourette, *A History of Christian Missions in China* (London, 1929), 294-95.

57. Henri Cordier suggested "he must have often regretted the lines he wrote" in the November 26, 1856, issue of the *North China Herald*, predicting the imminent demise of the Manchus, the government that later decorated him twice with high ranks. See "Necrologie," *T'oung Pao*, XVII (1916), 624-25.

58. Speer, *Missions and Modern History*, II, 59-64, presented some material to support his view that "the missionary enterprise has little to gain and a great deal to lose from the confusion of spiritual religion and political administration ... like the Taiping insurrection." Latourette, *Christian Missions in China*, 299-300, pointed out that the Protestants did not suffer immediately because they were still restricted to the treaty ports, but that harm was done to Catholic communities scattered through China. Timothy Richard believed that Christianity inherited a "legacy of ill-will" because people identified it with the lost rebellion. *Forty-Five Years in China: Reminiscences* (London, 1916), 185. To which Martin would probably reply, "A rebellion that succeeds is never forgotten ... all others are consigned to the limbo of abortions." *Cycle*, 127. Teng believed that the

rebellion "adversely affected Christianity," particularly in its reception along the Yangtze Valley, but that it should "not be held solely responsible for the anti-Christian movement." *The Taiping Rebellion,* 408-9.

59. Martin, *Cycle*, 133. This was written in 1895 or 1896.

60. *Ibid.*, 141. See also W. A. P. Martin, *Siege in Peking* (New York, 1900), 46, and W. A. P. Martin, *The Awakening of China* (New York, 1907), 162.

61. Martin, *Awakening,* 157.

62. Was he less sure of "providence" in later years? In *Cycle,* 143, he spoke of a "chance spark at Canton."

63. CL, IV, Ningpo, Martin to Board, #101, January 1, 1857.

64. W. A. P. Martin, "Recent Treaty," *Home and Foreign Record,* IX (November, 1858), 338.

65. *Ibid.*

66. Martin, *Cycle,* 147, and CL, IV, Ningpo, Martin to Board, #141, April 12, 1858.

67. CL, IV, Ningpo, Martin to Board, #141, April 12, 1858, and #146, May 9, 1858.

68. CL, IV, Ningpo, Martin to Board, #141, April 12, 1858. Allan Thomas Price, "American Missionaries and American Diplomacy in China, 1830-1890" (unpublished Ph.D. dissertation, Harvard University, 1932), 257. He noted that missionaries had often informally discussed the need for privilege of unlimited travel and residence, liberty of conscience for the Chinese, the need for representation in Peking, and either the suppression or legalization of opium.

69. Hsü, *Rise of Modern China,* 257.

70. Martin, "Recent Treaty," 339.

71. W. A. P. Martin, "Two American Embassies" (unpublished book-length manuscript), I, 111.

72. *Ibid.,* I, 25.

73. *Ibid.,* I, 32.

74. Martin, "Recent Treaty," 339; "Two Embassies," I, 119-20.

75. Martin, *Cycle,* 162, and F. W. Williams, *The Life and Letters of Samuel Wells Williams* (New York, 1889), 260-61.

76. Hsü, *Rise of Modern China,* 258.

77. *Ibid.,* 255.

78. Martin, *Cycle,* 181.

79. S. Wells Williams, "The Toleration Clause in the Treaties," *The Chinese Recorder* (May-June, 1880), 227.

80. The term used for the Catholic church in China.

81. Williams observed that Chinese willingness to grant this request to the Russians whom they had known as "quiet, gentlemanly, learned members of the Russian Mission, in Peking for many years" led some Protestant missionaries at the Shanghai Conference, 1877, to conclude that the matter of religious toleration was "brought forward and encouraged by the Chinese Commissioners themselves." Williams, "The Toleration Clause," 223-24. This misunderstanding was apparently due to a statement written by Reed to several missionaries in Shanghai and later published in *Spirit of Missions*, XXIV (March, 1859), 148-51.

82. F. W. Williams, *Life and Letters*, 271, and S. W. Williams, "The Toleration Clause," 225.

83. S. W. Williams, "The Toleration Clause," 225.

84. Martin, "Two Embassies," I, 197.

85. *Senate Executive Documents*, 36th Congress, 1st Section (1859-60), X, No. 30, 357. Reed to Lewis Cass, Secretary of State.

86. F. W. Williams, *Life and Letters*, 273.

87. S. W. Williams, "The Toleration Clause," 227.

88. S. Wells Williams, "The Chinese and the Treaties," *The Foreign Missionary*, XVIII (July, 1859), 51-52.

89. S. Wells Williams, "Narrative of the American Embassy to Peking," *Journal of the North China Branch of the Royal Asiatic Society*, Old Series, III (December, 1859), 342.

90. Dennett, *Americans in Eastern Asia*, 574.

91. Frederick Bruce to Lord J. Russel, *British Parliamentary Papers*, LXIX (1860), China; State Paper 2685, 1. He commented that he was surprised that an intelligent person like Martin could hold such a naive view.

92. CL, IV, Ningpo, Martin to Board, #151, June 1858, and #156, July 9, 1858. Price, "American Missionaries," 273, pointed out that before 1858, reciprocal pledges for freedom of religion in an absolute or limited form were made in ten treaties between the United States and other countries for the benefit of American citizens in other countries, and that in 1855 the Senate voted to include this type of provision in future treaties. However, no American treaty signed before 1858 included a unilateral pledge on religious liberty by one signator.

93. W. A. P. Martin, News article in *New York Times*, October 12, 1858, 1:1, 2.

94. W. A. P. Martin, News article in *New York Times*, October 20, 1858, 2:3.

95. CL, IV, Ningpo, Martin to Board, #156, July 9, 1858.

96. Martin, *Cycle*, 181.

97. W. A. P. Martin, "Relation of the Chinese Government to Mis-

sions," *The Missionary Review of the World*, XIX, Old Series (August, 1896), 608.

98. Martin, *Cycle*, 441.

99. W. A. P. Martin, "The American Treaty Violated," *North China Herald*, February 11, 1860.

100. *Ibid.*

101. W. A. P. Martin, "Attitude of the Chinese Government Toward Christian Missions," *The Missionary Review of the World*, IX, New Series (November, 1896), 844; Martin, *Cycle*, 183.

102. S. Wells Williams, "The Chinese and the Treaties," 51.

103. Martin, *Cycle*, 441-42.

104. *Ibid.*, 184, 189.

105. Martin, "Recent Treaty," 340.

106. CL, IV, Ningpo, E. B. Inslee to Board, #160, July 30, 1858.

107. CL, IV, Ningpo, Annual Report 1858, #176, October, 1858.

108. His four sons, all born in Ningpo, were Pascal (October 29, 1850-March 5, 1882), Winfred Robert (March 22, 1852-February 21, 1915), Newell A. (September 17, 1854-November 15, 1941), and Claude. Little information is known about the latter, except that he was two years old in April, 1858. CL, IV, Ningpo, Martin to Board, #141, April 12, 1858.

109. CL, IV, Ningpo, Martin to Board, #198, May 6, 1859.

110. CL, IV, Ningpo, Martin to Board, #202, June 3, 1859.

111. Martin, *Cycle*, 190-91.

112. F. W. Williams, *Life and Letters*, 302.

113. Martin, *Cycle*, 193.

114. F. W. Williams, *Life and Letters*, 277.

115. CL, V, Shanghai, Culbertson to Board, #145, n. d.

116. CL, V, Shanghai, Culbertson to Board, #147, July 14, 1859.

117. Helen Nevius, *Our Life in China* (New York, 1869), 183-90.

118. Thompson, *Griffith John*, 81-107.

119. Martin, *Cycle*, 445.

120. Lü Shih-ch'iang, *Chung-kuo kuan-shen fan-chiao ti yüan-yin* (The Origin and Cause of the Anti-Christian Movement Among the Chinese Officials and Gentry, 1860-1874) (Taipei, 1966), 202-60.

121. English Synopsis of *The Origin and Cause of the Anti-Christian Movement Among Chinese Officials and Gentry* (*1860-74*) (Taipei, 1972), 43.

122. CL, IV, Ningpo, Martin to Board, #224, August 30, 1859.

123. CL, IV, Ningpo, McCartee to Board, #227, October 29, 1859.

124. Several reasons were listed: 1) Peking is not a treaty port; 2) it is an "exclusive city"; 3) we need to send two missionary units; 4) the project is too expensive; 5) all we will have is the opinion of one man — more information is needed; 6) Tengchou is a better first port to enter. CL, IX, Outgoing to Martin, #133, September 10, 1859.

125. CL, IV, Ningpo, Rankin to Board, #230, November 1, 1859.

126. Furlough was considered almost a "semi-resignation." The Board had written Martin to the effect that his return to the field, even as was the case with other missionaries, was an "open" question to be decided when the time came "in view of all the providences of God." CL, VIII, Outgoing to Martin, #32, August 3, 1858.

127. CL, IV, Ningpo, Martin to Board, #233, November 16, 1859.

128. CL, IV, Ningpo, Rankin to Board, #252, and Martin to Board, #254, February 27, 1860.

129. CL, IV, Ningpo, Martin to Board, #254, February 27, 1860.

130. *Ibid.*

131. Martin, "Two American Embassies," I, 86-87.

CHAPTER FIVE

The Presbyterian
Message in Ningpo

SCHOLARS HAVE DEVOTED considerable attention to the Western missionary as an interpreter of Western civilization to China. Jessie Lutz has observed that

> Along with the teachings of Jesus, Chinese converts were often asked to accept other ideals and customs from the West; sanitation practices, concepts about the role of women and relations of the sexes, abstinence from alcoholic drink, individualism, standards of medical care. . . .[1]

Far less frequently has anyone seriously attempted to analyze the Christian Gospel preached in China, to trace its roots in Western culture, and to show the nature of its relationship to the "secular" message brought by Western missionaries. Scholars have apparently assumed that readers are so familiar with this that no elaboration is required. There are some documented examples of missionaries explaining to Christian audiences what they preached to the unconverted, but unfortunately, there were likely significant differences between these explanations and what was actually communicated to the non-Christian Chinese.[2]

In the case of a missionary as prolific in his literary endeavors as was W. A. P. Martin we are left with no doubts concerning the exact nature of the Gospel he preached at Ningpo. Furthermore, by examining his most noted work, *Evidences of Christianity,* produced during his years at Ningpo, it is possible to trace the source of his thought and see how it was modified by contact with the Chinese environment.[3]

Martin had a scholarly bent, and as soon as he had gained a grasp of Ningpoese, he gave a series of evening lectures to the city congregation of the Presbyterian church. His audience was largely "educated men, some of whom were teachers and preachers in the service of other missions."[4] Entitled *T'ien-tao su-yüan* (Evidences of Christianity),[5] this book attained more popularity in China than any other missionary book. It ranks of first importance for an understanding of the Presbyterian Christian message as it was articulated in nineteenth-century China.

From 1854 to 1912 *T'ien-tao su-yüan* went through thirty or forty editions in Chinese as well as many in Japanese and Korean.[6] It was part of the language study program for new missionaries who came to China, not only with the Presbyterian Board, but with other mission societies as well. *Evidences of Christianity* was also used in theological schools for the instruction of Christian preachers. In 1907, previous to the China Centenary Conference, it was voted "the best single book" published in Chinese in a poll conducted by the Christian Literature Society.[7]

Evidences of Christianity was the only presentation of the Gospel to which thousands of high Chinese officials and intellectuals, initially in Ningpo and later in north China, were ever significantly exposed. When Martin served as an interpreter on American diplomatic missions to Tientsin and Peking (1858-1860), and during his later years (1864-1894) teaching in and administering the government-sponsored T'ung Wen Kuan (Peking University),[8] he took advantage of his many contacts to distribute *Evidences of Christianity* in the highest government circles. A classical Chinese revision of the book was prepared in 1912 at the request of the North China Tract Society, which aimed to put a copy of the work in the hands of every government official.[9] Mandarin editions were also distributed to the common people in north China.

Whenever anyone thought of Martin and his period of sixty-six years of active residence in China, he immediately associated him with his famous publication. Arthur Smith, his colleague of many years, observed, "To have produced a volume with such a history would have been worth the life of any missionary."[10]

The author has given us a description of how he constructed *T'ien-tao su-yüan.*

> Arranging the topics in my own mind, I made them the subject of
> my evening discourses — not merely presenting my views, but
> discussing them with my hearers. Each morning I put into shape
> the matter which had been rendered warm and malleable by the
> discussion of the previous evening. I followed no authority, trans-
> lated no page of any textbook, and rarely, if ever, referred to one
> in the course of my lectures. Matter and form grew out of the
> occasion, the result being a live book, adapted to the taste as well
> as to the wants of the Chinese.[11]

Although Martin claimed to follow no particular textbook,
the first of the three parts of *Evidences* was arranged "much after
the plan of [William] Paley's *Natural Theology*."[12] Apparently, the
original unpublished text which he called *Evidences of Christianity* was almost immediately augmented by two other works by
Martin, *Natural Theology* and *Revealed Theology,* which constituted parts one and three of the published *T'ien-tao su-yüan*.[13]

The apologetic nature of this work was evident from the
outset. Fan Yung-tai, a friend of Martin's who wrote the preface for
the first edition in 1854, observed that the Doctrine of the Mean
and the Christian faith did not conflict but were in perfect harmony. In his own introduction Martin picked up on this keynote,
suggesting that the *ta-tao* (great doctrine) was not the property of
either East or West — its origin was in Heaven with a personal
God who, he argued, might be referred to as *shen, t'ien-chu,* or
shang-ti.[14] Martin further added that, contrary to what the
Chinese thought, Westerners were not all merchants and destitute
of knowledge of the *tao*. Some, he pointed out, were scholars from
many countries who had labored hard to learn about Chinese life
and culture in order to preach a faith that had its origins in the
East.[15]

The author divided the material in *T'ien-tao su-yüan* into
three sections according to the already mentioned classifications of
natural theology, evidences of Christianity, and revealed theology.
Section I contained seven chapters in which Martin appealed to
heavenly bodies, the five elements, living things, the human body,
the principle of life (soul), insects and animals, and all of creation
to demonstrate the existence of God. The first appeal, then, was
not to revealed truth but to an orderly world and the reliability of
man's rational capability of perception. This was almost exactly
the plan used by Paley in his *Natural Theology*.[16]

Martin's first appeal was to the heavenly bodies — the three lights — to illustrate the orderly nature of the universe and to emphasize that it consisted of matter activated by the principle of life.[17] He explained scientifically how the sun, planets, and earth were thought to have originated in the contraction and spinning movements of the original stuff of the universe. Finally, he pointed to God as the hidden source of the gravitational principle which produced this creative activity.[18]

The author next observed that ancient Chinese and Western theories[19] used to explain the nature of the universe did not reflect scientific reality, but that he would refer to a combination of physical elements — metal, wood, water, fire, and earth — to prove God's existence. He showed in detail how only the presence of a living creator could produce the marvelous interdependent functioning of these five elements in the universe. He often utilized simple scientific illustrations, unfamiliar to his listeners, but not difficult to comprehend.[20] His very use of the concept, if not all the content, of the "five elements" appealed to the Chinese mind.

As Martin began to deal with the origin of life in Chapter III, the format of the text became more polemical, reflecting something of the "give and take" of the discussion in which the lectures originated. In each instance Martin's apologetic was directed toward a specific Chinese concept. A hearer argued, for example, that *li* (reason or principle) had given birth to all things and asked,

> What is the principle of anything if not its nature? What anything is by nature is Heaven's mandate; and Heaven is the Lord. Therefore, to say that principle gives birth to anything is no different from the theory that the Lord gives birth to it.[21]

Martin replied that the nature or principle of anything adheres in matter and can hardly give birth to that thing. God the creator, he explained, has put a distinctive and unique principle in each part of His creation, but He must be distinguished from it.[22]

He mentioned the Chinese theory that the *t'ai-chi* (great ultimate) had given birth to the *yang* (male principle) and *yin* (female principle) which together produced all the rest of creation.[23] Without condemning this view as superstitious or idolatrous, he observed only that it had no foundation in fact. Weather, environment, mutations, and survival of the fittest, he stated, were better explanations for the many different species of animal and plant life in the world than was the interaction of *yin* and *yang*.[24]

When he presented the design of the human body as further evidence of God's creative ability, he drew a distinction between the popular Chinese proverb, *t'ien sheng jen* ("Heaven gives birth to man") and the concept of creation, which implied careful planning. He described the human body, showing its complex detail and the interdependent functioning of each part. Martin may have been tempted to use Paley's famous example of the watch to reinforce his emphasis on design,[25] but instead he pointed to what was obviously more familiar to his Chinese audience — a well-planned house or a metal tool.[26] In the course of his argument, he used the illustration of Socrates, who called the attention of his disciples to a jade craftsman who, although he could carve a beautiful human figure, was not able to give it any life. How different, Martin explained, from God, who could not only plan and execute but was able to impart life.[27]

Man's psychological nature was another significant aspect of Martin's natural theology. His starting point was that the human body had no life unless indwelt by a *ling-hun* (soul). He taught that each person has only one "soul," but that the soul had five properties: consciousness, self-consciousness, memory, thought, and imagination. He presented thought as particularly important in separating man from even the highest level of animal, such as the orangutan.[28] The author used many simple illustrations to indicate the interdependence among the five properties. For example, he compared memory without thought to undigested food, and thought without memory to dysentery.[29] The several stages in the process by which silk is produced were given as an example of the indispensable nature of each of the "spirit properties."[30]

There were four "heart properties": desire, emotion, discrimination, and moral judgment. Each of these, as in the case of the "spirit properties," was further subdivided in great detail to show how God directed the working of man's heart and mind. Martin particularly emphasized that moral judgment was a result of the Divine law written on the human heart.[31]

This portion of the first section of *Evidences of Christianity* closely reflected Dugald Stewart's *Outline of Moral Philosophy*, where, in Part I, Stewart described the intellectual powers of man — including, as did Martin, external perception, memory, imagination, judgment, and reasoning. Part II was entitled "The Active and Moral Powers of Man" and included an analysis of his appetites, desires, affections, self-love, and moral faculty. Although undoubtedly indebted to Stewart in the development of this portion of his work, Martin did not bother his Chinese readers with any of the philosophic speculations of Western thinkers.[32] One difference between the work of the two men was that Martin made an occasional appeal to Scripture to support his assertions, while Stewart completely separated natural and revealed theology.[33]

Martin's use of *ling* and *hun,* apparently to carry the meaning of Stewart's "intellectual powers" and "moral powers," probably confused the Chinese who associated a wide variety of concepts with these terms. Missionaries had united the two words into a combination not used by the Chinese and assigned the meaning "soul" to it. Martin started with this coinage in his analysis and then re-divided the expression as he groped for terms to express common Western psychological concepts seldom used, at least in these combinations, by the Chinese.

Martin was indebted to both Paley and Stewart in analyzing the unique instincts of fish, birds, and beasts.[34] He showed how the mating cycles of fish, for example, cannot be explained by learning, memory, or thought processes, but only by natural disposition.[35] The Chinese term for this, *t'ien-hsing* ("heavenly" disposition), is not a Christian expression but lent itself, along with all its associated concepts, for use in Martin's argument. In effect, he linked his presentation to a ready-made doctrine of Chinese natural theology easily understood by even unsophisticated readers. The specific content which he presented was new, but not the concept with which he framed it.

Martin ended this chapter by emphasizing that though man and the animal world were different, they stood in an hierarchical relationship to each other. "Animals are subject to man and man is subject to heaven. Animals use their bodies to serve man, and man uses his heart to serve God."[36] He perceived this unity among heaven, man, and the animal world, each in its own place and with its own responsibility, as a Scriptural emphasis with deep roots in both ancient and contemporary Chinese thought.[37]

Having used multiple arguments to establish the existence of God, Martin went beyond the usual province of an introduction to natural theology — certainly beyond Paley — to talk about God's nature. He argued from the world-wide unity of nature and man to the concept of one God over all — self-existent, with no beginning or end, and possessing the attributes of omnipresence, omnipotence, and omniscience.[38] He quoted from many portions of Scripture to buttress his statements, but only after he had fully appealed to the nature of the universe and the nature of man to deduce the nature of God. His method was to "investigate man in order to understand God."[39] Could this God be approached by mortal man? Martin answered "yes," pointing out that Mencius had said that evil man could prepare himself by fasting and ablutions to sacrifice to *shang-ti.*[40]

Martin had apparently read extensively about the work of the Society of Jesus in China under the Ming dynasty and liked to think of himself as a Protestant Matteo Ricci.[41] One of Ricci's more important works had been a treatise entitled *A True Disputation about God* which, in its apologetic approach and format, has distinct similarities to the natural theology section of *Evidences of Christianity.*[42] Although deeply indebted to Paley, Stewart, and other contemporary apologists, Martin may also have been unconsciously patterning his book after that of the great Jesuit.

Section II of *T'ien-tao su-yüan,* probably the original *Evidences of Christianity,* also has seven chapters. Chapter one explains man's need for revelation, chapter seven deals with doubts hindering an understanding of the faith, and the intervening chapters analyze five types of evidence: prophecy, miracles, the spread of the Christian faith, the transforming power of Biblical doctrines, and the wonderful nature of the *tao* (doctrine).

Martin strongly stressed that natural theology did not preclude the need for special revelation through the Holy Scriptures. He affirmed that although man was related to both heaven and earth,[43] he was ignorant of God, his own nature, sin, and redemption. Nothing in the world's religions, he declared, could be compared to the Bible and the answers it gave to man's deepest questions.[44] He pointed out how its unity, its consistency, and the applicability of its truth to all men attested to its Divine origin. He stressed that, in contrast with other books, the Bible told both the good and the bad about the men and women it described. The God it portrayed was not a local deity, constantly changing and being superseded by new objects of worship, but was unchanging and controlled the entire earth.[45] Although he was writing to Chinese readers, he left no doubt that man's plight was universal.

Martin's phraseology, far from being a wooden translation of an American model, appealed constantly to Chinese concepts. When Jesus was on earth, He was "filial" in relation to His family and to God — He "honored the King's law." In His incarnation He descended to man's "dust."[46] Throughout, Martin placed stress on the fact that the Christian faith was a religion of morality and rectitude.[47]

In discussing the major Biblical evidences for the Christian faith Martin first emphasized the importance of prophecy, showing how the New Testament fulfilled predictions uttered by the Old Testament saints in ways that defied human fabrication. He observed that these were unique to Christianity and constituted a formidable proof of its reliability.[48]

Miracles were not performed, Martin asserted, in order to astound men but to provide evidence of God's unity in the Old Testament, and of Jesus' deity in the New Testament.[49] He admitted that Confucius did not even wish to talk of the miraculous, but he affirmed that what Jesus did often seemed strange only because it was new and outside of men's previous experience.[50]

In the second place, Martin devoted several pages to the resurrection of Christ as the supreme miraculous testimony to the reliability of the Christian faith.[51] He presented the resurrected Christ Himself as the continuing miracle. He had worked only three years, but His influence had changed the world; although no one had served as Jesus' teacher, He had taught all the world; He never left Palestine to go abroad, and yet the entire world had heard of Him.[52]

In common with other nineteenth-century apologists, Martin gave great evidential importance to the historic triumphs of Christianity as it was propagated throughout the world.[53] The fact that the Christian faith had penetrated over two hundred countries was presented as a sure indication of God's protection and blessing. Other religions, he claimed, had not spread this extensively and were presently in a state of decline. Whatever measure of success they had attained in some areas of the world he attributed to accommodation — as when Buddhism entered China — or to dependence upon political and military power.[54]

Martin contended dubiously that historically the Christian faith had not relied upon anything but the spiritual zeal of its followers for its advancement. In his view the removal of religious restrictions in Japan and China was one further indication of this force at work. He marveled how God had providentially granted great material resources to Christian countries so that they could sponsor missionaries and build merchant fleets to bring them to their destinations. By contrast, he observed, non-Christian countries were getting progressively weaker and had very few ships.[55] He predicted that under the impetus of this advance, China's *Pu-sa* would be no more remembered in a few years than the old deities once worshipped in early European history.[56]

According to Martin, the outward geographic expansion of Christianity was paralleled by the inward transformation of character which it brought everywhere. Martin noted how God created man with a good nature and commanded him to walk in the true way. Although civilization was primitive, man's moral state was good. As man improved his physical state he soon deteriorated morally and wandered far from God. Many holy sages appeared to rectify this situation, but their strength and wisdom were insufficient. At this critical juncture, God sent Jesus into the world to enlighten mankind, to change their evil into good, and to save them.[57] As men believed and learned the truth of the Bible, they were restored to God's will, their governments were reformed, and they developed an interest in science. When science had developed, their countries became strong and able to spread the Christian faith to other countries.[58] America's drive across the continent to the Pacific Ocean was cited as a prime example of the energy generated by the Christian faith.[59]

Martin pointed out that the introduction of the Gospel to the islands of the Pacific had commenced the same transformation all over again. Evil customs such as cannibalism, human sacrifice, and idolatry were put away as superstitious people received the "efficacious pill" of the Gospel.[60] He noted that similar changes had occurred in India and Burma.[61]

When Martin applied his convictions about the progress of

Christianity to China, he was not as optimistic. He quickly dismissed Buddhism and Taoism because of their crude idolatry and their recourse to doctrines of hell and heaven to frighten and seduce men.[62] Confucianism, although correct and beautiful in his view, was not complete, for it had completely neglected the Divine dimension in its doctrines of the *wu-lun,* the five human relationships.[63] Man, made in God's image, was first responsible to Heaven. The Christian faith embraced not five but six relationships.[64] Martin argued that this firm foundation in God's will and grace was the prerequisite to a change in human morality.

In the final chapter of Section II, Martin answered a number of the more common objections that had been raised against Christianity. The first question dealt with conflicts between the age of the earth as presented in the Bible and in the Chinese classics. The former, based on deductions from genealogical records, had been thought to be about seven thousand years, while the latter seemed to imply forty or fifty thousand. Martin proposed no definite solution, but he claimed that the Chinese records with respect to *t'ai-chi,* the *yin* and *yang,* P'an Ku, "the first man, whom the Bible calls Adam," and the ancient kings, Yao, Wu, and Shun, were not clear enough for one to form any reliable comparative judgment.[65]

Some of his Chinese audience had questioned the Biblical assertion that the human race was a unity. Martin replied that differences in race, color, and language were not as important as the universality of human nature and the human body, and were probably related to climate and spatial separation. He pointed to China's many languages to illustrate the world problem and noted that European and Indian languages both came from Sanskrit. He observed that the Biblical Eden was in Asia and therefore very close to the first four centers of civilization in India, China, Babylon, and Egypt.[66]

Martin dealt briefly with the theory of evolution. He acknowledged that scientists believed that man and animals came from one line. He went on to state, however, that despite general consensus with respect to evolution — a gradual "creation" in contrast to a "sudden" one — several things could still be affirmed: the wonder of creation; the origin of human and animal life from the earth; and man's unique possession of a soul. How could man be man, he asked, if God had not given him a soul? Martin had undoubtedly accepted some type of theistic evolution as he attempted to accommodate his faith to the impact of the evolutionary hypothesis which had dominated scientific articles since the time when Darwin published *Origin of Species* in 1858.[67] He did not insist that the six days of creation be interpreted as literal, twenty-four-hour days. To him, the order of creation was far more important than the amount of time it might have taken.[68]

In reply to the query, "Why was Jesus born in a small country like Palestine?" he gave several answers: the monotheism of the Jewish people had uniquely prepared them to receive the Messiah; the land of Palestine, bordering as it did on three continents, was a convenient place from which to preach the Gospel; Jesus' birth in Palestine symbolized the fact that He had not come to reveal His majesty and that the Christian church did not depend upon political might to make its way in the world.[69]

A very important question that Chinese people must have raised constantly was, "If I follow this way, must I turn my back on Confucius?" Martin's basic principle was that "Confucianism and Christianity may be distinguished in terms of breadth and narrowness, but not in terms of truth and error."[70] "How then," he asked, "can you talk about turning your back on it?" Without spelling out any details involved in this relationship, he went on to point out that Jesus was the God-Man — at once both teacher and Lord. He had come to redeem men by His sacrifice, not to wield political power or to change men's customs.[71] Jesus' first and last objective was to relate men to God.

The final section of the *T'ien-tao su-yüan* may have been used for catechetical instruction. Martin quoted Scripture liberally to present the basic doctrines of the Christian faith: the text and versions of the Bible; the future life; the effect on man of the sin of Adam and Eve; redemption and regeneration; development of Christian morality; and perseverance in prayer.

He prefaced this doctrinal section with a brief chapter explaining inspiration, the nature of the Bible's reliability, scribal errors, differences between the Old Testament and the New Testament, and the scope and character of the content of Scripture.

He first discussed the doctrine of the future life, utilizing both Scripture and "common sense." Divine justice with its rewards for man's good and evil conduct, he affirmed, indicated a time of future judgment.[72] Otherwise there was no justice in the universe, and all attempts at a moral life were worthless.[73]

Martin argued that the fact that man was composed of a body and soul was another evidence for a future life. He observed that the soul controlled the body and was able to operate independently of it during a man's temporal life. Was it not reasonable then, he asked, to infer that it continued to exist after the death of the body?[74] Man's spirit came from heaven's spirit, which was not in any way controlled by a body.[75] He denied transmigration which blurred the distinction between man created with a soul in God's image, and animals which were extinguished at death.[76] He concluded his argument with instruction concerning the resurrection of the body, the future judgment, and the new heaven and new earth.[77] Martin avoided use of the term *ti-yü* for hell and spoke only of the *huo* (misery) which would come upon the souls of those who had done evil.[78] When Martin explained the origin of sin, he repeatedly reminded his readers that man's nature had originally been good.[79] Evil in the world, he asserted, did not originate with man's strange customs or ignorance, but from his deliberate disobedience to God's command. This initial rebellion caused man to lose his heavenly nature and resulted in a life controlled by sin.[80] Although man outwardly appeared good, he was not virtuous and needed to be redeemed and related again to God from whom he had been separated by sin. Even the small child, Martin observed, revealed his inherited tendency to sin. He made it very clear, however, that man was not punished for Adam's sin, but for his own deliberate transgressions.[81]

Having elaborated on the sin of the human race, Martin proceeded to talk about how Jesus provided a Divine redemption. He repeatedly called attention to Old Testament declarations and cultic symbolism which foreshadowed the coming sacrifice for sins. He used the Gospel accounts to show how Christ had obeyed God's will and thus fulfilled the role of the Second Adam.[82]

At this point, the unnamed reader raised the question, "How can Jesus save if He is the descendant of Adam and implicated in the sin of our ancestors?" Martin replied that, on the one hand, Jesus was fully man and able to face man's moral dilemma and that, on the other hand, He was God and thus able to save. He explained that the virgin birth was God's means for Jesus to be born as a man free from the entanglement of the inherited sin of the human race.[83]

Could not God have forgiven man's sin without the death of Christ? Martin answered that this was impossible, since God, unlike man, possessed a sense of holiness and must satisfy both His mercy and His justice. He illustrated this teaching with a story which Chinese people, whose traditional religions emphasize harmonious relationships more than the letter of the law, probably found difficult to comprehend. A Greek king had ruled that the sin of adultery would be punished by removing the offender's eyes. When he found that his own son was guilty, he sought to show mercy and yet meet the requirements of the law, and solved his dilemma by extracting one of his son's eyes and one of his own. Martin applied this by noting that the "country's law" permitted a relative to serve as an offender's "middleman," and that this was the relationship in which Jesus stood to God and man in satisfying both Divine mercy and Divine justice.[84]

Martin next discussed the Holy Spirit's work in applying the objective redemption provided by Christ to the life of the individual believer. He compared man's relationship to God with the earth's orbit around the sun.[85] If the earth would fall from this orbit, darkness would prevail, living things would die, and all the seasons would be confused. Even if the earth should be restored to its proper orbit, God would have to re-create life. Man has lost his original place in God's economy, and the harmony of his life has been ruined. Through Christ he can be restored to the proper relationship, but it is the work of the Holy Spirit to give new life and to re-create man's original nature.[86]

Martin emphasized that by the "new birth" God re-created man's original nature and directed him away from his sin — pride, selfishness, jealousy, and covetousness — to a path of love and glorification of God.[87] Man's conscience, never destroyed but misdirected in the same way that a compass might be by the steel on a ship, was now redirected toward willing obedience to God's purposes.[88]

Consonant with his reformed faith which emphasized the sovereignty of God, Martin believed that the converting work of the Holy Spirit preceded faith and was the means by which it was received.[89] Unfortunately, throughout this section of the book, he quoted Scripture passages without explaining them sufficiently and used Scripture allusions that must have been confusing to all but the most Biblically literate Chinese.[90]

On the other hand, he devoted a great deal of attention to the development of a moral life, a topic of high priority for his Chinese readers. True morality, Martin argued, was the fruit of the Holy Spirit, but, far from being automatic, it required understanding of Biblical principles, obedience, and discipline. The aim of the moral life, he affirmed, was to be like Jesus, a result encouraged by meditation on Jesus and His virtues.[91]

In contrast to the Chinese stress upon interpersonal relationships, Martin emphasized pietistic ethics concerned largely with individual acts and attitudes rather than with social morality. He did not, however, spell out details concerning the precise things which he felt a Chinese Christian should not do, apparently leaving this to the individual conscience guided by the Holy Spirit and the Bible.

Adherents to Chinese religions found strange the Christian use of verbal prayer. The Chinese Emperor visited the Altar of Heaven to beseech heaven's blessing and to avert disaster. Chinese priests presented the people's requests to the various deities, and individual believers utilized a variety of incantations and chants in hopes of obtaining what they needed.[92] Martin, therefore, devoted an entire chapter to the need of Christian believers to persevere in prayer. Prayer, he taught, served several functions: it enabled believers to know God better, to fellowship with Him, to thank Him, to praise Him, to seek His forgiveness, and to petition for His protection.[93] Martin placed very little emphasis on prayer as a means of getting things from God, although he did not neglect this aspect entirely.

How did prayer relate to predestination? It was the means, Martin affirmed, by which God accomplished the goals which He had previously determined.[94] Nor did God need men to pray so that He might know their needs — prayer was basically the way in which He related Himself to man.[95]

Martin discussed three types of prayer: public, family, and private. In contrast to what might have been expected from one living in a family-oriented society, he put major stress on the duty of private prayer.[96]

Prayer, he emphasized, was as natural as breathing. It required no special words, clothes, ceremonies, incense, or sacrifices and could be done standing, sitting, or kneeling.[97] He concluded his instruction by analyzing the Lord's Prayer and appending three sample prayers that could be used for repentance, evening and morning devotions, and for grace at meals.[98]

Martin's discussion of the meaning of the "holy sacraments," baptism and communion, as seal, sign, and symbol of faith was very traditional, but he used it as an occasion for talking once more about the relationship between Christianity and Confucian tenets. After observing that "each country has its own rites and ceremonies, and that Jesus neither adds to nor subtracts from them,"[99] he posed the question, "Can the traditions passed down to us by our ancestors be observed along with the Christian rites?" To this query he replied, "You may observe those that do not contradict the Bible, but you must reject those that do." He supported this conclusion by quoting the Ten Commandments, noting specifically that there was no difference between idolatry and worship before the ancestral tablet, or between sacrificing to idols and presenting food to the spirit of dead ancestors.[100]

In very discreet and polite language he empathized with Chinese views that saw failure to bow and to sacrifice as unfilial conduct producing dire consequences. He reminded his readers that Lü, one of Confucius' disciples, had said that "life and death, prosperity and all things" were under Heaven's control. If this were so, Martin argued, then one's first obligation was to God, the originator of all life and the being responsible for parents and their care for their children.[101]

Although Martin believed there was no need to offer food sacrifices to the ancestors, he stated that Chinese Christians should fix and clean the graves, put up the pictures of departed loved ones, and take flowers to the burial sites. But above all, worship and praise for God should be the truest way of expressing gratitude for life. He closed his argument by affirming that when a person has understood the truth, he will be able to discern for himself which of the ancestral rites to observe and which to abandon.[102]

Martin devoted the last chapter of his book to the doctrines of the Trinity. Several of his colleagues at Ningpo believed that he had lapsed from the orthodox Christian doctrine into either tritheism or Sabellianism, a doctrine which affirmed only one Divine person but three functions. His presentation in this chapter, possibly revised over the years, afforded no clear grounds for these charges. He recognized that the subject was a mystery and that no explanation would fully satisfy. He was convinced, however, that the doctrine of the Trinity was Biblical, and that, as with many other things in life, it was to be believed even if not fully understood. He affirmed that God is one in three, and three in one.[103]

In conclusion, several things may be noted about *T'ien-tao su-yüan*. Martin, although not overtly following any particular books, had absorbed several systems of thought which he gave to the Chinese along with his Biblical doctrine. Paley's *Natural Theology*, Dugald Stewart's *Outlines of Moral Philosophy*, and numerous works on the evidences of Christianity were the most dominant. The fact that he was influenced by such works was not unique, but, in contrast with his missionary peers, he embodied his thought, whether original or derivative, in a coherent, succinct, logical book that gained wide currency throughout the Chinese Empire.[104]

Martin's own Presbyterian Confession of Faith and Calvin's *Institutes* furnished most of the substance for dogmatic portions of his work, particularly in Section III.[105] The order of discussion was not usually the same, and a few doctrines from the Confession, such as effectual calling, adoption, assurance of grace and salvation, the sabbath, marriage, divorce, and the duties of the civil magistrates, were omitted. Nothing was said about the second advent of Christ nor His millennial reign, but these are also noticeably absent from the Confession of Faith and the *Institutes*.

A product of his age, Martin identified his Christian faith with Western civilization and used the latter as an evidence of the former. The easy spread of Western culture and the Gospel in the islands of the South Pacific contributed to his abounding optimism that China would soon become a Christian nation.

Although much of his factual information and his intellectual point of departure were Western-oriented, Martin utilized Chinese terminology, illustrations, and concepts to gain a "point-of-contact." The book does not read like a translation — it is thoroughly immersed in the Chinese context.[106] Martin interacted with his readers' viewpoints, sought to meet their objections, and used examples from and allusions to their own literature to elucidate what he believed. Non-Chinese illustrations, usually either historical or scientific, were of such a nature that the central idea could easily be grasped.

Some Christian concepts — man's relationship to the universe and to his fellow man, his moral nature, the ethical dimensions of the Christian life — were more easily understood by the Chinese than the being of the Triune God, the nature of sin, the psychology of the human personality, the redemptive work of Christ, and the relationship of the Gospel to Chinese customs. Whether the message he proclaimed was more or less obscure, Martin felt confident that he was responding to needs within the human heart that reflected the Divine influence and were imperfectly met by the three Chinese religions. He had little patience with Buddhism and Taoism, but he admired the moral qualities of Confucian teaching.

The message he proclaimed was modified to some degree in its *form* but not in its *content*. The doctrines he taught and the morality he enjoined were those of the historic Christian faith. He made no essential changes, although he espoused the principle that a Chinese Christian need give up only those indigenous rites which conflicted with the Gospel. His terminology — especially for heaven, hell, and the Scriptures — was Buddhist in origin, but he put Christian content into it.

In many portions of his work he confused imparting information with communication; his message was undoubtedly overloaded with long Scripture quotations, technical terminology, and vague allusions, and it would be impossible to determine exactly how effective his communication was. Chinese scholars admired his ability to "turn a phrase," and their honor and respect for his obvious knowledge of Chinese language and literature were possibly confused with understanding and acceptance of the mysterious Christian doctrine.

T'ien-tao su-yüan accentuated the positive and spoke appreciatively of Chinese life and society. Martin condemned idolatry as an accretion brought by Buddhism, but he did not denounce other Chinese beliefs and customs — geomancy, the five elements, the *yin-yang* duality, opium, infanticide, and polygamy.[107] He wished to emphasize the central core of the Gospel message — man's restoration to a right relationship with God through the sacrifice of Christ — and to let its application to China be worked out in the liberty given by the Holy Spirit.

Several things are apparent from Martin's notable effort to communicate the Christian faith to the Chinese: 1) any real communication must speak meaningfully to an audience's cultural heritage and in symbols with which it is familiar; 2) overloading even good information will impede communication; 3) in such an attempt a missionary will probably introduce, often unconsciously, alien systems of thought and emphases along with Biblical doctrine; and 4) the presentation of Biblical teaching will be selective and partial, according to the messenger's tradition and educational background.

Notes

1. Jesse G. Lutz, ed., *Christian Missions in China: Evangelists of What?* (Boston, 1965), vii.

2. *Ibid.,* 11-12. The editor selects portions of a speech given by Griffith John at the General Conference of the Protestant Missionaries of China, May 10-24, 1877, which he retitles "Salvation from Sin, the Great Need of the Chinese."

3. The only analysis of this book with which I am familiar is one in Japanese by Yoshida Tora entitled *Investigation of Evidences of Christianity* (Tokyo, 1960).

4. W. A. P. Martin, *A Cycle of Cathay* (3rd ed.; New York, 1900), 70.

5. The literal meaning of the Chinese title is "to search out the origins of the heavenly doctrine."

6. Albert Porter, "An American Mandarin," *Outlook,* August 24, 1907, 887. In 1910 alone 21,260 copies were sold in Japan. Arthur Smith, "The Life and Work of the Late Dr. W. A. P. Martin," *The Chinese Recorder,* XLVIII (February, 1917), 118.

7. Arthur Brown, "The Death of the Rev. W. A. P. Martin," Minutes of the Board of Foreign Missions of the Presbyterian Church in the U.S.A., XXXIV, 321.

8. Literally — "Interpreters' School," although usually referred to as Peking College, or even Peking University.

9. China Letters of the Board of Foreign Missions of the Presbyterian Church in the United States of America, XI, Peking, Annual Personal Report, 1913, 1. Record Group 82-5-12. China Letters are subsequently abbreviated "CL."

10. Smith, "Life and Work of Martin," 118.

11. Martin, *Cycle,* 70.

12. *Descriptive Catalogue of the Publications of the Presbyterian Mission Press* (Shanghai, 1861), 6. Charles Denby, United States Minister to China, had received the impression that *Evidences* was a translation of Paley. Charles Denby, *China and Her Peoples* (2 vols.; N. Y., 1906), I, 217.

13. CL, IV, Ningpo, Martin to Board, #17, July 17, 1854, and #72, September, 1855, mentioned three books — *Evidences of Christianity, Natural Theology,* and *Revealed Theology.* If these three are not the three parts of the published work, then the other two books have been lost.

14. *Evidences,* 1a,1-2;1b,1;5a,5-6. (The first number refers to the page, "a" or "b" to the side of the double leaf, and the final number to the line.) The first and third names are indigenous terms into which missionaries sought to pour a Christian meaning. *T'ien-chu* is the distinctive Catholic term, less susceptive to initial misinterpretation. Throughout Section I Martin also used the word *t'ien* (heaven) to carry the meaning of a personal God, although its precise denotation in the Chinese Classics is ambiguous. See William Theodore de Bary, Wing-tsit Chan, and Burton Watson, eds., *Sources of Chinese Tradition* (2 vols.; New York, 1964), I, 5-6, 34-35, 44-47, 100-4, 485-87, and 503-9. The term *Evidences* is not used after this footnote.

15. 3b,9-5a,1. Note his emphasis on *tao,* scholars, study, and propagating an Eastern faith. He did not call Westerners by the term "missionaries."

16. Frederick Ferré, *Natural Theology Selections — William Paley* (New York, 1963), xi-xv. "Once then we know by natural theology that there is an intelligent mind behind the intricacies of the universe, then we may well leave to revelation the disclosure of many particulars which our research cannot reach respecting either the nature of this Being . . . or his character and design. . . ." 86. Martin studied Paley in his first year at New Albany Theological Seminary. See *Plan of a Theological Seminary for the Presbyterian Church in the Western States Located at New Albany, Indiana. As Revised, Amended, and Adopted October 1840* (Louisville, 1847), 20. Wilson Smith has observed that Paley's books on moral philosophy and natural theology "were once as well known in American colleges as were the readers and spellers of William McGuffey or Noah Webster in the elementary schools." *Professors of Public Ethics, Studies of Northern Philosophers Before the Civil War* (Ithaca, 1956), 215-16.

17. 1a.

18. 3a,7;4a,3.

19. The Chinese have talked of the five elements — metal, wood, water, fire, and earth — and the Greeks of water, fire, wind, and earth. DeBary, *et al., Sources*, I, 184, 198-99.

20. For example, if there were no air to conduct sound, everyone would be functionally deaf and dumb, 6a,4-10. He explained the way in which water is evaporated to form clouds which produce rain, 7a,1-5.

21. 10a,5-6.

22. 10a,6-11a.

23. 11a,6-11b,9.

24. 12a,3-12b,8.

25. Ferré, ed., *Natural Theology*, xiv.

26. 14a,6-14b,3.

27. 12b,10-13b,4.

28. 18b,9-19a,5.

29. 18a,7-9.

30. 20a,4-6.

31. 23b,4-5.

32. Dugald Stewart, *Outlines of Moral Philosophy* (Edinburgh, 1793), 28-143.

33. 24a,4-8.

34. 24a,9-28a,3. He claimed that their bodily structures were wonderful but basically similar to the marvels of the human body. Paley tended to emphasize this more than he did their instincts.

35. 26b,8.

36. 27b,8-9.

37. DeBary, *et al., Sources*, I, 206. "The Idea that Heaven, earth and man, in their nature and in all their workings, form an inseparable trinity is fundamental in Han thought." C. K. Yang, *Religion in Chinese Society* (Berkeley, 1967), 250.

38. 28a,6-30a,10.

39. 30b,7. *t'ui-jen chi-shen.*

40. 31b,10-32a,1.

41. *Ch'ou-pan I-wu-shih-mu* (Management of Barbarian Affairs), T'ung-chih, XVII, 25-26. In debating what their view ought to be toward Martin's translation of Henry Wheaton's *Elements of International Law*, some Chinese officials commented that "he wishes to imitate men like Ricci in making a name in China."

42. Vincent Cronin, *The Wise Man from the West* (New York, 1955), 215.

43. A neat Chinese proverb — "He wears heaven on his head and the earth is beneath his feet."

44. 38b,10.

45. 43a,5-46b,5.

46. 42a,10. This is a Buddhist term.

47. 46b,4.

48. 52b,1-3.

49. 53b,2-7.

50. 53a,10-53b,2,and 54a,7-8.

51. 59a,9-60b,9.

52. 60b,9-61a,6.

53. This note is prominent in Ebenezer Dodge, *The Evidences of Christianity* (New York, 1869), v; Mark Hopkins, *Evidences of Christianity* (Boston, 1890), 335-45; Albert Barnes, *Lectures on the Evidences of Christianity in the Nineteenth Century* (New York, 1868), 109-50.

54. 62a,1-62b,3.

55. 62b,10 and 63a,1-63b,2-8.

56. 64a,2-7.

57. 65a,3-65b,6.

58. 65b,7-66a,9.

59. 63b,4-6.

60. 66b,2. The Chinese term is *ling-tan* (spirit pill).

61. 67a,6-7.

62. 67b,5-10.

63. 67b,2-3. He called Confucianism *cheng*, meaning upright, straight, orthodox, correct, etc. The five relationships are ruler-minister, father-son, husband-wife, elder brother-younger brother, friend-friend. Karl Reichelt, *Religion in Chinese Garment* (New York, 1951), 47.

64. 68a,4-5; 68a,8-69a,2.

65. 69a,4-70a,1.

66. 70a,3-70b,9.

67. 71a,6-71b,1. The edition of *T'ien-tao su-yüan* used in this study is undoubtedly a reproduction of the last edition of 1912. This would appear from the author's statement that America had forty-five states, 63b,5. The forty-fifth and forty-sixth states (Arizona and New Mexico) were added to the Union in 1912. Some of Martin's views, particularly on science, obviously reflect a period later than the first edition of 1854. His other beliefs and attitudes are consistent with the general missionary approach revealed in his Ningpo letters from 1850 to 1860. Most of his many revisions were stylistic in nature.

68. 72a,1-3.

69. 72a,3-9.

70. 73a,9.

71. 73b,1-6.

72. 78a,1. Divine justice is *t'ien-li,* a Chinese expression associated with the very nature of things.

73. 78a,1-80a,6. This line of reasoning is good natural theology, fits the Biblical data, and harmonizes with the Buddhist teaching of karma. C. H. Plopper, *Chinese Religion Seen Through the Proverb* (Shanghai, 1935), 223. Martin quoted the Chinese proverb, *yu ch'ien-yin pi yu hou-ko.* "If there is a previous cause, there certainly will be a later result."

74. In this section he came perilously close to Buddhist doctrine which stated that a man's spirit leaves him when he is sleeping. 80a,6-80b,9.

75. 81a,6.

76. 82b,9-83a,8.

77. 83a,9-86a,8. Judgment, immortality of the soul, and even a new world would not be as strange to the Chinese mind as the resurrection of the body. Reichelt, *Religion in Chinese Garment,* noted that "resurrection of the body is never mentioned in the thought systems existing from China's ancient period." 20.

78. 85b,5. From this context alone it would appear that the judgment of which he spoke extended from death to the day of resurrection. D. Z. Sheffield expressed fear to his Board, the ABCFM, that some new missionaries might adopt a belief in "probation for the heathen." He thought that many English missionaries accepted this view. A.B.C. 16.3.12.XII, #181, 4. Sheffield to Judson Smith, November 5, 1886. It is probable that Martin tended toward this view in his early ministry.

79. 86a,1;87a,10;90b,1;92a,6-7. Chinese sages and philosophers have differed as to the nature of man, but, with the exception of Hsün Tzu, the dominant view has been that it is good. DeBary, *et al., Sources,* I, 88, 100. Martin only made passing reference to this dispute, but he was obviously thinking about it. 92a,6-92b,1.

80. 90a,6-92b,2. By this Martin did not mean that man no longer had God's law written on his heart, 92a,7. The compass was still there, but it needed to be redirected.

81. 90b,5-9;89b,6-8.

82. 93b,5-94b,10;93b,4.

83. 94b,10-95a,1;96b,4-97a,1.

84. 97b,8-98b,4.

85. He referred to man as a *hsiao-t'ien* (small heaven). This fit very well with the Chinese concept of man as an integral part of the universe.

86. 100b,6-102a,1.

87. *Tsui*, the common term used for sin, meant "crime" in ordinary conversation.

88. 105b,4-10.

89. 107a,8-107b,2.

90. One of these was "steadfast anchor . . . a hope that enters into the veil. . . ." Hebrews 6:19, RSV; 108a,2. He used the term "centurion" in 107b,2. No Biblical references were used for any of his Scripture quotations, making it virtually impossible for Chinese readers to find the proper context.

91. 114b,2-4;117a,2-10;120b,7-8;115b,8-116a,5.

92. Yang, *Religion in Chinese Society*, 15. He noted that an analysis of five hundred "prayer slips" included the following requests: healing of diseases, marriage, traveling mercies, wealth, lawsuits, progeny, family problems, lost articles, moving (household), business affairs, crops, domestic animals, and official position.

93. 121b,9-122a,5.

94. 122b,9-123a,3.

95. 123a,4-7.

96. He gave nearly three times as much space to private prayer as he did to family prayer. 124b,9-125a,3, and 125a,3-125b,4.

97. 125b,2-8.

98. 125b,9-127b,10.

99. 128a,2.

100. 129b,7-130a,6.

101. 130a,6-131a,2.

102. 131a,2-8. Martin was much more tolerant of the ancestral rites in his English writings, undoubtedly hoping to modify the strict views of many of his colleagues. For the place of these views, elaborated more fully in his English writing, see Chapter X, "Strategy for the Conversion of China."

103. 131b,1-9;133b,7-134a,4.

104. Hampden C. DuBose, *Preaching in Sinim, or The Gospel to the Gentiles with Hints and Helps for Addressing a Heathen Audience* (Richmond, Virginia, 1893), went into great detail on the need of the Chinese people for "natural theology." He described how the five elements, human physiology, natural history, astronomy, and the "book of nature" in general should be used where there had not been an adequate preparation for the Gospel such as was found through the presence of Jews in the Roman Empire. 135, 137-39, 141-44, 154-68, and 169-89.

105. Martin's favorite teacher at New Albany Theological Seminary

had been John Matthews, professor of theology. His only textbook in classroom instruction was the "Confession of Faith of the Presbyterian Church." See LeRoy Halsey, *A History of McCormick Theological Seminary of the Presbyterian Church* (Chicago, 1893), 33, 45-46.

106. How much credence is to be given to statements that *T'ien-tao su-yüan* was "written in Chinese without assistance" and that it is "one of the best Wenli books ever written by a foreigner"? "Obituary of W. A. P. Martin," *North China Herald,* December 23, 1916, 304. At no point in this work does Martin acknowledge Chinese literary help in such a clear manner as he does in his *Christianity and Other Creeds.*

107. Some of these were mentioned with disapproval but only in the context of dealing with a larger issue.

CHAPTER SIX

A Developing Crisis — Secular or Institutional Missionary?

FOR WILLIAM and Jane Martin and their four sons the period of furlough from 1860 to 1862 was a pot-pourri of many activities. One of William's primary concerns was to arrange for the education of his two oldest sons, Pascal and Winfred, in Phillips Academy at Andover, Massachusetts. He traveled extensively to promote the cause of missions, which, because of the Civil War, faced a crisis both in finances and in the recruitment of new candidates.[1] He also took special training in telegraphy at Philadelphia, hoping that he might teach its practical benefits to Chinese students.[2]

Some of Martin's furlough time was spent in scholarly activities. He had joined the American Oriental Society in 1858 just a few years after its founding and was now able to attend his first meetings.[3] In recognition of his work as an interpreter with the American diplomatic missions in North China, Lafayette College at Easton, Pennsylvania awarded him an honorary degree in July, 1861.[4]

Lessons from his ten years of service in China, particularly those learned during his most recent experiences in North China, crystallized into a new strategy during Martin's time in America, a strategy summed up officially in a report which he sent to the Board shortly before he sailed again for China,[5] and which guided his thinking in subsequent years. Briefly, he proposed to establish a high-grade school to train Chinese Christians in literature, theology, science, and medicine. Training ministers would be its principal task, but such a school would also train educators, doctors, and scientists who would serve as "auxiliaries in the work of evangelization." Their work, Martin hoped, would "strikingly exhibit the superiority of Christian civilization"; hence, it would prove a "formidable obstacle to the success of our cause" if such training were left to other agencies.[6]

W. A. P. Martin, his wife, and their two younger sons, Newell and Claude, arrived back in China in mid-summer, 1862, after an eighty-five-day trip from New York and around the tip of Africa.[7] Even during the relatively short period of their absence many momentous changes had occurred in China.

The British and French, following their initial reprisal at Taku in July, 1859, had regrouped and forced their way into Peking in October, 1860, to ratify the agreements reached earlier in Tientsin. This treaty fully opened the way for foreign diplomatic residence at Peking.[8] More important, these new arrangements between China and the Western powers marked the end of the tributary period and the beginning of the treaty era in Sino-Western relationships. The years immediately following the signing of the Peking Convention were called the "T'ung-chih Restoration," named after the ruler who succeeded Hsien-feng, who died in 1861 in Jehol where he had retreated in shame and disarray after the allied invasion of Peking in 1860.

This was a period of reform when particular attention was paid to pacification of rebellions,[9] a restoration of the war-suspended civil examinations, a reconstitution of local civil administration in many areas of the empire, the rehabilitation of the economy, an effort to select and instruct men of talent in the old Confucian principles, and a new approach to foreign affairs. Western learning was not rejected, but accepted according to the principle of "Chinese learning as the basis; Western learning for practical use."[10]

Feng Kuei-fen, a Soochow scholar, was probably the first to use the phrase *tzu-ch'iang*, "Self-strengthening, that more than any other would symbolize the age."[11] Tseng Kuo-fan, the Chinese general-scholar most responsible for military victory over the Taiping rebels, and Li Hung-chang, holder of many government posts, chief of which was Governor-General of Chihli from 1870 to 1895, each argued for both the adoption of Western technology, and for the reaffirmation of the old Confucian virtues of sincerity, good faith, courage, and righteousness. Railroads, shipyards, telegraph systems, coal mining, military and naval build-up, Western learning in general, and scientific and linguistic studies in particular, were all acceptable, but only as long as the *li* — proper behavior within the hierarchical system of a rational and universal natural order — was maintained.

This combination of Western technology and studies with Chinese values found several institutional expressions,[12] the most important of which was the Tsungli Yamen, established in 1861 to care for "foreign affairs."[13] The Tsungli Yamen was really an ad-hoc branch of the Grand Council designed to deal with the immediate emergency. Its scope went beyond foreign affairs to promote schools, science, Western industry, and other aspects of modernization. It continued as an institution till the time of the Boxer Rebellion, but its usefulness was diminished by the fall in influence of Prince K'ung in 1870, and particularly by the development of the Superintendents of Trade at Tientsin and Shanghai whose function was to divert diplomatic contacts from Peking to these other sites, and thus to obviate the arrangements for foreign envoys to reside in Peking as established by the Peking Treaty of 1860.[14]

When the Martin family arrived in Shanghai in 1862, they expected to stay only a few days. The "finger of God," however, directed differently.[15] W. S. Culbertson, pillar of Presbyterianism in Shanghai, died suddenly on August 25, 1862, while the Martins were there, and William yielded to the entreaties of his younger brethren to help them temporarily in their work.

Protestant mission work had begun on a permanent basis in Shanghai in the mid-1840's.[16] Joseph Wight and Culbertson, representing American Presbyterians, arrived in 1850, and by the time Martin was delayed there in 1862, there was a sizeable community, not only of missionaries but of other foreigners engaged in commerce and diplomacy. Before his own arrival, Martin thought the "Shanghai mission all a mistake and the field a hopeless one."[17] Once upon the scene, he was more impressed. Shanghai, he decided, was the only "old city of this old empire which has received the impulse of a new life."[18] He noted that its population, attracted by the security of a foreign protectorate, had risen from 200,000 to one million in fifteen years, and that the trade of its port ranked first in all the East. He believed that the tremendous infusion of refugees who spoke many vernaculars and were more energetic than the local citizens provided a potential strategic base from which to evangelize all China.[19]

Having found good pragmatic reasons to be in Shanghai, Martin set to work with "the greatest of zeal and industry."[20] Aided by his Ningpo assistants he reopened the two Presbyterian chapels,[21] took over management of the press, moved from Ningpo only two years earlier, made plans to reinvigorate the school program, and sought to revive the local Presbyterian church which had added no converted members in ten years.[22]

Martin knew that better preaching, better teaching, and better administration in the Shanghai mission — the keys to his leaving it on its own — depended on the missionaries there obtaining a good foundation in the basics of the Chinese language. Therefore, beginning October 1, 1862, he organized all of the Presbyterian missionaries and one or two others into a class to learn the classical Chinese characters, convinced that he could save them "years of hard and perhaps fruitless labor."[23]

The ground of his confidence was *The Analytical Reader: A Short Method for Learning to Read and Write Chinese* on which he had begun to work while still in Ningpo. Utilizing a character-count method developed by William Gamble at the Presbyterian press, he further improved this "spelling book" which introduced his students to the basic vocabulary needed for both ordinary and religious use.[24]

By early October, Mrs. Martin was extremely ill, and despite her periodic improvement it was clear the family could not continue long in Shanghai, even though the Executive Committee in New York and his colleagues on the field urged Martin to delay at least a year before leaving.[25] It was not clear yet where they would settle. Martin preferred Peking, but since the capital was not an "open city" covered by the treaties, there was apprehension that the Chinese government would object. His only hope of living and working there would depend upon the questionable clause in the Chinese text of the French treaty of Tientsin.[26] He was spurred by the fact that the capital

> . . . now swarms with Jesuits who are straining every nerve to

> preoccupy it to the exclusion of Protestants, and if they could do this it might be a source of great calamity to our missions in general. I go to the capital with no intentions to spend my time in fighting *them,* but feeling that my presence will be a protest against their usurpations.[27]

Ever since their arrival in Peking following the signing of the latest treaty, the Protestant missionaries seemed almost obsessed with the many signs, past and present, of the Roman Catholic presence at the center of the Empire.[28] They noted the cemetery with burial plots of twenty-six priests, the Jesuit observatory on the eastern wall, and the present energetic refinishing of the old cathedral, built some two hundred years before any Protestant had been on the scene.[29] One missionary commented smugly that

> They [Protestants] will use no crooked means of obtaining the favor of the great. Should it be given to them, they will be thankful. But in order to get it, they will not compromise themselves with the national idolatry, nor, should they enjoy it, lean on the arm of flesh rather than on the power of God.[30]

The most irksome thing, of course, was that the Roman Catholic missionaries could preach freely[31] while the Protestants were permitted to live in Peking only if they had valid non-evangelistic work.[32]

The Peking Convention of 1860 had enlarged the number of "open ports" to include Tientsin, and Martin proceeded first to this large northern city, leaving his family there while he went on ahead to spy out the land. Through the help of S. Wells Williams and Anson Burlingame, American Minister to China, he obtained temporary summer quarters in a temple three miles outside the West Gate of Peking.[33] By autumn Martin had located a larger dwelling, adequate both for living quarters and a school, in the southeastern part of the city near the Tsungli Yamen. Poor communications with home made rapid Board approval of this new step impossible, and he borrowed funds both for the purchase price and the necessary repairs from Williams.[34]

By the beginning of October, 1863, Martin had a rough idea of the strategy he wished to pursue at Peking. He regarded preaching as his most important task, but official fear of Christianity in Peking made it unwise to hold meetings in streets, "heathen temples," or other public places where noisy crowds might assemble. He wished to maintain a low profile and hold only quiet home meetings and personal conversation until the "toleration clauses ... are completely operative."[35] He recalled that the "headlong temerity of a Dutch missionary," who was expelled from Peking in 1862, had caused a reactionary tendency toward Christian preaching.

Not that he was without friends. The United States Minister, Anson Burlingame, suggested he could obtain for him a "post of great influence — purely of a missionary kind," and even Frederick Bruce, the British minister, whom Martin knew but from whom he expected nothing but opposition, seemed willing to help. Chinese officials with whom he had made an earlier acquaintance through his diplomatic work welcomed him warmly. Although he professed irksome the official etiquette which their friendship demanded, he understood the need to be like Paul who had "certain of the chief of Asia which were his friends."

These contacts encouraged him to believe that his efforts for Christ might reach the Emperor himself. John Burdon, of the Church Missionary Society, told him that his *Evidences of Christianity* had been shown to the Prince Regent. Rejoicing that "Caesar's household has been penetrated," Martin expostulated, "what a blessed thing for China if the young emperor, now eight years old, would grow up with the Christian predilections of the King of Madagascar."[36] Sharing Matteo Ricci's earlier vision of the conversion of the Emperor, he commended him to the "prayers of the children of America," observing that

> If he grows up a blood-thirsty tyrant, his reign will be a curse to many millions, but if it please God to give him an enlightened and liberal mind he may prove a Joshua to lead this great people out of the desert of Paganism into the Canaan of truth. . . . Some of his great officers have read Christian books, and when he becomes older, no doubt he will desire to read them for himself. . . . Pray for this dear child.[37]

Martin enthusiastically shared his vision of Peking's strategic importance for missionary work with the still reluctant Executive Committee of his Board in New York. First, he claimed, it was a center for the "family of nations" — Koreans, Mongolians, and Tibetans who could return to their homes and evangelize their countrymen. Second, Peking was "the chief seat of pagan worship for the whole of Eastern Asia." In the third place, there were two million members of the Manchu race who could be evangelized through Mandarin Chinese. Finally, Martin argued, the fall of the Taiping insurgents, whose success he had so confidently predicted in the 1850's, had given new life to the reigning dynasty to whose national integrity the West was now fully committed.[38]

During these years in Peking William Martin continued to tread the well-worn missionary paths that he knew so well from his initial term in Ningpo. Evangelism, "the main work of the missionary," was high on his list of priorities.[39] The Presbyterian quarters were ideal for this since they were "surrounded by a large population of trades people, who are more accessible to missionary efforts than the employees of government. . . ."[40] While the chapel was being refurbished, the first formal Presbyterian worship service was held in the home of Mr. Ts'ao, the senior catechist. The small chapel, which held only sixty, was enlarged to seat over double that number by April, 1864, and services were held four times a week.

A Scotch missionary, W. C. Burns, who sometimes worked independently and at other times was affiliated with the English Presbyterians, frequently helped Martin at these services. A revivalist with extensive experience in both Scotland and South China, he lived a very simple life, and apart from a good meal once a week at Martin's home, close to his own very cheap dwelling, he subsisted on a few cents a day.[41] Burns had come to Peking to seek official relief for Chinese converts undergoing persecution, but most of his time was spent preaching to Chinese, edifying the missionary community, and translating works like *Pilgrim's Progress* and *Peep of Day,* a children's book, into Chinese.[42]

Crowds at various chapel services in the early days concerned Chinese officials. On one occasion, Wen-hsiang, the Manchu Grand Councillor, called Martin in and asked him to warn all missionaries to "proceed cautiously, avoid opposition, and keep their operations somewhat in the background." Martin passed the message on to his colleagues, but did not let it deter him from expanding his own preaching activities by renting still another chapel on a large street near one of the city gates.[43] He referred to this chapel as a *zayat,* a term indicating that it was probably used more for religious conversation than for evangelistic proclamation.[44]

Mrs. Martin, although occupied with educating her two children, Newell and Claude,[45] was an able assistant in evangelism and teaching. Within the first year of their residence in Peking, she had started a class for women and girls in their home. A Presbyterian catechism was used for regular instruction, and weekly sermons were delivered by the Chinese assistant, Mr. Huang.[46] Separate women's meetings helped to avoid "the promiscuous assemblage of men and women," a practice which, as Mrs. Martin noted, Emperor K'ang-hsi in his famous edict declared to be "most offensive in the eyes of the Chinese, and which alone will prevent them ever universally adopting Christianity, even should there be no other reason for rejecting it."[47]

Results at the various meetings were not spectacular. Initially, large crowds came out of curiosity to see and hear the strange foreigner, but with the exception of the Sunday morning service at the central chapel, they began to dwindle. One person was baptized the first year and six in each of the next two years. Divided equally among Chinese and Manchus, they ranged in age from mid-teens to old men. Martin was particularly grateful that only one was financially dependent upon the mission, a good omen for the prospects of a self-supporting church. Trained more systematically in Scripture doctrine in regular Bible classes following the morning worship, these converts were organized into a church.[48] Some of the church members did not last, and Martin confessed that with people seeking admission "from all motives but the right one," it was difficult to separate the chaff from the wheat.

Most of those attending the chapel, as well as those baptized, were from the poorer class, although Martin was encouraged by frequent intelligent inquirers with high social connections. Among these he mentioned a physician from the Imperial Medical College, a young officer whose yellow belt showed his relationship to the Emperor, and an old Mandarin who came to the chapel meetings waited on by four servants.[49] The latter had prepared a list of sixteen questions including inquiries on creation, "last things," astronomy, and geography. Without doubt, however, "the gentry of Peking, being mostly connected with the government, are more disposed to stand aloof from intercourse with foreigners than those of other cities."[50]

Martin carried on much less evangelistic itineration about Peking than he had in the environs of Ningpo. In fact, he limited his country treks to one ambitious undertaking of five weeks that led him from Peking through inland China to Shanghai. Although he had some scientific objectives for his journey, the religious motives were still dominant.[51] This pioneer venture into areas which he claimed had never before been penetrated by a foreigner, proved his hypothesis that the "empire is open to the very centre."[52] He preached on Sundays, distributed tracts and sold books at village fairs, and conversed with Mandarins and country folk alike. When he reached K'aifeng, he proclaimed the Gospel of the Messiah to the small remnant of a Jewish community who were without a rabbi, intermarried with the Chinese, illiterate in Hebrew, ignorant of their monotheistic faith, their synagogue destroyed by their own hand, and desperately poor.

His concern for this isolated community of the ancient people of God continued long after his journey. He sought to persuade Joseph Schereschewsky, a converted Jew, then a missionary with the American Episcopal Mission in Peking, to visit them.[53] In a less evangelistic tone, he urged rich Jews in Shanghai to provide financial aid to rebuild their synagogue in order to continue a "witness of the true God" in central China.[54]

Martin's participation in the early Presbyterian parochial school experiment on the American frontier as well as his educational experiences in Ningpo caused him to see the need for a Christian academy in Peking that would educate "preachers, physicians and engineers" to diffuse Christian truth throughout China.[55] How else, he reasoned, could he get beyond the common man being evangelized in the chapel and reach government leaders? He had described this vision to friends at home during his first furlough, but his hopes were not fulfilled until May 6, 1864, when he opened a day school with four young men and two small boys as a nucleus.[56] The Board at home, particularly hampered by lack of funds during the Civil War, could give no real encouragement to this venture, but Robert Hart, a close friend since Ningpo days, gave him 1500 taels a year from Customs revenue to run the school.[57]

Because children of the official class received the traditional education, Martin's school, which he named Truth Hall Academy, largely attracted children from the poorer classes. A few of the students roomed at the mission compound, but most continued to live at home. They all took their meals at the school, and the poorest were clothed with mission funds,[58] but Martin viewed this as "aid rather than support."[59] Ranging in age from ten to twenty-one years, the students were thought to have even greater potential for the future evangelization of the North than those in the school in Ningpo had for South China. In a remark that may have reflected his own frontier experiences and perspective Martin observed,

> Less haughty and more docile, they are not inferior in talent to some of the wealthier families and are far more likely to exert themselves having the stimulus of necessity in addition to other motives.[60]

The idea was to seek the conversion of these non-Christian youths so that they might become "evangelists for the north." Each year a number of the students were intellectually ready to accept the Gospel message, but there were few public professions of faith.[61]

Martin put great emphasis upon geography, mathematics, science, and Chinese classics in the school's curriculum. In fact, the so-called Christian studies were only taught on Sunday, a practice which William Morrison, who later succeeded him, termed a "peculiarity of the school here."[62]

Lack of Board support for Truth Hall Academy discouraged Martin greatly. He could understand the financial and personnel problems produced by the "stormy years" of the Civil War, but after "a gracious Providence has restored to us the blessings of peace and union have we no more men and money to devote to the Master's cause in this great empire?"[63] Money — at least for the school — was not as critical a problem as manpower. He did not even use all that Hart donated annually, and although he wanted to erect a large church building in Peking,[64] he was satisifed to build a new chapel, the Hall of Truth, by the south gate. The real crisis was in men. Nearly every letter appealed anew for a medical doctor as well as for a general missionary. He wanted men like

Calvin Mateer, John Nevius, Hunter Corbett, or even D. B. McCartee to join him in entering the open doors at the capital,[65] but these hopes were never realized.

An important non-mission project in which Martin became involved during his early years in Peking was the translation of the Sacred Scriptures into Mandarin, the popular language of Northern China. Nearly all Protestant translations up to this period were either into the classical language or one of the local vernaculars — such as those of Ningpo, Amoy, or Foochow. An early Mandarin version of parts of the Bible had been translated by a Jesuit, C. P. Louis de Poirot, in the mid-1750's and had been used in the Peking area.[66] In 1856, Walter Medhurst of the LMS put the New Testament of the Delegates' Version into the Southern Mandarin language current in Nanking.[67]

In 1861 the Shanghai Corresponding Committee of the British and Foreign Bible Society suggested the need for a version in Peking Mandarin,[68] and a committee was established with Joseph Edkins (LMS), W. A. P. Martin, S. I. J. Schereschewsky (Protestant Episcopal Church in America), J. S. Burdon (CMS), and Henry Blodget (ABCFM) as members.[69] By 1864 the American Bible Society appointed all of the same men to their China Committee, in order that work on the Mandarin version could proceed with the greatest unity.[70]

Martin's views concerning Bible translation appear to have taken a more literal turn since his tentative support of the LMS version in the late 1850's. In surveying the various attempts to render the Scriptures into classical Chinese, he steered a careful course between literalism and excessive freedom. The LMS translation was "elegant and scholarly" but "sacrifices too much to grace of diction." Bridgman and Culbertson's work, however, "combines a conscientious respect to the inspired original, with due regard to the proprieties of the Chinese language." More important, he claimed that the latter translation also avoided allusions to "superstitious legends, amatory poems and cynical or lascivious epigrams."[71] These principles guided him as he approached his work on the Mandarin New Testament.

The great advantage of written Mandarin was that it very nearly coincided with the spoken vernacular of Northern China. Martin called it the "poor man's Bible" or the "common" Bible.[72]

He noted that the Empress Dowager had commanded that certain well-known passages from the Chinese classics be put into Mandarin in order to instruct the young emperor more easily.

> What the Chinese thus do with their own sacred books, for the benefit of one who is called the Son of Heaven shall we not do with the Holy Scriptures, for the benefit of the people that many of them may become the children of God.[73]

Based on Medhurst's southern Mandarin version, the work proceeded much more quickly than it would have had it been a completely new translation.[74] By October, 1864, little more than six months after they had started, the Committee, members doing much of its work individually,[75] had finished the rough draft of the historical portions of the New Testament; the Gospel of John, mostly Martin's work, was already being printed.[76] A year later, the first edition of John was exhausted, and one half of the New Testament had gone to press.[77]

At this point an old controversy arose in a new form. Alexander Williamson, formerly a missionary in Shanghai and now a special agent for the National Bible Society of Scotland, reached Peking after an extensive trip distributing the Scriptures in North China. He reported his great embarrassment at the people's confusion over the various names for God and recommended that Protestants use *t'ien-chu* ("Heavenly Lord"), the Roman Catholic term. Bishop Smith of Victoria had made a similar proposal several years earlier, but it had failed to receive any significant support.[78]

Missionaries in Peking discussed Williamson's proposal, and in the fall of 1865 a group consisting of Edkins, Martin, Collins (CMS), Dudgeon (LMS), and Blodget and Goodrich (ABCFM) signed a statement advocating *t'ien-chu* for "God" and *sheng-shen* for Holy Spirit.[79] This statement, accompanied by an explanatory letter, was sent to each major mission station in China to elicit widespread missionary approval. Williamson made the same proposal at monthly prayer concerts at Tientsin and Chefoo and gained significant support.[80]

Most of South China, "controlled by the fixed usage of older stations," as Martin put it,[81] was adamantly opposed to this compromise measure. Martin's explanation of the matter, probably the same that he had given to the Executive Committee of his mission board, reached the missionaries at Ningpo. He indicated that *t'ien-chu* was already used widely by Protestants in preaching and in tracts. He believed the term was unequivocally free from any "tinge of paganism," that it was already widely understood throughout the Chinese Empire because of the work of the Roman Catholic Church, and that its use would commend the Bible to Catholics for their support. He had high hopes that adopting *t'ien-chu* would unite the warring factions of Protestantism, sharply divided between *shang-ti* and *shen*.[82]

Dr. McCartee, who incorrectly saw Martin as the prime figure in this movement, reacted violently to the proposal. He pressured the Bible society, and the China Committee was asked to suspend work on the Mandarin version until the issue was settled. The American Bible Society referred the problem to a translation subcommittee of scholars, including Dr. Woolsey of Yale College.[83]

Submitted April 28, 1867, their report discouraged the use of *shang-ti* for "God," but left the possible use of *t'ien-chu* open. It reaffirmed a fifteen-year-old recommendation that any published editions should be small until agreement on a common term could be reached. It recommended that the Mandarin version "deserves the patronage and assistance of our society."[84]

This report opted for freedom and, as such, did not satisfy all of the missionary community. It did enable the translation to continue, and in 1872 the Mandarin New Testament was completed. The American Bible Society edition used *chen-shen* ("true God") and the British and Foreign Bible Society issued one edition with *t'ien-chu* and one with *shang-ti*.[85] The Old Testament translation was rendered by Schereschewsky, and a complete Bible published in 1878.[86]

Widely accepted in North China,[87] the Peking Mandarin version was "to Chinese in half the empire what Wycliffe's Bible was to the English and Luther's to the Germans."[88] Martin continued on the China Committee until well into the 1870's, although his responsibility in translation concluded just before his return to America in the summer of 1868.[89] His contribution to the actual translation of the New Testament does not appear to have been as great as that of the others,[90] even though he viewed it as the "fourth major literary work he had done."[91] The Gospel of John, for which

Martin prepared the rough draft, was the first portion to be printed, indicating his desire "to get on with the work" and his impatience with lack of progress.[92]

This was neither the end of the term controversy nor of the need for more revision and for more versions of the Sacred Scriptures. Progress to this point was commendable, and both the variety of translations and the heat of the arguments indicated a vitality in the Christian movement. Unfortunately, a dynamic approach to translation and the need to train and use Chinese as the major translators were not yet acknowledged principles. As a result it could probably be correctly said that "the Bible as we know it has not yet been placed in the hands of the Chinese; and that, as a natural consequence, Christianity has never yet had a fair chance in China."[93]

Chapel preaching, itineration, starting a Christian academy, and translating the Scriptures were missionary tasks which gave W. A. P. Martin great satisfaction, but even while he was engaged in these activities, opportunities pointing in another direction appeared and created a serious identity crisis.

The first of these opportunities had come before Martin even reached Peking. While he lingered in Shanghai, he began to translate Wheaton's *Elements of International Law* into Chinese.[94] His diplomatic activities in North China had convinced him that Chinese officials could use some knowledge of Western law in their international relations. Peter Parker, at Lin Tse-hsü's request, had translated a few paragraphs from Vattel's work, *Le Droit des Gens* (International Law), but such a small amount was obviously insufficient,[95] and in Martin's view "to introduce it [Vattel] to the Chinese would not be unlike teaching them the Ptolemaic system of the Heavens."[96] Far better than the out-dated Vattel (1758) was Wheaton's treatise of 1836 which "brings the science down to a very recent day and is generally recognized as a full and impartial digest."

Henry Wheaton was well qualified to write on international law. From 1815 to 1827 a successful lawyer in the United States, he spent the next twenty years of his life as an American diplomatic representative in Europe. His most significant position was as Minister Plenipotentiary at Berlin. In 1847 he returned to America to accept the post as Lecturer on International Law at Harvard.[97]

Elements of International Law, the first work of any note on the subject in English, was published in 1836 and received widespread acclaim, with many favorable reviews appearing in England, France, Germany, and the United States.[98] It was received as a standard textbook in all nations, and became required reading for the training of diplomatic interpreters in Western countries.

Concerning this, his first secular translation, Martin observed,

> I was led to undertake it, without the suggestion of anyone, but providentially I doubt not, as a work which might bring this atheistic government to the recognition of God and his Eternal Justice; and perhaps impart to them something of the Spirit of Christianity.[99]

He mentioned the project to George Seward, United States Consul in Shanghai. When Wen-hsiang, the Grand Secretary, confused by diplomatic problems with France early in 1863, asked Burlingame to recommend a Western authority on international law, the United States Minister mentioned Wheaton's book to him and consented to have portions of it translated. Soon after this, Burlingame learned of Martin's effort from Seward and arranged an interview with Chinese officials when Martin came to Peking.[100] Chinese interest was further spurred when Ch'ung-hou, whom Martin had briefed on the translation at Tientsin in July, 1863, offered to write and recommend the work to Wen-hsiang.[101]

On September 10, 1863, Martin met with members of the Tsungli Yamen to discuss his translation.[102] They were favorably impressed and hoped that it included several important sections which Robert Hart, the Inspector-General of Customs, had already introduced to them. They promised Martin literary help in completing the translation and five hundred taels to subsidize the cost of printing and publication.[103] Subsequently, a specially appointed Commission of four men — all of literary competence and one a scholar working in the Hanlin Academy — were assigned to help him. Martin told them he was not interested in any remuneration but added, "You will, of course, give me a decoration for it."[104]

Martin clearly perceived that the Chinese viewed Wheaton as a book about ethical philosophy rather than international law.

To it they wished to apply Confucius' maxim: "cull out the right and observe it; cull out the wrong and correct it." The price of their liberty to reject or follow the law could be seen, he added, in the burned-out summer palace, a monument to their violating a truce and imprisoning Harry Parkes. For "such ignorance the best remedy is 'to teach it with thorns.'"[105]

As Martin already understood, the Chinese readiness to have Wheaton translated was like the Trojans receiving gifts from the Greeks.[106] On August 30, 1864, the ministers of the Tsungli Yamen memorialized the throne:

> We, your ministers, find that this book of foreign laws does not entirely agree with our own laws, but there are in it occasional passages which are useful. For example, in connection with the case of Danish ships captured by Prussia outside of Tientsin, we used some sentences from the book, without expressly saying so, as arguments. The Prussian minister acknowledged his mistake without saying a word. This seems a good proof. He [Martin] says that this book should be read by all countries having treaty relations with others. In case of dispute it can be referred to. . . . We, your ministers, guarding against such frequent requests with books and possible attempts to make us follow them, have told him that China has her own laws and institutions and that it would be inconvenient to refer to foreign books. Martin, however, points out that although the laws of the Tsing Dynasty have been translated into foreign languages, China never attempted to force Western countries to practice them. It cannot be that just because a foreign book has been translated into Chinese, China would be forced to practice it. Thus, he [Martin] pleaded repeatedly.[107]

There are differing opinions as to why Martin translated Wheaton's masterpiece. The Chinese, not convinced that his motives were entirely "disinterested benevolence," surmised rather perceptively that he wished to make a name for himself. Others have since been suspicious of his motivation. The French *charge d'affaires* in Peking complained to Burlingame that Martin was a trouble-maker and must be stopped from giving "the Chinese an insight into our European international law."[108] Present-day commentators in the People's Republic of China believe that Martin's work was praised "because the foreigners wanted the Manchus and Chinese officials to observe the letter of the 'unequal treaties.'"[109] S. Wells Williams, however, believed that its effect could be the opposite — it might stimulate China to reach the level of Western law and thus eliminate the need for certain aspects of the "unequal treaties," such as extraterritoriality.[110]

The Chinese provided Martin with a room near the Tsungli Yamen[111] and with help from Chinese colleagues, and he finished his translation of Wheaton by mid-April.[112] At least three hundred copies were printed and, at the suggestion of Hart, sent to officials both at provincial centers and at the treaty ports.[113] "The first copy taken from the Chinese Empire" was sent to the Secretary of State, William Seward, who commented, "The learning and zeal of the Chinese government in connection with this matter cannot be too highly commended."[114] *Elements of International Law* was "promptly reprinted" in Japan and thus helped introduce the subject to China's neighbor.[115]

The Executive Committee of the Board of Foreign Missions expressed doubt that Martin's translation, which took six months of his time in Peking, was "direct missionary work," but he countered that "it will not stand second in influence to the translation of the Bible." Furthermore, he added, "I am laying the government under an obligation, which may result in good to the mission."[116] Martin also defended his literary work by recounting his opportunities to distribute religious books to his translation helpers, and to converse with them on the "subject of Christianity." They visited him at his home, noted with delight a play toy enabling them to catch metallic fish with a magnetic rod, and then visited his chapel to examine the books available for distribution and the Scripture texts pasted on the walls.[117]

Apart from such pragmatic considerations, how could Martin justify his translation of Wheaton, even as a type of secular missionary service? Part of the answer can be found in his English preface.

> To its [international law's] fundamental principle, the Chinese mind is prepared to yield a ready assent. In their state ritual as well as in their canonical books, they acknowledge a supreme arbiter of human destiny, to whom kings and princes are responsible for their exercise of delegated power; and in theory, no people are more ready to admit that His law is inscribed on the human heart.

> The relations of nations, considered as moral persons, and their reciprocal obligations as deduced from this maxim, they are thoroughly able to comprehend.[118]

Since Martin believed that God's law was "inscribed on the human heart," he might have been expected to utilize Chinese concepts of law that were vestiges of natural revelation. This might have produced an original work, similar in form to *T'ien-tao su-yüan,* building upon Chinese assumptions that "harmony, [and] not abstract justice was the ideal." Such a harmony "rested upon mutual self-respect and adherence to a policy of live and let live in conformity with the natural moral order."[119]

This, however, was not Western policy. Theodore Woolsey, whose noted work, *Introduction to the Study of International Law,* Martin later translated, observed that "Christian states," in their conduct toward nations on perhaps a higher level but outside their form of civilization, "have acted on the principle that there is no common bond of obligation between them and the other party, observing so much of international law as suited their policy or sense of right at the time."[120]

At a later time Martin did appeal to historical vestiges of international law existing in China among a family of independent, sovereign states, produced by the disintegration of the Chou Dynasty in the fifth and sixth centuries before Christ. He observed that the relationships among these equal states, recorded in the *Rites of the Chou Dynasty,* were similar to international intercourse among European states in the nineteenth century, and thus a type of precedent for China in its confrontation with the West. He elaborated in detail a variety of laws governing exchange of envoys, the conduct of war, the rights of neutrals, and the negotiation of treaties. These facts, he affirmed, proved that "the States of Ancient China had a Law written or unwritten, and more or less developed, which they recognized in peace and war."[121]

However, he failed to note in his investigation that this unwritten legal code "condemned forced contracts between states," the very thing that the West had perpetrated against China in the "unequal treaties."[122] He only sought to establish the *existence* of international law, particularly those features familiar to himself as a Westerner. He did not seek a deeper understanding of the principles to be derived from the *content* of indigenous Chinese law. By the same token, Wheaton's work, although helpful in a number of specific incidents, dealt with many questions of little concern to the Chinese — extraterritoriality, tariff limitations, jurisdiction by consular officials, and most-favored-nation stipulations — while overlooking the weightier matters of Imperial audiences and "diplomatic accreditation."[123]

Martin's translation, actually a paraphrase, both utilized existing terminology for concepts of law, and also developed new terms.[124] Not everyone was pleased with the accuracy of his work, nor with the quality of his Chinese, but most agreed that it was still a "splendid performance."[125]

Whatever imperfections it had, the translation of Wheaton's *Elements of International Law* into Chinese was a landmark both for Martin and for the Chinese. It eventually led to his position with a government educational institution and enhanced his prestige in all future service. And the Chinese had given their official imprimatur to a whole new set of Western concepts which exposed them to the idea that "the nations of the West have principles by which they are guided, and that force is not their only law."[126]

During his initial years at Peking Martin also prepared a book on natural philosophy. Intended to serve as a textbook in Truth Hall Academy, this seven-volume work had two main purposes. First, it was to compensate for a lack of such subject matter in the Chinese educational system which even the earlier Jesuit works on astronomy and mathematics did not satisfy. Second, it was to "bring down the whole edifice of superstition," a job, not for "a blind Samson, but science with her eyes open."[127]

Martin's interest in this approach was not new. It will be recalled that his graduation speech at Indiana Seminary was "The Uses of Physical Science as an Equipment for a Missionary."[128] While at Ningpo he somewhat took the back seat to older medical missionaries like Drs. McCartee and MacGowan who used this method quite extensively. After he had established Truth Hall Academy in Peking, he appealed to his Board for someone to teach science, and when no one was provided to fill the need, Martin tried to meet it himself. In one of his first letters from North China he asked the Board to purchase a "philosophical museum" for his personal use,[129] and he later sent a much larger order for a "philosophical apparatus" for classroom teaching.[130]

In desiring to introduce science into the Celestial Empire, Martin followed the illustrious train of many notable predecessors — the famed Jesuit, Matteo Ricci, Alexander Wylie, Joseph Edkins, Dr. Benjamin Hobson, Li Shan-lan, later to be his colleague at the T'ung Wen Kuan, and many others.[131]

Not a translation, but an original work that was very probably greatly indebted to the course he took at Indiana University, Martin's *Natural Philosophy* had a simple aim — to establish "that fundamental truth, the being and unity of God as the author and law-giver of Nature."[132] Negatively, this book would strike a blow against superstition.

> The system of state education had for ages been confined to belles-lettres, ethics and politics. The highest scholars knew no more why a stone falls to the ground or why water rises in a pump than did those of Europe before Newton and Torricelli. With them levity is a force as real as gravity; cold and darkness no less than light and heat. They find a ready explanation for all phenomena in the 'play of dual forces.' Their chemistry has not emerged from the chrysalis of alchemy. . . . The power that shakes these pillars will bring down the whole edifice of superstition. It is not a blind Samson that can do it, but science with her eyes open. Hence the emphasis I lay on scientific education. . . .[133]

What the Jesuits had done earlier in astronomy and mathematics was, in Martin's opinion, very valuable. He believed, however, that the new thirst for Western knowledge in the 1860's demanded a work that would impart knowledge useful in day-to-day life, besides giving simple scientific theory. And *Natural Philosophy* was a practical work. Altogether it consisted of seven volumes, each concerning a particular subject: hydraulics, gasses, heat, electricity, dynamics, chemistry, and mathematics. Each contained many pages of practical science illustrations, and a third of each volume was devoted to an explanation of the drawings.

Martin spent two years writing this book. Robert Hart, to whom it was dedicated, arranged to have it printed at government expense in 1868. A special edition of ten copies, "bound in yellow satin," was prepared for the "august eyes" of the Emperor himself. This simple, practical book, whose English title might better be rendered "Introduction to Science," went through many Chinese editions and was reprinted in Japan as well.[134]

Gnawing financial pressure was a constant fact of life for the Martin family. The Presbyterian Board, limited in money by the exigencies of the Civil War, found it difficult to meet his personal needs and the demands of his expanding work. Thus Martin often sought to make ends meet by finding work at which he could make money. Since March, 1865, he had been spending two hours a day teaching English in the T'ung Wen Kuan, a government school to train interpreters, and it was a very profitable project. The income of 1350 taels received at this very part-time job nearly doubled his missionary salary and was only slightly less than the total Peking budget which he had submitted in October, 1863.[135] He did not intend to continue teaching at this school, agreeing with Hart that "it is a pity that an architect should be employed in carrying brick and mortar."[136] At a later time, however, this job afforded him the opportunity to be an "architect" and lured him from his direct missionary post.[137]

Despite his disavowal of "secular writing" in 1859, his earlier contacts with the *New York Times,* developed during his work with Reed and Ward, afforded potential for additional income. He received twenty or thirty dollars for each letter commenting on news from the capital, and gave this money to the mission treasury.[138] For a man engaged in increasing responsibilities with the government, this work had its precarious side. "While not liking much to deal in such politics as might endanger my position," he commented, "I yet feel at liberty to notice promising events."[139]

Martin's involvement with the T'ung Wen Kuan commenced at the same time that Great Britain, America, France, and Russia began working together, and with China, in a relatively harmonious manner to restore China to health. Specifically, this meant that the Western powers took "no active intervention in the Civil War," made no encroachment on China's territory, and provided "neutral support and moral aid in all just demands on the Chinese government."[140]

Martin commented upon the various events that signaled this new era — the peaceful disposition of the Lay-Osborne flotilla, the Pin-ch'un diplomatic mission to Europe, expansion of the T'ung Wen Kuan, and the Burlingame mission — in detail in many articles in the *New York Times*.[141] He was a particularly active propagandist for Anson Burlingame, ex-United States Minister to China, and his journey on behalf of the Chinese Empire.

The Martin and Burlingame families were often together for holidays and social events.[142] Martin's regard for Burlingame was based, however, on more than pleasant personal associations. He frequently lauded Burlingame's sensitive attitude.

> In the darkest days of our national conflict and without the support of a single man-of-war, he caused our flag to be respected, and, in connection with Sir Frederick Bruce, he initiated a policy which, if acted on, will remove the old jealousies of the Treaty Powers, and combine their influence in the laudable enterprise of fostering a new civilization in this ancient empire.[143]

When Burlingame prepared to leave Peking to return to America in 1868, he went to the Tsungli Yamen to give his farewells, accompanied by Martin who interpreted for him. Burlingame's chance remark that he would be glad to help the Chinese in their relationships with the Western powers was seized upon, discussed at some length by both the Americans and the Chinese, and finally resulted in his appointment by Imperial decree to become Minister Plenipotentiary of the Chinese Empire.[144]

The Chinese were very happy with such an arrangement. The time had arrived for revision of the British Treaty of Tientsin, and China feared that Great Britain would force further progress — railways, telegraphs, new concessions for missionaries, mining, and many other things — on them. If Burlingame, whom they appeared to sincerely admire and trust, would represent them in foreign capitals — a new use for the policy of *i-i chih-i* ("playing off barbarians against one another") — he would be able to "dissuade European and American governments from forcing the pace of Westernization."[145] Burlingame, provided for with a handsome salary of eight thousand pounds a year plus expenses, and accompanied with "a Chinese and a Manchu co-envoy" as well as numerous interpreters and aides, left China for the United States early in 1858.[146]

Martin viewed this "formal adoption of the diplomatic usages of Western nations" — along with the acceptance of his translation of Wheaton, the Pin-ch'un mission, and the expansion of the T'ung Wen Kuan — as evidence that "China was progressing faster than Japan in adopting liberal attitudes."[147]

Burlingame's penchant for oratorical rhetoric created the impression that China need not be pushed along the path of progress — she had, in fact, already arrived![148] British circles, nettled because this was an American project and apparently unaware of the leading part played in its conception and implementation by British citizens, Robert Hart and J. McLevy Brown, were very critical. A *London Times* article, severely criticizing United States support for the mission, was reprinted in the *New York Times*. Martin answered it in six long articles written from his furlough headquarters in New Haven under the pseudonym "Perry Plus."[149]

First of all, he attacked the idea that Burlingame's appointment was anti-British in its inspiration. Sir Rutherford Alcock, the new British minister, had telegraphed his country's leaders giving his approval and urging their endorsement.[150] Second, he elaborated in great detail the signs of progress in China. The *Times* of London declared that all this was forced, to which Martin agreed, noting, however, that the Chinese were not passive but adjusting on their own terms. Their resistance to such things as "steamers, railways and telegraphs,"[151] he affirmed, was because they were truly progressive — "they wanted to build them themselves."[152]

In the third place, Martin extolled the virtues of the accord which Burlingame had made between the United States and China. He began by rehearsing past agreements. The Treaty of Wanghia "was not conducted on the basis of mutual advantage," but, in his view, in 1858 the enlightened Western representatives at Tientsin "promoted the welfare of China as the common interest of Christendom ... advancing no claim, that was not founded on justice ... [and] employed moral suasion to effect their ends in preference to physical force."[153] Martin was convinced that this had melted the Chinese "ice of suspicion" and had led to the ensuing period of cooperation. Asserting that "we have had our turn, and it is right that the Chinese should have theirs," Martin extolled the Burlingame Treaty provisions which gave status to Chinese in the United States — the right to a seat on street cars in San Francisco, removal of a discriminatory mining tax, and access to American schools.[154]

Martin fortified his arguments by painting a favorable portrait of the men responsible for China's foreign policy. Though they were not perhaps convinced that the earth was round, he pictured them as "men of culture, urbane and hard working . . . in Christendom, or out of Christendom, it would not be easy to meet with a more dignified body of men than these Chinese Mandarins."[155] He pointed out that they were interested in such wide-ranging issues as the plight of Chinese in California and Peru, the coolie trade from Macao, the superiority of moral suasion over military force, and procedures in embassy missions.[156]

J. Ross Browne, Burlingame's replacement as United States Minister, wrote a long letter to the Secretary of State refuting Martin's contention that China had a "progressive spirit and enlightened statesmanship."[157] Browne differed with Martin on many details but he was mainly concerned that

> The representations made by Dr. Martin have materially contributed to the formation in the United States of an erroneous estimate of Chinese progress, and it cannot be denied that a representative government like ours is to a great extent governed in its policy by public sentiment. For this reason . . . I feel it my duty to correct some of the errors into which Dr. Martin seems to have fallen.[158]

He charged that Martin had erred in attributing China's "shattered condition" to acts of injustice perpetrated against her by the Western powers. Rather, he claimed, her present state was "due to [her] own weakness," as Martin himself had suggested at the time of the Taiping Rebellion when he referred to the government as "illiberal, effete and pagan."[159] He suggested that Martin's excessive praise derived from vested interest as a "salaried officer in the pay of the Chinese government . . . his employers."[160] His animus to Martin did not stop here — he declared that Peking College (another name for the T'ung Wen Kuan) was "non-existent," and concerning the translation of Wheaton that Martin and others had cited as an evidence of progress, he observed that the Chinese never "contemplated accepting its obligations."[161]

Martin did not believe with some that the Burlingame Mission, instead of promoting the modernization of China, could have the opposite effect of "lulling the Chinese into indifference" or of frightening them into a retreat.[162] Nor was he as naive as he had been in 1858 when he took everything at face value. He was not really sorry that force or its threat were available in 1858. For better or for worse, force provided the option to use milder methods at the present time.

The infectious enthusiasm of Burlingame,[163] the liberal statements of high officials with whom Martin had increasing contact, his on-the-scene perception of subtle changes for the good, his own generous assessment of human nature, a conviction that China deserved better treatment,[164] and his optimistic expectation of the spread of God's Kingdom in China, all led Martin to believe that moral suasion would *gradually* bring about the desired progress. He also knew well that force could easily be evaded once the pressure was let up. Thus he postulated as a full grown reality what he saw and felt in its embryonic stage, and because he was speaking of it from this perspective, he was misunderstood both by those at a distance and by colleagues near at hand. Missionaries as a group tended to dislike Burlingame's cooperative approach,[165] believing with Ross Browne that now, as in the past, China must be forced to recognize old agreements and to grant new ones. Otherwise, in Browne's view, she would feign an air of cooperation to gain time that would finally help her resist the Western package — merchant, missionary and everything else.[166]

Thirty years later Martin confessed his disillusionment. He recognized that a treaty had been signed and certain gains realized. The mission had visited America, France, Germany, and Russia, and then, after Burlingame's death in St. Petersburg, two newly appointed Chinese co-envoys had stopped in Belgium and Italy on their way back to China in October, 1870. Martin noted, however, that the co-envoys were not awarded any posts of diplomatic significance after their return and that hopes of progress were dashed both by more missionary riots, for which he blamed the Chinese, and by resistance to changes in and through the T'ung Wen Kuan.[167]

Martin's personal identity crisis came to a head late in 1867. After great difficulty the T'ung Wen Kuan had expanded[168] into more than an interpreters' school, its faculty had been increased, and Martin, by this time well-known as the translator of Wheaton's work, was invited to take the "chair of International Law and Political Economy." His teaching responsibilities would not begin for two years, but he was put on full salary and was at liberty to return to America first if he desired.[169] He does not appear to have delayed long in responding affirmatively to this invitation, but he did refer it routinely to the Mission Board, thanking them for their attitude in leaving the decision up to him.

The Executive Committee asked him if he did not know of the mission rule that missionaries should not seek "secularizing employments from a love of lucre."[170] Denying that a teaching post was like a *consulship*, he affirmed that the "duties are thoroughly consonant with my calling and such as a missionary might well consent to perform in the interests of his work even if unpaid."[171] Such a position was "missionary work," he claimed, "for it would secure a post of advantage in which I may by the blessing of God promote the cause more effectively."[172]

What would he do with his salary?

> It brings some accession of means just at a time when our older boys are entering college and our younger boys might be sent home for education. It meets therefore our exigency for which charity has made no provision. I do not feel it my duty to decline it.

Martin's rather testy reply indicates some tension with the Board. While the Civil War was raging, he had contributed the money he earned to the mission treasury — now he felt justified in using it to meet his own needs. He claimed that this job would not disrupt his relations with the Board. He was glad that they were finally sending him a colleague, W. T. Morrison, and he affirmed his willingness to continue as a Presbyterian missionary, serving without salary.[173]

No doubt he was a bit disillusioned with Presbyterian lack of enthusiasm for missions and regretted that "we do not go forward as the ABCFM." "But," he added, "the fault is not yours — the blame rests with the churches, the seminaries, and the times."[174]

Six years of "unremitting brain work" in Shanghai and Peking had taken their toll, and Martin reported to the Board that he "felt the need of respite." He told them that if they would cover only a portion of the passage cost, with no responsibilities for salary and other expenses, he could return to America with his family like an "old ship to run into dock and refit for another course." The Martins left Peking on June 25, 1868, and sailed from Shanghai on July 17, 1868.[175]

During W. A. P. Martin' second term of religious work in China he had engaged in many normal missionary projects — preaching, translating, writing, and founding a Christian school. Increasingly, however, he spent time teaching in the interpreters' school, interpreting for friends in the American legation, promoting the cooperative policy, and commenting on many aspects of Chinese life. In his third term in China, although he purposed to go back to his missionary work "with more vigor," his commitments and interests would rapidly become even more independent.

Notes

1. China Letters of the Board of Foreign Mission of the Presbyterian Church in the United States of America, VIII, Outgoing to Gamble, #91, March 6, 1862. China Letters are subsequently abbreviated "CL."

2. W. A. P. Martin, *A Cycle of Cathay* (3rd ed.; New York, 1900), 299.

3. These were held October 16-17, 1861, at New York. He delivered a lecture on "The Ethical Philosophy of the Chinese" and presented informal talks on Yedo, the Nestorian faith, and various orthographic alphabets used to transcribe Chinese vernaculars. *Journal of the American Oriental Society,* VII, Proceedings of October 16-17, 1861, xliii-xliv.

4. Norma Farquhar, "W. A. P. Martin and the Westernization of China" (unpublished M.A. thesis, University of Indiana, 1954), 67.

5. The report comes from CL, IX, Martin to Board, #4, April 28, 1862.

6. At about the same time John Nevius urged the Board to establish a theological seminary, but he gave no outline of his plan. See his letter to the Board of October 2, 1862, in Helen Nevius, *John L. Nevius* (New York, 1895), 230-41.

7. CL, V, Shanghai, Martin to Board, #254, June 11, 1862.

8. Immanuel C. Y. Hsü, *The Rise of Modern China* (New York, 1970), 263-65.

9. As noted in Chapter IV, the Taiping Rebellion, the most serious of the internal conflicts, did not end until 1863.

10. See Joseph R. Levenson, *Confucian China and Its Modern Fate: A Trilogy* (Berkeley, 1968), I, 59-78, for an astute analysis of this phrase and its implications during this period of Chinese history. The expression was popularized in the 1890's, but the idea was current much earlier. S. Y. Teng and John K. Fairbank, eds., *China's Response to the West: A Documentary Survey, 1838-1923* (New York, 1966), 50.

11. Teng and Fairbank, *China's Response,* 50.

12. John Fairbank, *Trade and Diplomacy on the China Coast: The Opening of the Treaty Ports, 1842-54* (Cambridge, 1953), and *Chinese Thought and Institutions* (Chicago, 1957). This is one expression of what he has called hybridization or synarchy, with its parallels to Chinese and barbarian relations in earlier Chinese history and society.

13. Teng and Fairbank, *China's Response,* 48.

14. Hsü, *Modern China,* 327.

15. W. A. P. Martin, "Return to China," *The Foreign Missionary,* XXI (December, 1862), 210-11; CL, V, Shanghai, Martin to Board, #268, September 3, 1862; #273, September 30, 1862.

16. Kenneth Latourette, *A History of Christian Missions in China* (London, 1929), 250-51.

17. CL, V, Shanghai, Culbertson to Board, #258, July 18, 1862.

18. CL, IV, Shanghai, Martin to Board, #273, September 30, 1862.

19. *Ibid.*

20. CL, V, Shanghai, Gamble to Board, #269, September 3, 1862.

21. They had been established earlier but Culbertson's literary work, Farnham's supervision of a building program for the press, and Gamble's job running the press meant no one was available for the work of evangelism.

22. CL, V, Shanghai, Martin to Board, #273, September 30, 1862.

23. CL, V, Shanghai, Martin to Board, #274, September 18, 1862.

24. W. A. P. Martin, *The Analytical Reader: A Short Method for Learning to Read and Write Chinese* (Shanghai, 1863). This is a later edition of what he worked on in Shanghai.

25. CL, VIII, Outgoing, Board to Martin, #125, December 16, 1862; V, Martin to Board, #275, October 6, 1862; V, Roberts to Board, #296, June 20, 1863.

26. CL, VIII, Outgoing, Board to Martin, #125, December 16, 1862.

27. CL, V, Shanghai, Martin to Board, #294, June 7, 1863.

28. They were not the first missionary family to reach the Imperial City. William Lockhart (LMS), Joseph Edkins (LMS), John Burdon (CMS), and Joseph Schereschewsky of the Protestant Episcopal Church in

America had arrived in Peking from 1861 to 1863. Alexander Wylie, *Memorials of Protestant Missionaries to the Chinese* (Shanghai, 1867), 112, 187, 222, 253.

29. Henry Blodget, "The City of Peking," *Church Missionary Gleaner*, XIII (May, 1863), 54-55; William Lockhart, Letter, *The Chronicle of the LMS* (January, 1867), 12; "Dottings from Peking," *Church Missionary Gleaner*, XII (September, 1862), 108.

30. "Dottings," *CMG*, 108.

31. Protestant missionaries apparently did not yet realize how the benefits of the "French treaty" could also apply to them by the "most-favored-nation" clause.

32. "Peking — Its Present State," *Church Missionary Gleaner*, XII (November, 1862), 130.

33. Martin, *Cycle*, 230.

34. CL, VII, Peking, Martin to Board, #40, October 1, 1863. The total expenditure was 1300 taels, a relatively inexpensive charge due to the fact that one of the wives of the former owner had committed suicide there. Martin, *Cycle*, 230. Martin held the property from Williams in the form of a lease, paying him 140 taels ($200) per year in interest. CL, VII, Peking, Martin to Board, #68, April 12, 1864. The repairs made were common for most mission residences — putting in a chimney, glass windows and wood tile on the floor. Jane Martin, "Missionaries in the Capital of China," *The Foreign Missionary*, XXII (May, 1864), 302; CL, X, Peking, Martin to Board, #151, October 31, 1864; Martin, *Cycle*, 231.

35. CL, X, Peking, Martin to Board, #151, October 31, 1864.

36. CL, #34, July 25, 1863.

37. W. A. P. Martin, "Something About the Little Emperor," *The Foreign Missionary*, XXIII (December, 1864), 175.

38. CL, X, Peking, Martin to Board, #151, October 31, 1864.

39. W. A. P. Martin, "Progress at Peking," *The Foreign Missionary*, XXIII (October, 1864), 122.

40. W. A. P. Martin, "Journal of the Rev. William A. P. Martin, D.D., at Peking," *The Home and Foreign Record*, XV (March, 1864), 59.

41. *Ibid.*; Martin, *Cycle*, 240.

42. Jane Martin, "Missionaries in the Capital of China," *The Foreign Missionary*, XXII (May, 1864), 301. She identified him to her young readers as "the friend of McCheyne," a well-known Scotch minister.

43. Martin, *Cycle*, 238.

44. *Zayat* is a Burmese term denoting a wayside shelter found in Burman villages. See Robert Torbet, *Venture of Faith* (Philadelphia, 1955), 35; Martin, "Progress at Peking," 123.

45. Margaret Wylie to her brother, Anderson, February 10, 1866. Harris Collection, Indiana University Archives.

46. CL, X, Peking, Martin to Board, First Annual Report, #151, October 31, 1864.

47. Jane V. Martin, "Tartar Women Hearing the Gospel in Peking," *The Foreign Missionary*, XXV (April, 1866), 276.

48. CL, VII, Peking, Martin to Board, Second Annual Report, #242, October 1, 1865; Third Annual Report, #243, October 1, 1866; Martin, *Cycle*, 238.

49. Martin, "Missionary Matters at Peking, China," *The Foreign Missionary*, XXIII (July, 1864), 53, and "Progress at Peking," XXIII (October, 1864), 124.

50. Martin, "Missionary Matters at Peking, China," 53.

51. He wished to learn about the Jewish colony at K'aifeng and to make some observations on the cities, rivers, and canals of the interior. His careful descriptions on these subjects were written up both in popular magazines and scholarly journals. See, for example, W. A. P. Martin, "A Colony of Jews," *New York Times*, October 22, 1866, 2:1-2; "Inland Journey from Peking to Shanghai," *New York Times*, August 29, 1866, 2:1-2; "The Rivers of China," *New York Times*, May 23, 1867, 2:1-2; D. C. Gilman, "Geographical Notices," *American Journal of Science*, XLVII (January-May, 1869), 98-103; and W. A. P. Martin, "Early Inventions of the Chinese," *Journal of the American Oriental Society.* Proceedings at Boston, May 19, 1869, liv.

52. Martin, *Cycle*, 265, 274; CL, VII, Peking, Martin to Board, #286, March 24, 1866; Martin, "Notes of an Inland Journey from Peking to Shanghai — Including a Visit to the Jews in Honan," *The Foreign Missionary* (October, 1866), 140.

53. Martin, "Notes of an Inland Journey from Peking to Shanghai — Including a Visit to the Jews in Honan" (April, 1867), 291-92.

54. W. A. P. Martin, "The Jewish Monument at Kaifungfu," *Journal of the North China Branch of the Royal Asiatic Society*, XXXVII (1906), 6.

55. Martin, *Cycle*, 235.

56. Martin, "Progress at Peking," 124.

57. Martin, *Cycle*, 235. In letters to the Board Martin identified his benefactor only as an "English friend in China" who has a "public fund under his control." CL, VII, Peking, Martin to Board, #75, August 31, 1864.

58. CL, VII, Peking, Martin to Board, Second Annual Report, #242, October 1, 1865; Third Annual Report, #243, October 1, 1866; Fourth Annual Report, #499, October 1, 1867.

59. CL, VIII, Peking, Morrison to Board, #191, September 30, 1868.

60. CL, VII, Peking, Martin to Board, Second Annual Report, #242, October 1, 1865.

61. *Ibid.*

62. CL, VIII, Peking, Morrison to Board, #191, September 30, 1868.

63. CL, VII, Peking, Martin to Board, Second Annual Report, #242, October 1, 1865.

64. From the time of his arrival in Peking, Martin had proposed "the immediate erection in Peking of a church of considerable size, at a cost say of 3000 dollars." Confessing that he was not "hurrying along slowly" in advocating such an ambitious scheme, he declared he could get most of the money from private sources. Martin, "Missionaries in the Capital of China," *The Foreign Missionary*, XXIII (May, 1864), 303.

65. CL, VII, Peking, Martin to Board, #217, November 24, 1865.

66. Marshall Broomhall, *The Bible in China* (London, 1934), 79-80.

67. *Ibid.*, 80; Wylie, *Memorials*, 36.

68. Although the Chinese written language is the same throughout China, each spoken Chinese "dialect" has a different syntax, idiom, and pronunciation.

69. American Bible Society. Unpublished manuscript. Essay #16, IV-G-3b. Mandarin Versions, 58.

70. *Ibid.*; Letter, Martin to Holdich, March 17, 1864, and April 12, 1865, American Bible Society Archives; CL, Peking, VII, Martin to Board, #68, April 12, 1864; Minutes of Committee on Versions of the American Bible Society, III, 193-94.

71. W. A. P. Martin, "Chinese Versions of the Bible," *Bible Society Record*, VIII (July, 1863), 108-9. Were his opinions influenced by a recent American Bible Society gift for the printing of the Bridgman and Culbertson version, also strongly supported by the Presbyterians?

72. CL, VII, Peking, Martin to Board, #71, July 19, 1864, and #499, October 1, 1867.

73. Letter, Martin to Holdich, July 30, 1864. American Bible Society Archives.

74. CL, VII, Peking, Martin to Board, #242, October 1, 1865.

75. Blodget revealed that there were four steps in their procedure: 1) rough drafts of different books were prepared by each translator; 2) these copies were circulated for individual criticism; 3) a revised text embodying these criticisms was prepared and revised again by the committee; 4) the final text was determined by majority vote. ABS, unpublished manuscript, Essay #16, IV-G-3, 64.

76. CL, X, Peking, Martin to Board, #151, October 31, 1864.

77. CL, VII, Peking, Martin to Board, #242, October 1, 1865.

78. ABS, unpublished manuscript, Essay #16, IV-G-3, 16.

79. *Ibid.*

80. The exact amount is uncertain. Martin stated that "the brethren in Shantung, will it is believed, concur in this movement. . . ." CL, VII, Peking, Martin to Board, #242, October 1, 1865. McCartee indicated that at Chefoo only Mills supported it. CL, VII, McCartee to Board, #226, December 21, 1865. The problem is complicated by the fact that some missionaries frequently shifted their positions. CL, VII, McCartee to Board, #272, February 21, 1866.

81. CL, VII, Peking, Martin to Board, #242, October 1, 1865.

82. CL, VII, Peking, Martin to Board, #324, June 27, 1866. *T'ien-chu* was a neutral term which had no superstitious connotations to the Chinese. It was the choice of Franciscan and Dominican missionaries in the seventeenth century. The Jesuits, who desired to accommodate to Chinese thinking, preferred *shang-ti*.

83. Letter, McCartee to Holdich, January 4, 1866, ABS Archives; Minutes of Committee on Versions, III, 222, ABS Archives.

84. ABS, unpublished manuscript, Essay #16, IV-G-3, 19-20.

85. *Ibid*., 63. The *t'ien-chu* version was a concession to J. S. Burdon, 69.

86. Editions reflecting the different preferences for "God" were printed. ABS, unpublished manuscript, Essay #16, IV-G-3, 68-72.

87. W. E. Soothill, *A Typical Mission in China* (New York, 1906), 197, called it "the most popular edition in the empire."

88. Broomhall, *Bible in China,* 84.

89. CL, VII, Peking, Martin to Board, #153, June 10, 1868.

90. ABS, unpublished manuscript, Essay #16, IV-G-3, 66.

91. CL, VII, Peking, Martin to Board, #153, June 10, 1868. The others were *Evidences,* Wheaton, and *Natural Philosophy.*

92. A copy of this 1864 Mandarin edition of John is in the ABS Library in New York.

93. Herbert A. Giles, "The New Testament in Chinese," *The China Review,* X (December, 1881), 158.

94. Martin, *Cycle,* 221.

95. Hsü, *Modern China.*

96. W. A. P. Martin, trans., *Wan-kuo kung-fa* (Elements of International Law) (Peking, 1864). Preface as quoted in William V. Kellen, *Henry Wheaton: An Appreciation* (Boston, 1902), 40-41.

97. Richard Henry Dana, ed., *Elements of International Law* (3rd ed.; New York, 1866), v-vi.

98. Elizabeth F. Baker, *Henry Wheaton, 1785-1848* (Philadelphia, 1937), 148.

99. CL, VII, Peking, Martin to Board, #44, October 1, 1863.

100. Diplomatic Despatches, China Despatches, Vol. 21, Burlingame to William Seward, October 30, 1863.

101. Martin, *Cycle,* 222.

102. *Ibid.,* 233. He suggested that the first meeting was in November, 1863, but he indicated certain areas of general agreement had already been concluded before October 1, 1863, when he submitted his quarterly report. CL, VII, Peking, Martin to Board, #44, October 1, 1863. The precise date occurs in W. A. P. Martin, "Peking News," *New York Times,* January 8, 1864, 4:5,6.

103. Martin, *Cycle,* 234. CL, VII, Peking, Martin to Board, #44, October 1, 1863, and #71, July 19, 1864.

104. Martin, *Cycle,* 234. Undoubtedly a less blunt request than it sounds in English and yet indicative of Martin's increasing passion for official recognition.

105. W. A. P. Martin, "Peking News," *New York Times,* January 8, 1864, 4:5,6. Martin's rhetoric in 1864 was much more strident than in 1896 when he wrote *A Cycle of Cathay.*

106. Martin, *Cycle,* 235.

107. *Ch'ou-pan i-wu-shih-mu* (Management of Barbarian Affairs), T'ung-chih, XXVII, 25-26. The portion used here was translated by T. F. Tsiang in "Bismarck and the Introduction of International Law into China," *The Chinese Social and Political Science Review,* XV (April, 1931), 101. Tsiang's point in this article is that Bismarck by his war with Denmark in 1864 provided the occasion for China's use of legal provisions outlined in Wheaton.

108. Martin, *Cycle,* 234. He apparently felt that it would be easier to deceive the Chinese government if it were ignorant of Western law.

109. Victor Purcell, *The Boxer Uprising* (Cambridge, 1963), 73.

110. Diplomatic Despatches from China, XXII, S. Wells Williams to William Seward, November 23, 1865.

111. *Ibid.,* XXI, Burlingame to William Seward, October 30, 1863.

112. CL, VII, Peking, Martin to Board, #68, April 12, 1864.

113. *Ch'ou-pan i-wu-shih-mu,* T'ung-chih, XXVII, 26; Martin, *Cycle,* 234.

114. Peking Legation Archives, XXXII (1864-65), #147, 129, William Seward to S. Wells Williams, August 9, 1865 and #147, 133, William Seward to Williams, August 14, 1865.

115. Martin, *Cycle,* 234; George Wilson, ed., *Classics of International Law,* XIX: Richard H. Dana ed., 8th Edition of Henry Wheaton,

Elements of International Law (Oxford, 1936), 607. One edition with Japanese diacritical marks was published in Kyoto in 1865 and a new edition was issued in Tokyo in 1876.

116. CL, VII, Peking, Martin to Board, #46, November 23, 1863.

117. W. A. P. Martin, "Journal," *The Foreign Missionary*, XXIII (July, 1864), 53.

118. W. A. P. Martin, trans., *Wan-kuo kung-fa* (Peking, 1864), 1.

119. Cyrus Peake, "Recent Studies in Chinese Law," *Political Science Quarterly*, LII (March, 1937), 138.

120. Theodore Woolsey, *Introduction to the Study of International Law* (New York, 1868), 20.

121. W. A. P. Martin, *The Lore of Cathay* (2nd ed.; New York, 1912), 427-49. He has been widely regarded as the first foreigner to investigate China's ancient system of international law. Peake, "Recent Studies in Chinese Law," 122; Roswell S. Britton, "Chinese Interstate Intercourse Before 700 B.C.," *American Journal of Law*, XXIX (October, 1929), 618.

122. Peake, "Recent Studies in Chinese Law," 137.

123. Immanuel Hsü, *China's Entrance into the Family of Nations* (Cambridge, 1960), 138-39.

124. *Ibid.*, 135-36. See Hung-ta Ch'iu, *Chung-kuo kuo-chi-fa wen-t'i lun-chi* (A Collection of Essays on Questions of Chinese International Law) (Taipei, 1972), 24-28, for a technical discussion on terminology and concepts used.

125. Hsü, *China's Entrance*, 129.

126. Arthur Smith, "The Life and Work of the Late Dr. W. A. P. Martin," *The Chinese Recorder*, XLVIII (February, 1917), 119.

127. Martin, *Cycle*, 236.

128. Albert Porter, "An American Mandarin," *Outlook*, August 24, 1907, 885.

129. CL, VII, Peking, Martin to Board, #44, October 1, 1863.

130. CL, VII, Peking, Martin to Board, #457, June 13, 1867. This included a galvanic battery, pulleys, double acting air pump, mountain barometer, thermometers, prisms, small model steam engine, leyden jars, electric toys, etc.

131. T. H. Tsien, "Impact on China Through Translation," *Far Eastern Quarterly*, XIII (May, 1954), 312; Cyrus H. Peake, "Some Aspects of the Introduction of Modern Science into China," *ISIS*, XXII (1) (December, 1934), 179-80.

132. CL, VII, Peking, Martin to Board, #499, October 1, 1867.

133. Martin, *Cycle*, 236.

134. *Ibid.*, 237. He suggested once that Mateer, who had prepared himself more thoroughly in this area, should write a book to replace his,

but with less opportunity for specialization than Martin, Mateer never got around to it. See Daniel Fisher, *Calvin Wilson Mateer: Forty-Five Years a Missionary in Shantung, China* (Philadelphia, 1911), 166-67.

135. CL, VII, Peking, Martin to Board, #242, October 1, 1865, and #208, November 5, 1863. Martin's basic board salary at this juncture was 700 taels with 144 taels allowance for two children. The total budget, including these salary amounts, was $1459.

136. CL, VII, Peking, Martin to Board, #217, November 24, 1865. He commented, "I accepted with a view to do good and to relieve the finances while the War was on. And I could save money for the school. Now a friend has given to this, so I will resign at the end of the year."

137. See Chapter 7 for a full discussion of Martin's role in the T'ung Wen Kuan.

138. CL, VII, Peking, Martin to Board, #71, July 19, 1864.

139. CL, VII, Peking, Martin to Board, #133, April 25, 1865.

140. Q [pseud.], "The Cooperative Policy," *New York Times*, April 23, 1864, 2:2,3. He probably used the pseudonym to protect his relationship with the Chinese government.

141. Q [pseud.], "Lay-Osborne Flotilla," *New York Times*, January 30, 1864, 4:1-2; Q [pseud.], "The Chinese Embassy," *New York Times*, August 27, 1866, 2:4-5.

142. See letters of Jane Burlingame to her sister, January 11, 1864, May 7, 1864, June 18, 1867, and July 17, 1867, in Burlingame Papers, Box 3, Manuscript Division, Library of Congress, Washington, D.C.

143. W. A. P. Martin, "The Prince of K'ung," *Harper's New Monthly Magazine*, XXXII (April, 1866), 586.

144. Martin, *Cycle*, 374, and Martin, "The Chinese Embassy," 1:1-2.

145. Hsü, *Modern China*, 357-58.

146. *Ibid.*

147. Martin, "The Chinese Embassy," *New York Times*, February 18, 1868, 1:1-2.

148. Martin, *Cycle*, 376.

149. Perry Plus [pseud.], "The Chinese Embassy," I, *New York Times*, October 23, 1868, 4:1. An editorial remark in this same issue of the *Times* (6:3) commented that a "series begins today by a gentleman whose long residence and public position in China have made him familiar with politics and public men of the Empire."

150. *Ibid.*, and Perry Plus [pseud.], "The Chinese Embassy," II, *New York Times*, October 26, 1868, 2:1.

151. He was well aware of how Tseng Kuo-fan reacted negatively to these innovations when he answered a specific inquiry sent to all provincial authorities by the Tsungli Yamen as they were preparing a "position paper" on treaty revision. Hsü, *Modern China*, 357.

152. Perry Plus [pseud.], "The Chinese Embassy," III, *New York Times,* October 28, 1868, 2:1.

153. This is a rather stange interpretation of the Tientsin Treaty.

154. Perry Plus [pseud.], "The Chinese Embassy," IV, *New York Times,* November 3, 1868, 2:1.

155. Perry Plus [pseud.], "The Chinese Embassy," V, *New York Times,* November 9, 1868, 2:1.

156. Perry Plus [pseud.], "The Chinese Embassy," VI, *New York Times,* November 20, 1868, 2:1.

157. Diplomatic Despatches, China, XXVI, #48, J. Ross Browne to Secretary of State Fish, June 28, 1869, 1.

158. *Ibid.*

159. *Ibid.,* 2, 3, and 9.

160. *Ibid.,* 3.

161. F. W. Williams, *Anson Burlingame and the First China Mission to Foreign Powers* (New York, 1912), 298.

162. Martin, *Cycle,* 376-77; Hsü, *Modern China,* 359. Burlingame's mission "encouraged the growth of conservatism in China. . . . They became more complacent and less responsive to outside stimuli."

163. F. W. Williams, *A Sketch of the Relations Between the U.S. and China* (New York, 1910), "His friendliness and hope and optimism were thought by the Chinese and foreigners alike as too good to be true." 60.

164. *Ibid.* Williams observed that the Treaty "recognizes China as an equal among nations — not the old doctrine that because she is not a Christian nation she should not be placed in the roll of nations," 64. An editorial in the *Pall Mall Gazette,* Boston, August 19, 1868, commented of Article 4 giving to Chinese religious liberty in America that, "heathenism and idolatry are placed upon a footing with Christianity, and joss and his colored-paper flummery are to be held as sacred as the temples of the Most High God. . . ." Burlingame Papers.

165. Diplomatic Despatches, XXVI, China, includes a letter from M. J. Knowlton of Ningpo, June 10, 1869, asking for missions to benefit from the "real reciprocity" promised in the treaty. Allan Price, "American Missionaries and American Diplomacy in China, 1830-1900" (unpublished Ph.D. dissertation, Harvard University, 1932), 337, 359-60.

166. For a debate on the pros and cons of Burlingame's approach see Appendix III and V in F. W. Williams, *Anson Burlingame.* Hart expressed his opinion in "Note on Chinese Matters," Browne replied, and George Seward summed up his support of Burlingame in a letter to Secretary of State Fish.

167. Martin, *Cycle,* 379. See F. W. Williams, *Anson Burlingame,* 64.

168. See Chapter 7 for a full discussion of this school.

169. CL, VIII, Peking, Martin to Board, #117, February 4, 1868.

Hsü, *Modern China,* 328. Hsü claimed that "in 1867 Martin returned to the U.S. for two years of advanced work in international law and political economy at the University of Indiana, where he earned a doctorate." This statement is wrong on at least two counts: Martin went home in July, 1868, and returned to China in 1869; he never received a doctorate at the University of Indiana; most of his time was spent in the Atlantic States. He may have studied law informally at Yale under the direction of Theodore Woolsey. His sons, Pascal and Winfred, were students at Yale at this time, and it would have been easy for their father to do independent study with Woolsey's help.

170. CL, VIII, Peking, Martin to Board, #153, June 10, 1868.

171. *Ibid.*

172. CL, VIII, Peking, Martin to Board, #128, March 30, 1868.

173. CL, VII, Peking, Martin to Board, #153, June 10, 1868, and #128, March 30, 1868.

174. CL, VII, Peking, Martin to Board, #117, February 4, 1868.

175. CL, VIII, Peking, Martin to Board, #153, June 10, 1868, and #117, February 4, 1868.

CHAPTER SEVEN

Pioneer of Modern State Education in China

WILLIAM MARTIN'S second furlough in the United States was brief and intense.[1] The articles he had written for the *New York Times*, *Harper's Magazine*, and various church publications had given him the reputation of a scholar, providing frequent opportunities to lecture and speak about China.[2]

He returned to China in the summer of 1869 with mixed emotions. His wife and all four of his boys remained in America.[3] Rumors abounded that China would not ratify the treaty that Burlingame had made with the United States on her behalf. A hurried letter from Robert Hart had already warned him of the pending demise of the T'ung Wen Kuan.[4]

When he arrived in Shanghai, he found that many of his fears seemed justified. "The college has collapsed," he hastily wrote to Dr. Williams in Peking, "and I have to look about for some mode of meeting the expenses of my family at home." He had heard that his old friend might be leaving his diplomatic post and requested that he be recommended to succeed him. Such a position, he stated, "would enable me to devote a good deal of my time as I desire to the preparation of books for the benefit of the Chinese."[5]

After he reached Peking some of his optimism returned. The report of the death of "the Peking College" was premature, he wrote, adding that the government still supported it, even though it had been blamed for recent floods. He admitted that there had been failures, largely because the students were too old and Chinese had not been used as the language of instruction.[6] As for

169

the Burlingame Treaty, he decided that the Chinese government was merely delaying its ratification until it understood the fine print.[7]

The state of disarray into which "Peking University," as Martin often called it, had fallen was well stated by J. Ross Browne, the American Minister to China,

> In effect, about thirty poor Chinese, most of them middle-aged men, were commencing the study of European languages, without any previous training whatever that could possibly qualify them to understand the elementary principles of Arts and Sciences. This was simply the *Tung-wen-kwan*, or language school, established in 1862 for the purpose of creating native interpreters.[8]

Browne could certainly not be faulted for this perception; the Peking T'ung Wen Kuan had been barely surviving since its inception in 1862. In January, 1861, Prince K'ung had memorialized the Throne requesting that the Emperor

> . . . command the viceroy and governor at Canton and Shanghai to find natives acquainted with foreign letters, and to send them, with a good supply of foreign books, to the capital with a view to the instruction of youth to be chosen from the Eight Banners.[9]

This memorial grew out of the Chinese desire to understand more about the "barbarians" and from provisions in the British and French Treaties of Tientsin stipulating English and French as the languages for intercourse with the Chinese nation.[10] In addition to the initial interpreters' school in Peking, similar schools were started in Shanghai (1863), Canton (1864), and at the Foochow Shipyard (1866).[11]

Since their arrival in China in 1807, Protestant missionaries had established a wide variety of educational institutions, and it was only natural that the Chinese officials should turn to them as best equipped to help develop the T'ung Wen Kuan.[12] John Burdon of the Church Missionary Society was the first instructor in English, and he was succeeded first by John Fryer, who would later start the Polytechnic Institute in Shanghai, and then by Martin. Martin's invitation came through Anson Burlingame, the American Minister, who had originally planned to make him president of a school which he proposed to fund with the surplus of a Chinese indemnity given to reimburse Americans for property destroyed at Canton.[13] At first, Martin was not inclined to accept the invitation at the T'ung Wen Kuan but then agreed, providing that it would require no more than two hours of his time daily.[14] He gloated over this turn of events that found the government turning to outsiders for teaching help.

> Humbling, was it not? Yet the logic of events was destined to convince China that not only in languages, but in everything that makes a nation great and strong, she would have to accept the teaching of foreigners.[15]

Even the two hours a day was a drain on his energy, and, seeing no great prospects of the school expanding, he prepared to resign. He was reluctantly persuaded to reconsider by Ministers Tung and Tan of the Tsungli Yamen, who correctly prophesied that some of his few, poor English students might someday teach the Emperor of China.[16] Despite his decision to stay on, he was convinced that "a missionary is liable to exert a better influence when independent of a pagan government." He also knew that this work had "interfered seriously with *more useful,* and I may add, more sacred employments."[17] A friend, whom he had tentatively approached to succeed him, refused the offer as "liable to turn him aside from preaching the Gospel." Many years later Martin mused, "Which was right? Perhaps neither, perhaps both."[18]

And so he held on, grateful that he was saving the Board the amount of his salary — an amount that could maintain his own developing school — and that he did have opportunities to impart his faith.

> By the rules of the school, the teacher is not permitted to make use of the Bible, as a textbook; but there is no effort made to prevent the young men reading it in private, nor is there any restriction imposed on the communication of religious truth orally or by means of other books.[19]

After Martin became president, a classroom placard forbidding teaching the Bible was removed by the proctors, who were responsible to the Tsungli Yamen for administering the school.[20] Some of the English essays assigned to the students were on Christian themes. Despite these various direct emphases, Martin's hopes were more that his students — the country's potential leaders — would imbibe enough Christianity to affect future national policy than that they would "mature into the fruits of conversion."[21]

In 1866 the government made plans that would radically alter the character of the school.[22] Martin explained the new proposals to his mission board in some detail:

> Young men of talent are to be drawn from all the provinces of the Empire. Professors have been invited from Europe, and liberal appropriations made for books and apparatus, so that this little school, under the sunshine of imperial patronage, suddenly expands into the proportions of a college or rather of a university. I am to be relieved of my present charge, and the chair of International Law and Political Economy is offered to me — a post which on account of its influence on the leading minds of the nation I have not thought it wise to decline. . . . The organization of this new college with a view to renovation of the educational system of the country, is altogether the most cheering indication of progress that has occurred since the opening of the capital and country by the signing of the existing treaties.[23]

The "imperial patronage" of which he spoke was the Throne's approval of memorials that would expand the school's curriculum to include "astronomy, mathematics, chemistry, physics, biology, geography, geology, mineralogy, metallurgy, mechanics, anatomy, physiology, political economy, and international law."[24] The memorial itself only specified "astronomy and mathematics," since there would be less adverse conservative reaction to these two disciplines which had "been introduced into China and accepted as early as the seventeenth century."[25]

Prince K'ung's original memorial had indicated that the "young men of talent" mentioned by Martin would be members of the Hanlin Academy, an association of scholars who supervised all the literary activities of the Imperial court, but very strong opposition by Wo-jen, Manchu president of the Academy and tutor to the Emperor, defeated this portion of the proposal. Martin regretted this reversal but was satisfied with the prospect of increasing the student body from the Eight Banners and from the schools in Shanghai and Canton.

Wo-jen, who vehemently criticized the entire memorial on social, racial, and religious grounds, was only the most notable voice of the conservative clique, which was composed of critical censors, Hanlin scholars, and the literati, who were anti-foreign to the core. The target of their vilification was the *yang-wu* element

— those who dealt with foreign affairs. These men, among whom were the notable leaders, Tseng Kuo-fan and Li Hung-chang, were hardly liberals, but they were prepared for some non-Confucian adjustments to the present exigencies.

The Empress Dowager appeared to be neutral on the surface but leaned to the side of the obscurantists. Despite the general anti-modernizing climate which she and the conservatives fostered, the expanding vision for the T'ung Wen Kuan, along with the development of the Tsungli Yamen and the Maritime Customs, indicated that China was beginning to take a forward look.

After its modification, the biggest problem confronting the school was the faculty that Robert Hart had induced to come to China during his furlough in England. Of the five, only one, Monsieur Billequin, whom Martin referred to as the "father of Chinese chemistry," was satisfactory.[26] The most objectionable was Johannes Von Gumpach, a "charlatan, who mistook notoriety for fame, and sought to obtain money without earning it."[27] An opponent of the Newtonian theory of gravitation who denied the elliptical orbits of the planets and believed every heavenly body to be a living being, he was hardly qualified to be "head of the Department of Astronomy." Martin piously hoped that his pupils would be "guided by their textbooks rather than the fanciful theories of their master."[28]

When the T'ung Wen Kuan was reorganized, Martin was asked to be Professor of International Law and Political Economy. This appointment led Von Gumpach, no friend of his, to comment indignantly in response to the English title page of *Natural Philosophy* which read "By W. A. P. Martin, D.D., Professor of Hermeneutics, Political Economy and International Law in the University of Peking," that "he knows absolutely nothing of International Law and is completely ignorant of Political Economy." Von Gumpach added that "Hermeneutics" could only refer to "Biblical Exegesis," and observed that Martin's use of this term

> conveys to the American and English public the false impression as though the Manchu government had actually carried its liberality to the extent of founding a Chair for the highest teaching of Christianity in the 'national university of China.'[29]

Von Gumpach also sarcastically derided the academic pretensions of the school, noting that it had been called "the University of Peking," "The College of Western Sciences, Arts and Literature," and "The New University of Peking."[30] Martin's work on *Natural Philosophy* was "Printed for the University," he observed, and yet, inasmuch as Martin admitted in the English preface that the work was prepared "for the use of advanced pupils in Mission Schools," how could the T'ung Wen Kuan be considered a University?[31]

From 1866 to 1869 the T'ung Wen Kuan went downhill, leading to Ross Browne's extremely negative evaluation. What was the answer to this malaise? Robert Hart strongly recommended that Martin be promoted to head up the floundering institution. After first giving him an examination to demonstrate his competence in mathematics, the Tsungli Yamen officially invited Martin to become "president" of the school.[32] On November 26, 1869, in an impressive ceremony attended by the student body, several officials from the Tsungli Yamen, and Dr. S. Wells Williams, the United States charge d'affaires, he was inducted into office.[33]

Martin submitted his resignation to the Presbyterian Board of Foreign Missions on December 1, 1869. This was not a sudden step but culminated many years of mental and spiritual conflict, and many factors entered into his decision. He was convinced, for one thing, that the field in Peking was more religiously barren than any other, and he had apparently considered a transfer to Shantung.[34] Furthermore, his board had sent him no help for over five years. He observed that during this period of Presbyterian inaction, the ABCFM had entered the field, and that talk had begun concerning comity arrangements that would assign Peking to them and Shantung to the Presbyterians. Since this seemed a distinct possibility, Martin concluded that he could no longer recommend that the Presbyterians send any reinforcements to Peking.[35]

Martin may also have feared that the Board would shift to a policy discouraging any broad educational work. In 1871, for example, John Lowrie, Corresponding Secretary of the Board, notified missionaries to be

> Careful not to aim at reproducing the kinds of labor that grow out of an advanced Christian state of society, whether it be seminaries, hospitals, printing presses, or anything else. For

> many years our work among heathen people will be the humble
> one of sowing the grain of mustard seed.[36]

These views, developed in the later 1860's when finances were still
very precarious, were incompatible with Martin's growing commitment to preparing China for the Kingdom of God through law,
science, and education.

To what degree was Martin motivated by a sense of responsibility to make the T'ung Wen Kuan work? He, Hart, Burlingame,
and others had "gone out on a limb," both in private conversation
and public communication, to assure Westerners that China was a
progressive country. For the school to fail completely, as it was
certainly in danger of doing in 1869, would be a big step back-
ward, and Martin and the others would lose face.

The position at the T'ung Wen Kuan also provided an
unparalleled opportunity for Martin to pursue his literary
work, and although he did not question missionary work in
general, he seemed to feel that in Chinese society, where
scholars were highly respected, the role of the teacher gave
him a natural context for Christian witness.

These multiple areas of discontent and concern, combined
with an unusual opportunity to pioneer — though possibly this
was exaggerated in Martin's own mind — and a salary exceeding
by nearly ten-fold anything the Board could do for him, all helped
him make his decision. The financial incentive may have added
some urgency to all the other considerations, since his family was
in America and facing critical financial needs. But, for his own
peace of mind, Martin saw his new position as a change of role
and not of function.

> I would like to be considered as possessing a life [missionary]
> membership . . . in spirit I am still a missionary and labor, as I
> believe, in what is *for me* the most effective way, for the good of
> this people. . . . One of the highest Mandarins, an Imperial Cen-
> sor, said in the presence of several others that he had declared
> when I was not present that 'if all missionaries were like Dr.
> Martin, he would himself be a Christian.' I quote this — not from
> vanity, God knows, but to show you that I *am not utterly sec-
> ularized,* or neglecting the opportunities that are given to me. The
> college is secular and cannot be otherwise, but in my hands by the
> blessing of God it will be at least less anti-Christian than it would
> otherwise be.[37]

Martin's choice was made somewhat easier by the fact that in his time there was little dichotomy in China between Christian schools and secular schools; the larger distinction was between traditional education and Western learning. Government and mission schools were both involved in the latter,[38] and the choice was simply whether one wished to train students in mathematics and science under Christian auspices and with religious subjects also included in the curriculum, or in a more secular institution. In the late 1860's, a secular school under government sponsorship and supported by the largesse which Robert Hart could supply from the resources of the Maritime Customs, seemed to have much more potential for continuity and expansion than was available in the financially precarious mission projects.

Why would the Tsungli Yamen want a foreigner to lead a government-sponsored Chinese school? Actually, this approach fit into an established pattern by which Chinese dynasties had utilized foreign participation in their governments.[39] This was the case with Hart at the Maritime Customs, and Maritime Customs funds supported the school. A foreigner would be able to give proper direction in a curriculum designed to prepare a new type of civil servant; no Chinese was at that point capable of fulfilling such a role. Moreover, the school allowed government leaders to make safe concessions to a new era, without jeopardizing old traditions. A Western-type school with its foreign director was a symbol of change to encourage the West that Chinese officials were sincere in their talk of progress. And from the Chinese perspective to have any foreigner under their control and to work with him in evolving a new approach was "to make use of foreigners but not to let them make use of us."[40]

Martin was well accustomed to Chinese life. He came with the high recommendations of Hart and Burlingame, two Westerners whom the Chinese greatly respected. His cooperative, tolerant, and friendly spirit assured them that he would be both loyal and flexible. Moreover, his translation of *Elements of International Law* had impressed them.

Shortly after his appointment, he had a mild scare. His earlier letter to the *North China Herald*, stating his doubt that China intended to honor the "religious toleration" clause of the Tientsin Treaty, had been discovered by a Chinese censor and sent to the members of the Tsungli Yamen, apparently in the hope that they would oust him. Officials seemed satisfied with his explanation that it had been written nearly ten years earlier, and nothing further was heard of the matter.[41]

Martin brought academic flair, "a high ideal of duty; very considerable literary skill; the gift of eloquence both in English and Chinese; a charming simplicity of manner combined with much natural dignity, and the complete confidence of his employers — the Tsungli Yamen — to his task as head of the school."[42] Although he was given "power to recast its organization in a more practical plan,"[43] he was not particularly known for his administrative ability and was content to allow Hart and the Tsungli Yamen to make many of the organizational decisions.[44] This freed him for teaching, writing, and control of academic affairs, his major interests.

When Martin took over at the T'ung Wen Kuan, the school had already passed through "seven years of infancy." The next seven years he called a "struggle to survive."[45] The first step for survival was to reorganize the curriculum into two separate courses of study, requiring five years and eight years respectively.[46] The five-year curriculum, designed for Chinese or Manchus holding one of the regular degrees, or sufficient literary accomplishment to take the examinations, did not include any foreign languages. The first two years, besides introducing Western mathematics, utilized classical Chinese mathematical books from the Han and Sung dynasties.[47] The next three years included a heavy dose of science, mathematics, political economy, and international law.[48]

The eight-year curriculum was for the "Bannermen of Peking," that is the Manchus and "all descendents of Mongol and Chinese soldiers of the conquest" of China.[49] The initial two years and most of the third were devoted exclusively to the acquisition of a foreign language — English, French, German, or Russian. Those who learned English used it in all of their subsequent scientific studies, while students belonging to the other language departments used Chinese as "a vehicle for scientific instruction, it not having been found practicable to institute parallel courses in several languages."[50] Geography and history were included in the third year of language study, and studies in science and mathematics largely composed the final five years.[51]

When Martin assumed his new responsibilities at the school, the student body numbered only forty or fifty.

> In the next two years the number of students drawn from the Eight Banners of Peking, hitherto limited to thirty, was doubled, and at the same time students were summoned from the schools for foreign languages in Canton and Shanghai, while some were sent up from the provinces of the interior, and the whole number raised to one-hundred which is the present limit.[52]

By 1888 student enrollment reached its peak of 125.[53]

Most of the students were enrolled in the eight-year course and came to the school at about fifteen years of age. The minority — usually about twenty percent — had attained some literary standing or were graduates of other schools and commenced immediately on the five-year curriculum.[54] Until 1870 most of the students had come from the Peking Bannermen. Intellectually they were not very promising, despised for going to a foreign school, and not too interested in anything but the Chinese studies, which might afford them a path to success.[55] After 1870, the proportion of Chinese students increased, until by 1893 it would appear that fifty-two percent were Chinese and only forty-eight percent were Bannermen.[56] Chinese students did not automatically improve the quality of the school. Young men with ability tended to follow the time-proven route to officialdom, and the high government stipends used to procure students for the T'ung Wen Kuan produced relatively easy living and a lax academic atmosphere.[57]

Martin, perhaps to justify the potential of the school, was more optimistic about the students. They were, he observed, "quick of apprehension and patient in application."[58] Their high academic potential was evident, he felt, since twenty had been admitted to compete for higher degrees in the examinations, three had already attained the second degree, and one had received the highest degree.[59]

Conservative critics, particularly from the censorate, an official body established to act as "watch dog" over government policy, continued to snipe at the school, accusing it both of poor discipline and inferior education. One suggested that Chinese teachers would be able to solve both problems better than the foreign teachers whose long tenure had made them lax. Replying to this charge, the Tsungli Yamen

> . . . defended Martin as president of the school and pointed out the difficulty of finding a Chinese to serve in that position who was familiar with both Chinese and Western learning and who could also meet the proposed requirement regarding scholarship and character.[60]

Some of the students were older. These "resident graduates"

> . . . having served a term or two in diplomatic or consular employ are permitted to reenter the college and revive their studies while waiting for a new appointment. They are usually given the charge of a class, with the title of tutor, or employed as official translators.[61]

Two of these resident graduates, with Martin's personal help and advice, were honored to instruct Emperor Kuang-hsü in English for half an hour every day at 4 A.M.[62]

One of Martin's major administrative responsibilities was securing and keeping a competent faculty. During most of his administration, there were eight or nine foreign and four Chinese instructors, as well as numerous tutors and assistant tutors. A Chair of Astronomy had been established before Martin assumed the presidency, but after the Von Gumpach debacle in 1867, the post remained vacant until Mark Harrington accepted Martin's invitation in 1877. Poor health forced him to relinquish this assignment after a short time, and he was ultimately succeeded by S. Marcus Russel of Queen's College, Belfast.[63] Martin wrote to John Fryer, an American teacher who had formerly taught at the T'ung Wen Kuan, asking him to return, but Fryer declined, replying that he was still under contract at the Kiangnan Arsenal.[64]

In 1871 Dr. John Dudgeon of the London Missionary Society was invited to teach Medicine and Physiology. The Tsungli Yamen refused, however, to either allow students to receive clinical training at the hospital or to establish a medical school. Their control over the students in this instance clearly infringed on Martin's authority in academic affairs.[65]

It required ingenuity and flexibility to match available professors with required course offerings. Professors often had to teach in two subject areas. Martin himself usually taught international law and political economy, but it was frequently necessary for him to teach some science courses. When his schedule did not permit this, "language professors . . . or even complete outsiders" would take these courses.[66]

The task of planning and obtaining improved facilities also fell to Martin. Much of what was available in 1869 had been constructed in 1866 when the school was expanded. Martin described it as resembling a military barracks — two rows of low houses accommodating both students and servants, and seven quadrangles, each with a main building flanked by smaller houses.[67]

When plans to meet construction costs from the $200,000 surplus which the Chinese government paid to the United States for American property destroyed in Canton did not materialize,[68] Martin persuaded Wen-hsiang, the Manchu Grand Secretary, to buy seven presses and four fonts of movable type and to erect "commodious buildings" for their use. By 1876 the government also provided funds for building a Chemical Laboratory and Museum.[69] After meeting formidable obstacles in trying to obtain a location not harmful to the "wind and water," permission was finally given to erect an observatory to facilitate teaching astronomy.[70] Despite the care that had been taken in selecting the site, Martin noted that the structure was "high enough to make property cheap in the neighborhood."

Gradually, Martin was able to build up the library of the T'ung Wen Kuan. Obtained both by purchase and by gifts from interested friends,[71] the collection eventually came to include over 7500 English and 2000 Chinese volumes, half of the Chinese volumes on mathematics.[72] A library reading room contained a good supply of newspapers and magazines in several languages.

The school's original purpose was to prepare men for government service as interpreters. This goal was first achieved when three students were sent to Europe with the Pin-ch'un mission in 1866, six to the United States with the Burlingame entourage in 1868, and two with Ch'ung-hou when he went to France in 1870 to apologize for Chinese acquiescence in the Tientsin massacre.[73]

After Kuo Sung-t'ao was appointed Chinese resident envoy to England in 1877, the pace of establishing diplomatic missions was quickened. Chinese legations followed rapidly in Germany (1877), the United States and France (1878), Russia and Spain (1879), and Peru (1880).[74] In 1879 Martin could list a total of sixteen graduates, holding ranks from four to nine, serving as interpreters at these various legations, and by 1888 the number had increased to twenty.[75]

Gradually, many T'ung Wen Kuan graduates came to occupy diplomatic posts more significant than that of interpreter.

> As early as 1888 some were to be found acting as Secretaries of legations in European capitals, and by 1896 a few had risen to the rank of consul-general and charge d'affaires. By 1907 two had served as envoys to Japan, one as envoy to England, one as envoy to France, and one as envoy to Germany, and in the years since that time graduates of the College have had a large place in the conduct of the foreign relations of China.[76]

Resident graduates, who had either returned from abroad or had taken part-time jobs in Peking immediately upon their graduation, served in the Imperial Household, on one of the Six Boards, and in other minor clerical positions.[77] By 1888 many of the graduates took jobs in the civil service, became District Magistrates and Prefects in many parts of China, entered the telegraph service, acted as interpreters for high provincial officials, and accepted other posts of prominence. Obviously, the impact of the school and of Western learning was being felt in Chinese diplomatic and political life, even though the conservative majority did little more than tolerate it.[78]

Martin possessed an ability to accommodate his Western thinking to the demands imposed by the Chinese environment. The curriculum he developed was Western-oriented but included some Chinese topics in mathematics, probably from suggestions given by the Mathematics Professor, Li Shan-lan, whom he admired greatly.[79] The school's pedagogical approach stressed the development of logical thinking, and Martin never tired of reporting samples of the examination questions used in the various departments.[80]

Martin's Christian testimony to students and colleagues alike was candid, but not obnoxious. He requested fellow professors not "to skip the religious lessons in their reading books" and stated that "a favorite subject for discussion was the creeds of the pagan and Christian worlds."[81] Students consulted him frequently on religious matters. He had no illusions about the results of this kind of missionary work. "Though deterred from professing Christianity by social considerations or lest it should prejudice their official career, most of them gave it their intellectual consent. . . ."[82]

The faculty and students of the T'ung Wen Kuan translating Western technical books into Chinese was a natural outgrowth of the institution's major goal to prepare men for "oral interpretation."[83] By 1888 over twenty works had been translated, or written as original contributions.

The procedure employed in the translation work was fairly simple. Martin or one of his colleagues made a rough oral translation of the English text to Chinese aides who wrote it in Chinese. After this had been further checked for accuracy of meaning, it was edited again by the Chinese translators.[84]

Two of Martin's works, *Elements of International Law* and *Natural Philosophy*, were written independently of the college but printed under government auspices, the latter at the T'ung Wen Kuan press. In addition to these two volumes, Martin was also involved in translating and producing nine books on science, international law, and political economy.[85]

To put Martin's notable literary achievements at the T'ung Wen Kuan in perspective, several things must be remembered. First, from 1600 to 1800 Jesuit missionaries, notably Ricci, had translated a number of European scientific works into Chinese, providing both a model and some basic vocabulary for later missionaries.[86] Second, Protestant missionaries, to a small degree before 1850, but much more after that date, translated many books in mathematics, astronomy, medicine, and other sciences. In fact, Li Shan-lan, who taught at the T'ung Wen Kuan, was the principal assistant to Alexander Wylie and Joseph Edkins in their translation work during the 1850's and 1860's.[87] Later, under the auspices of the School and Textbook Committee and the Educational Association of China, missionaries translated a large number of secular textbooks which they needed in their rapidly proliferating schools, and also appropriated those produced by the translation departments of the government schools.[88]

Third, the total translation effort at the T'ung Wen Kuan was far surpassed by that of the Kiangnan Arsenal which, during the period between 1880 to 1896 alone, published seventy-eight books.[89] Translation, however, was but one facet of the work of the T'ung Wen Kuan; instruction and training were continuing activities with only a little over two months of vacation each year.[90] In appreciation for the total service rendered by the foreign faculty, the Tsungli Yamen successfully memorialized the Emperor to grant "Mandarin rank of the third degree for the President [Martin] and of the fourth for professors Billequin and Vapereau."[91]

Martin's work at the T'ung Wen Kuan was both fulfilling and frustrating. His role in a government educational institution gave him a base for continuing to serve as news commentator with the *New York Times*,[92] organizing the Peking Oriental Society,[93] writing books and articles to acquaint the West with China,[94] and serving as an informal political confidante to the Chinese government.[95]

A fulfilling task which grew directly out of his administrative position in the T'ung Wen Kuan was his appointment by the Chinese government in 1880 to tour several foreign countries and report back on their educational systems. This trip, taking him to Japan, America, England, France, Germany, Switzerland, and Italy over a two-year period (1880-82), led him to emphasize the need for nations to learn from each other, and the value of comparative educational statistics.[96]

Despite the fact that his government position helped him accomplish some subsidiary goals, Martin's ultimate purpose that the T'ung Wen Kuan would lead to a complete reform in the educational system was not realized. He often spoke, for example, to the cabinet ministers about "engrafting science on the civil service examinations."[97] Two abortive attempts to do so were made on the provincial level in 1874 and 1885. In 1887, Li Hung-chang, prompted by the suggestions of a censor, proposed successfully that physical sciences and mathematics be included as examination subjects.[98] Martin felt that this would "inaugurate an intellectual revolution whose extent and results it would be difficult to predict."[99] Conservative influence was still so strong, however, that few scholars wished to use this alternative approach to obtain their degrees.

Neither had the T'ung Wen Kuan contributed measurably to advancing the Kingdom of God in China. It had produced no

Christian teachers for the new schools in China. A government school controlled by the Tsungli Yamen to prepare men for official state position, it was hardly a productive field for evangelism. Martin, although zealous in continued testimony concerning his faith, could not communicate enough of the Gospel to show its relationship to Western civilization. He was satisfied to work in this difficult situation which others with similar motivation would have found impossible. Timothy Richard, for example, although theologically more liberal than Martin, still insisted that he would not serve as President of Shansi University unless the Christian faith were taught in the classroom.[100]

William Martin continued his work with the T'ung Wen Kuan until 1895 when he resigned because of failing health and returned to America.[101] Although he was nearly seventy years old, his heart was still in China, and in January, 1897, he returned to Peking, little realizing that his work as an educational pioneer was not yet completed.[102]

When Japan had defeated China two years earlier, it was clear that the policy of "self-strengthening" — superficial modernization with no basic changes — had failed. More radical alterations than building armies and navies, teaching courses on science and mathematics, or even secret political alliances were needed.[103] From 1896 to 1898 conflicting reform ideologies contended for the Chinese mind. One repeated proposal was that China needed a new, comprehensive system of education. Japan's victory reinforced this idea, for when she inaugurated the Meiji era, educational reform was given top priority.[104]

Up to this time only piecemeal efforts, such as the several "interpreters' schools," had been made. In the early 1890's the government had established Nanyang University at Shanghai under the direction of John Ferguson and Peiyang University at Tientsin with Charles D. Tenney as President.[105] Provincial authorities had started numerous schools for local clientele, Chang Chih-tung's *Tzï-ch'iang hsüeh-t'ang* (Self Strengthening School) at Wuch'ang being one prominent example.[106]

The first official memorial for a comprehensive educational system was submitted to the Throne by Li Tuan-fen, Vice-President of the Board of Punishments, on June 12, 1896. This, and a similar memorial by Wang P'eng-yun, an imperial censor, were approved by the Emperor, and at his request detailed procedures, based on Japan's educational system, were submitted.[107]

Nothing of further significance happened until June 11, 1898, the beginning of the "One Hundred Days of Reform" during which the Emperor Kuang-hsü issued seventy-three edicts, thirty-six of which dealt with education, eight being specific proposals concerning the Imperial University.[108] The organizational structure provided for a Chancellor, to be appointed by the Emperor, and a Dean of the Faculty, a Chinese who would be appointed by the Chancellor. Foreign studies were included in the curriculum but were not to have such dominance that a foreign dean of faculty would be required.[109]

Sun Chia-nai, former President of the Board of Censors and then President of the Board of Civil Office, was made Chancellor. He consulted frequently with W. A. P. Martin concerning organizational details and followed his advice to use "scholarships" rather than "stipends" to support students.[110] He was impressed with Martin's ability and with the need to make a structural change that would provide for a foreign Dean of the Faculty. This change was made on August 9, 1898, and Martin was asked to fill the new position.[111] His salary was five hundred taels ($375) a month and his title was *tsung-chiao-hsi*.[112] His specific duty was to be in charge of the science curriculum in the University.[113] Two Chinese head teachers and two officials outranked Martin and had more comprehensive responsibilities in the administration of the school. Much less than when at the T'ung Wen Kuan would he seem to have rated the title "President," which he and others almost always used when describing his status.[114]

There was apparently some "in-fighting" before the appointment was made, and the United States Minister, Conger, reported that Li Hung-chang's support for Martin was a decisive factor.[115] Sun knew that Martin was a strong personality and advised that he "should have only clearly defined powers and should not be allowed to meddle in affairs beyond his jurisdiction."[116]

The volume and variety of the reforms during the "Hundred Days" were too much for the conservative clique. Fearful that their own position would be undermined, they incited the Empress Dowager to take over the government from Emperor Kuang-hsü on

September 21, 1898. Most of the reform edicts were annulled, but the commitment to a national education system — the Imperial University at Peking and the colleges, high schools, and elementary schools at lower levels — was not reversed.[117] Sun Chia-nai, Hsü Ching-ch'en, the Chinese dean, and Martin retained their positions. Martin was not sure why the new university survived. He thought support by Li Hung-chang and Jung-lu, adviser to the Empress, had been decisive. The latter had said, "to suppress the university would be a disgrace in the eyes of foreign nations."[118] A friend of Martin in Peking thought that only Martin's prestige had saved the school.[119]

Entrance exams were given beginning in December, 1898, and the physical facilities were readied for the university to open.[120] The formal convocation was held December 31, 1898, and classes convened January 28, 1899.[121]

At the beginning, there was a foreign faculty of eight and several of what Martin called "native assistants, mostly Christian graduates of mission schools."[122] Several of the foreigners and many of the Chinese had been connected with the missionary movement — either on the giving or receiving end — and one writer commented that the school had a "missionary spirit — [but was not] given to a proselytizing aim."[123]

To accommodate the religious convictions of the faculty, Sun Chia-nai permitted the foreigners the option of not observing the Confucian rites at the opening ceremony. However, "the Western faculty led by Martin, the dedicated missionary, chose to pay their regards to a very important symbol of Chinese culture."[124] This did not sit at all well with most missionaries in Peking who felt that it was idolatrous for Martin and his colleagues to "remove their hats and bow to the tablet of Confucius."[125]

When the Boxer hordes descended on Peking in June, 1900, all university life came to a halt, although none of the school's buildings were destroyed. In the chaotic conditions prevailing after the Western armies captured Peking, no educational work could be resumed. Martin went back to the United States on October 23, 1900, spent a year visiting friends and relatives and pursuing some literary work. He returned to his adopted land in September, 1901.

Even before the Imperial Court returned to Peking on

January 7, 1902, the Empress Dowager was proposing reforms similar to those she had rejected only three years before.[126] Expelling the foreigners had brought only disaster, and she was now willing, albeit superficially, to give reform a chance. On January 10, 1902, Chang Po-hsi was appointed Chancellor of Imperial University, and Martin was reappointed to his old position.[127]

Chang was a "moderate progressive . . . completely loyal to the Empress . . . [with a] reputation for efficiency, administrative ability, honesty and scholarship."[128] Within a short time he let it be known that he intended to dismiss the entire foreign faculty, and this "startling occurrence," as Martin called it, took place on February 26, 1902.[129] Chang named economy as the reason for this move. The foreign professors had demanded and received back pay for eighteen months, including the time of the siege and the allied occupation.[130] This depleted the educational funds and created a precarious financial situation. Chancellor Chang felt that the school might not be reopened for several months,[131] and he did not wish to have a high-salaried staff doing nothing.[132] Therefore, the faculty was appropriately lauded, given three months' bonus, and dismissed.

Additional reasons for these abrupt dismissals have been advanced. The *London Times* suggested that Martin might have been *persona non grata* because he had denounced the Empress Dowager and the government following the siege.[133] He had compared her to "Jezebel of Samaria," but his intemperate outburst would hardly have contaminated the entire faculty. Chang Po-hsi himself stated that it was time for Chinese educators to seek specialists to teach in Chinese schools. Missionaries, he noted, had not been experts in their fields, and had not always produced the best results.[134] Nationalism was beginning to develop in China, and Chang and others rightly felt that Chinese supervision and Chinese cultural patterns should replace foreign guidance and methodology.[135]

The indigenization of Chinese education was the avowed goal of Martin and his colleagues, but it was hard to take when it happened. Martin was as polite as Chang when the axe fell. He had never expected to be dean for more than a few years. Moreover, he had discussed reorganizational plans with the Chancellor and now hoped that "the effort to . . . expand [may] not prove abortive for the want of foreign advisers!"[136] At a reception given for him by the Peking Missionary Association on February 25, 1902, he showed some bitterness, stating that the country could very well disintegrate, and that if this should happen, it "would be providential and for the real good of the Chinese people."[137]

Foreign friends were not so discreet as Martin. Articles in the *North China Herald* publicly scolded the Chinese government for having "thrown him out like a worn-out sponge."[138] Martin was deeply disturbed, but when he returned to America in mid-March, 1902, he hardly felt that "he shook the dust of this ungrateful country from his shoes and left for home. . . ."[139] He would soon, in fact, be back.

When he arrived in Vancouver, B. C. in early April, 1902, he found awaiting him a telegram from Chang Chih-tung, Viceroy of Hunan-Hupeh, inviting him to return to China and head up a new university at Wuch'ang in Central China.[140] Martin had never met Chang, but, impressed with his accomplishments in education, industry, and politics, he accepted the position.

He arrived at Wuch'ang to take up his new position in September, 1902, and stayed there until 1905. Even though Chang had good intentions, "the university existed only on paper." Martin taught a few of Chang's mandarins[141] "the law of nations . . . [and] some notion of geography and history," but had few other responsibilities. Most of his time was taken up writing and visiting old acquaintances. The climate was bad, and he did not seem to like the city of Wuch'ang. However, these inconveniences were more than compensated for by a lovely home along the bank of the Yangtze and a generous monthly salary which came to him as "President of Wu Ch'ang University."[142]

The University's failure to materialize was not because of any dissatisfaction that Chang felt about Martin: Chang was ordered to Nanking to assume a new post within a month of Martin's arrival, and a month after that he was summoned to Peking to undertake still further responsibilities. Thus, Martin observed, his zeal exceeded his wisdom. Martin added,

> Viceroy Chang has been derided, not quite justly, as possessing a superabundance of initiative along with a rather scant measure of finality, taking up and throwing down his new schemes as a child

does his playthings. In these enterprises the paucity of results was due to the shortcomings of the agents to whom he trusted their management.[143]

For most of forty years W. A. P. Martin had been employed, fully or partially, by the Chinese government or its provincial leaders in educational enterprises. These various efforts — pioneering a new type of government school, translating Western books, pushing for educational reform, representing the Chinese government in its search for educational models, and participating in the development of the first national university — earned him the accolade "founder of modern state education in China."[144] Missionary schools run by Calvin Mateer and D. Z. Sheffield were equally innovative, but unrelated to the state. John C. Ferguson and D. C. Tenney developed the "most thorough and well equipped government colleges"[145] in the pre-Boxer period at Nanyang University (1897) and Tientsin University (1895) respectively, but they followed a trail which Martin had blazed thirty years earlier.

Notes

1. First, there were visits with his mother, sisters, and brothers, most of them scattered in posts of Christian ministry in Indiana, Illinois, and Ohio. The family was reunited with the two boys who had been left at home, and they all settled in New Haven, a base for travel to the churches and for study in International Law and Political Economy, possibly under the direction of Dr. Theodore Woolsey at Yale College. He also traveled extensively to many churches to report on the progress of Christian missions in China. W. A. P. Martin, *A Cycle of Cathay* (3rd ed.; New York, 1900), 241.

2. For example, he attended the meeting of the American Oriental Society in Boston on May 19, 1869, and delivered two major lectures — one, "On the Competitive Examination System in China," and another, "The Early Inventions of the Chinese." *Journal of the American Oriental Society*, IX, Proceedings at Boston, May 19, 1869, li-lv.

3. Mrs. Martin presumably remained at home to help her children in their adjustment to college in New Haven. She probably did not return to China until the spring of 1873. She still was not back in November, 1872, for in a letter to Professor Whitney in November, 1872 he spoke of his "domestic affliction." W. D. Whitney Collection, Library, Yale Univer-

sity. Also see *Annual Report* of the Board of Foreign Missions of the Presbyterian Church in the United States of America, XXXIII, 35.

4. Martin, *Cycle*, 241. Stanley Wright, *Hart and the Chinese Customs* (Belfast, 1950), 328.

5. Letter to Dr. Williams, September 6, 1869. Box 5 of Williams Family Collection, Library, Yale University.

6. Perry Plus [pseud.], "The Peking College," *New York Times*, December 2, 1869, 4:7.

7. W. A. P. Martin, "The Chinese Embassy," *New York Times*, December 1, 1869, 5:1.

8. Diplomatic Despatches, China, XXVI, No. 48, Browne to Secretary of State Fish, June 25, 1869.

9. Martin, *Cycle*, 266; Ssu-yü Teng and John K. Fairbanks, eds., *China's Response to the West: A Documentary Survey, 1832-1923* (New York, 1966), 48. "Bannermen" included the Manchus and all "descendents of Mongol and Chinese soldiers of the conquest" of China. H. B. Morse, *The Trade and Administration of China* (Shanghai, 1908), 62.

10. The precedent for this step was the Russian Language School in Peking but also an early "Official Bureau of Interpreters" in the T'ang dynasty and a "School of Interpreters . . . in the capital since the first reign of the Ming dynasty." Knight Biggerstaff, "The T'ung Wen Kuan," *The Chinese Social and Political Science Review*, XVIII (October, 1934), 309-10; Knight Biggerstaff, *The Earliest Modern Government Schools in China* (Ithaca, 1961), 98; G. Deveria, "Histoire du Collège des Interprètes de Péking," *Mélanges Charles de Harlez* (Leyden, 1896), 94-102.

11. Teng and Fairbank, *China's Response*, 75.

12. For a description of the work of missionaries in educational institutions see Kenneth S. Latourette, *A History of Christian Missions in China* (London, 1929), 214-15, 221, 267, 441-51.

13. Martin, *Cycle*, 297. For some of the details of this see Johannes Von Gumpach, *The Burlingame Mission* (Shanghai, 1872), 604-5. His source was Diplomatic Despatches, China, Burlingame to William Seward, November 18, 1863. Martin is only listed as a member of the board in this dispatch.

14. The salary was 1000 taels ($1330) annually, and later, when he was made Professor of International Law and then President, it was increased to 5000 taels ($6650).

15. W. A. P. Martin, "The Tungwen College," Appendix F of H. B. Morse, *The International Relations of the Chinese Empire* (3 vols.; New York, 1918), II, 472.

16. Martin, *Cycle*, 297-98.

17. China Letters, VII, Peking, Martin to Board, October 1, 1865.

18. Martin, *Cycle,* 298.

19. CL, VII, Peking, Martin to Board, #243, October 1, 1866.

20. Martin, *Cycle,* 325.

21. Compare statements in CL, VII, Peking, Martin to Board, #243, October 1, 1866 with #499, October 1, 1867.

22. Martin's official publications: *Cycle,* 301; "The Tungwen College," in Morse, *International Relations,* II, 474, and *Calendar of the Tungwen College* (Peking, 1879), 29, give this date as 1865, but CL, VII, Peking, Martin to Board, #499, October 1, 1867 as well as Biggerstaff, *Government Schools,* 108, and Teng and Fairbank, *China's Response,* 75, give it as December, 1866.

23. CL, VII, Peking, Martin to Board, #499, October 1, 1867.

24. Teng and Fairbank, *China's Response,* 75.

25. Martin, "The Tungwen College," in Morse, *International Relations,* II, 475.

26. *Ibid.*

27. *Ibid.*

28. Martin, *Cycle,* 304; Martin, "A University in Peking," *New York Times,* September 4, 1867, 2:1-2.

29. Von Gumpach, *Burlingame Mission,* 602. He poked fun at literal translations into English of polite descriptions of Martin in Chinese such as "pinnacle of the West" and "lord Martin." 599.

30. *Ibid.,* 595. Martin declared that he preferred "college." It was similar to American colleges in the mid-nineteenth century that were roughly equivalent to high schools. In some of his articles in the *New York Times* and in the preface to *Natural Philosophy* he called it a "university." Biggerstaff erroneously remarked that "Martin and Hart always referred to the T'ung-wen Kuan as 'the College.'" *Government Schools*, 140. Italics mine.

31. Von Gumpach, *Burlingame Mission,* 599-600.

32. Martin, *Cycle,* 294. The Chinese phrase "tsung-chiao-hsi" literally means "head teacher," but in the Tung Wen Kuan the *function* of this position was equivalent to the term "hsiao-chang," normally translated as "President" or "Principal." Biggerstaff, "The T'ung Wen Kuan," 324; Wu Hsüan-yi, "Ching-shih t'ung-wen-kuan lüeh-szi" ("A Summary History of the Peking T'ung Wen Kuan"), *Tu-shu yüeh-k'an,* II (January, 1933), 8.

33. Martin's appointment to this position was widely heralded in the United States, and in 1870, as a result, he was awarded an honorary LL.D. by New York University. Norma Farquhar, "W. A. P. Martin and the Westernization of China" (unpublished M.A. thesis, Indiana University, 1954), 233.

34. CL, X, Peking, Martin to Board, #198, January 4, 1870. He

stated that if he ever gave up his connection with the government, he would want to preach in Shantung.

35. *Ibid.* He reminded the Corresponding Secretary that he had told him this when he was still in America.

36. CL, John Butler to Board, #56, March 15, 1871. Lowrie's letter is included with Butler's.

37. CL, X, Peking, Martin to Board, #169, December 1, 1869.

38. Alice H. Gregg, *China and Educational Autonomy. The Changing Role of the Protestant Educational Missionary in China, 1807-1937* (New York, 1946), 11, 20-22.

39. John Fairbank, ed., *Chinese Thought and Institutions* (Chicago, 1957), 205.

40. Martin, *Cycle,* 342.

41. *Ibid.,* 357.

42. Wright, *Hart and Chinese Customs,* 329.

43. CL, X. Peking, Martin to Board, #169, December 1, 1869.

44. Wright, *Hart and Chinese Customs,* 329; CL, V, Shanghai, Culbertson to Board, #260, July 17, 1862. Culbertson commented that Martin's strong point was not his "executive ability."

45. W. A. P. Martin, "Statement of Martin on T'ung Wen Kuan to Secretary of State Fish," February 5, 1877. This is enclosed with Diplomatic Despatches, China, XL, #217, George Seward to Fish, March 13, 1877.

46. The eight-year curriculum was not finally approved by the Tsungli Yamen until late in 1876. Martin, "Statement to Fish," February 5, 1877.

47. *Calendar of the Tungwen College* (Chinese Text), 1879, 37.

48. *Ibid.* "Third year: physics, chemistry and theoretical mechanics; fourth year: differential and integral calculus, navigation, astronomy and practical mechanics; fifth year: international law, political economy, astronomy, geology, and mineralogy."

49. Martin, *Cycle,* 311; Morse, *Trade and Administration,* 62.

50. *Calendar,* 1879, 18.

51. *Ibid.* "Fourth year: arithmetic and algebra; fifth year: natural philosophy, geometry, plane and spherical trigonometry; sixth year: theoretical and practical mechanics, differential and integral calculus, navigation and surveying; seventh year: chemistry, astronomy, and international law; eighth year: astronomy, geology and mineralogy, political economy."

52. *Ibid.,* 32.

53. *Calendar of the Tungwen College,* 1888, 14.

54. Biggerstaff, "The T'ung Wen Kuan," 327.

55. Biggerstaff, *Government Schools,* 124.

56. *Ibid.,* 141.

57. *Ibid.,* 127.

58. Martin, *Cycle,* 314-15.

59. Martin, "Statement to Fish," February 5, 1877.

60. Biggerstaff, *Government Schools,* 142.

61. Martin, *Cycle,* 316.

62. *Ibid.,* 317. He stated that the Emperor and many of his princes and ministers had a great interest in learning English in anticipation of their using it at a New Year audience with foreign envoys which, unfortunately for continuing interest, never occurred.

63. *Calendar,* 1879, 33; Martin, *Cycle,* 311.

64. John Fryer to Martin, May 25, 1870. John Fryer Collection, Box 1, Miscellaneous Letters. Bancroft Library, University of California at Berkeley. The Kiangnan Arsenal included, among many other activities, a school for training translators.

65. Martin, *Cycle,* 320.

66. Biggerstaff, *Government Schools,* 133.

67. Martin, *Cycle,* 307.

68. *North China Herald*, II, May 9, 1868, and Diplomatic Despatches, China, XXXI, #126, Frederick Low to Secretary of State Fish, January 20, 1872. Enclosure #1 is a letter from Martin to Fish on this matter. Also see Martin, *Cycle,* 299.

69. *Calendar,* 1879, 33; Martin, *Cycle,* 308-9.

70. Martin, *Cycle,* 309-10. "Wind and water" is a literal translation of the Chinese term for "geomancy."

71. Letter of December 29, 1870, from Martin to Mrs. Couper, widow of a physician whom he had met on the *Mississippi* during his diplomatic days, gratefully accepting even a "single volume" of her husband's medical library. Found in Samuel F. DuPont Collection in Eleutherian Mills Historical Library. On occasion, needed books — some on Euclid, for example — were borrowed from the Kiangnan Arsenal Library. John Fryer to Martin, May 25, 1870. John Fryer Collection, Box 1, Miscellaneous Letters.

72. *Calendar,* 1879, 27; Biggerstaff, *Government Schools,* 134.

73. Martin, "The Tungwen College," in Morse, *International Relations*, II, 476; Biggerstaff, "The T'ung Wen Kuan," 334.

74. Teng and Fairbank, *China's Response,* 97.

75. *Calendar,* 1879, 15; *Calendar,* 1888, 4.

76. Biggerstaff, "The T'ung Wen Kuan," 335.

77. *Calendar*, 1879, 16.

78. Martin, *Cycle*, 327; Biggerstaff, *Government Schools*, 152-53, and "The T'ung Wen Kuan," 339-40. Martin conceded that its purpose was hardly to "renovate the whole mandarinate."

79. Martin, *Cycle*, 368-70.

80. *Calendar*, 1879, 21-23; *Calendar*, 1888, 5-7; News items by W. A. P. Martin in *Wan-kuo kung-pao*, XII, April 10, 1880, 325b, and May 8 1880, 334b-336b. See Adrian Bennett, "Missionary Journalism in 19th Century China: Young J. Allen and the Early Wan-kuo kung-pao, 1868-1883" (unpublished Ph. D. dissertation, University of California at Davis, 1970), 234. Examinations were held monthly, annually, and triennially. *Calendar*, 1879, 20.

81. Martin, *Cycle*, 325.

82. *Ibid.*, 326. He was grateful though that "the creed of a student never seemed to make any difference in his official prospects."

83. *Calendar*, 1879, 25, and Martin, *Cycle*, 319.

84. Farquhar, "W. A. P. Martin," 132. John Fryer used a similar procedure. See Adrian Bennett, *John Fryer: The Introduction of Western Science and Technology into Nineteenth-Century China* (Cambridge, Mass., 1967), 29. This method is specifically implied in the Chinese preface of Martin's Chinese book, *Christianity and Other Creeds*.

85. *Calendar*, 1879, 25-26; Biggerstaff, "The T'ung Wen Kuan," 332-33. The books he helped to translate are: *Guide Diplomatique* (de Martens) by Lien-fang and Ch'ing-ch'ang under his supervision in 1877; *Introduction to the Study of International Law* (Woolsey) by Wang Fung-tsao under his supervision in 1877; *Political Economy* (Fawcett) by Wang Fung-tsao under his supervision in 1880; *Universal History* (Tytler) by Ch'ang-hsiu and Yang-chu under Professor Cowles' supervision and revised by Martin in 1879; *Mathematical Physics*, 8 volumes, compiled by Martin with the assistance of Tu, Li *et al.*, 1884; *Droit International Codifié* (Bluntschli) by Martin assisted by Lien-fang and Ch'ing-ch'ang in 1880; "International Law in Ancient China" by Martin; *Chinese Students' Manual* by Martin; *Laws of Land Warfare* (Euopean Institute of International Law) by Martin.

86. Cyrus H. Peake, "Some Aspects of the Introduction of Modern Science into China," *ISIS*, XXII (1) (December, 1934), 179.

87. T. H. Tsien, "Impact on China Through Translation," *Far Eastern Quarterly*, XIII (May, 1954), 312-13.

88. The School and Textbook Committee was established by missionaries at the Shanghai Missionary Conference in 1877. See "The Shanghai Missionary Conference," *The Chinese Recorder*, VIII (May-June, 1877), 239-50. It was replaced in 1890 by the Educational Association of

China. This organization used Martin's translations of *Political Economy* and *Droit International Codifié. The Chinese Recorder,* XXIX (December, 1898), 606.

89. Bennett, *John Fryer,* 37. Fifty-five percent were in the natural sciences, twenty-six percent in the applied sciences, eight percent in history and the social sciences, six percent in vocabularies, and five percent in military and naval sciences. See Tsien, "Impact on China," 311, for a concise chart depicting the contribution by government and private agencies. The translation department of the Kiangnan Arsenal was an outgrowth of the Shanghai T'ung Wen Kuan, commenced in 1863.

90. *Calendar,* 1879, 17. The first semester began about twenty days after the Lunar New Year and continued until about July 20. The second semester opened about the end of August and continued until about ten days before the Lunar New Year.

91. Martin, "The Tungwen College," in Morse, *International Relations,* II, 477. A Chinese record of this is found in *Ta-ch'ing shih-lu,* Chapter 219, 10b.

92. He wrote many articles for the *New York Times* from 1863 to 1872, and then no further contribution appears until 1900. "Mr. Seward in China," January 26, 1871, 1:7-2:1.

93. An affiliate of the North China Branch of the Royal Asiatic Society, this scholarly group was organized with Martin as its first president. He wrote numerous articles for its journal through the years. W. A. P. Martin, "The Past and Present of the Peking Oriental Society," *Journal of the Peking Oriental Society,* I (May, 1886), 190.

94. During these years he wrote *The Hanlin Papers First Series* (1880), *The Hanlin Papers Second Series* (1894), and *A Cycle of Cathay* (1896) as well as a large number of articles in *Harper's Weekly, The Chinese Recorder, New Englander, Forum, Andover Review,* and *Revue de Droit Internationale et De Législation Comparée.* The excellent material contained in these books and articles was enhanced by his position as "President" of Peking University.

95. Martin, *Cycle,* 380-85, 396, 353; Renville C. Lund, "The Imperial University of Peking" (unpublished Ph. D. dissertation, University of Washington, 1957), 301. These two sources give several examples of his influence on critical matters.

96. The report of this journey was contained in Martin's Chinese work *Hsi Hsüeh K'ao-lüeh* (A Resume of Western Education) which is no longer available. See also "Notices of Recent Publications," *The Chinese Recorder,* XIV (September-October, 1883), 332. No indication exists that his report influenced the educational policies of the Chinese government.

97. Martin, *Cycle,* 319.

98. Teng and Fairbank, *China's Response,* 205.

99. W. A. P. Martin, *The Chinese, Their Education, Philosophy and Letters* (New York, 1881), 81-82.

100. Timothy Richard, *Forty-Five Years in China: Reminiscences* (London, 1916), 299-303.

101. His only other trip to the United States between 1869 and 1895 was apparently in 1880-82 while on the educational tour for the Chinese government. An old friend, Helen Nevius, reported that he was operated on for cancer during this brief furlough in the United States. Helen Nevius, Letter to Henry Rankin. This is preserved in Henry Rankin, "Notes on W. A. P. Martin," 6.

102. News item, *Missionary Review of the World*, Old Series XX (February, 1897), 137.

103. China concluded a secret alliance with Russia in 1896 which she hoped would protect her against future aggression. See Immanuel Hsü, *The Rise of Modern China* (New York, 1970), 413.

104. W. A. P. Martin, *The Lore of Cathay* (New York, 1912), 19.

105. Robert Coltman, *The Chinese* (Philadelphia, 1891), 176; Morse, *International Relations,* III, 547.

106. Lund, "The Imperial University," 49.

107. Tun-yung Lo, "Ching-shih ta-hsüeh t'ang ch'eng-li-chi" ("A Record of the Founding of the Imperial University"), in Hsin-ch'eng Shu, *Chin-tai chung-kuo chiao-yü shih-liao* (Source Materials on Modern Chinese Education), I, 158. Several missionaries, headed by Gilbert Reid, had proposed a comprehensive educational plan to Prince K'ung in August, 1895, that may have helped to stimulate Li Tuan-fen's memorial. Gilbert Reid, "Educational Reforms," *The Chinese Recorder,* XXVI (October, 1895), 476-77.

108. Lund, "The Imperial University," 71-76.

109. *Ibid.,* 82-83, 94.

110. *Ibid.,* 98.

111. *Ibid.*

112. Sun originally suggested six hundred taels a month, but Martin, undoubtedly anxious for this prestigious position, had offered to take this assignment for the same amount he had been paid at the T'ung Wen Kuan. See Lo, "Imperial University," 149-50.

113. Diplomatic Despatches, China, CIV, E. H. Conger to William Day, Secretary of State, August 5, 1898, stated that Martin will "also have charge of the Seal of the university, and the plan of organization will be entirely his own." Either this is overstated or Chinese sources do not give an accurate picture of Martin's role.

114. Lo, "Imperial University," 158. See Farquhar, "W. A. P. Martin," 170-72, for a brief discussion of this. *The Chinese Recorder,* XXIX

(September, 1898), 451, struck a happy medium by calling him "President of The Foreign Staff of the University." Certainly Martin's statement, "A University for the Empire was created and the Emperor selected me for its first president . . ." (*Cycle*, 2) is very misleading.

115. "China Selects an American — Dr. William A. P. Martin Appointed President of The New Imperial University," *New York Times*, September 23, 1898, 7:6. Martin's appointment earned him a promotion by the government from third class to second class. It also brought him an LL.D. from Princeton University in the spring of 1899. Honorary Degree File, Princeton University.

116. Farquhar, "W. A. P. Martin," 169.

117. Hsü, *Modern China*, 452-53.

118. W. A. P. Martin, *Siege in Peking* (New York, 1900), 54.

119. News item, *North China Herald*, February 26, 1902, 371.

120. The university was located in the "Horse Spirit Temple" in East Peking. Lo, "Imperial University," 158.

121. Lund, "The Imperial University," 117.

122. Martin, *Lore*, 20. He said that there were ten foreign teachers and twelve Chinese by the spring of 1900.

123. Lund, "Imperial University," 120-23.

124. "Peking University," *North China Herald*, February 6, 1899, 211.

125. *Ibid.*

126. Hsü, *Modern China*, 488-93.

127. Lund, "Imperial University," 153-54.

128. *Ibid.*

129. W. A. P. Martin, "The Imperial University, Peking," *The Chinese Recorder*, XXXIII (March, 1902), 143.

130. "Dr. Martin on China," *New York Tribune*, April 13, 1902, 3:4.

131. Classes opened on November 18, 1902. See Ting Chih-p'ing, *Chung-kuo chin ch'i-shih-nien-lai chiao-yü chi szi* (Record of the Last Seventy Years in Chinese Education) (Taipei, n.d.), 10-11.

132. *Ibid.* Early plans for the university called for foreign professors to receive three hundred taels a month and for Chinese professors to be paid thirty to fifty taels a month. Lund, "Imperial University," 83. It is not known whether there were compensating factors of wheat, oil, wood, etc. for the Chinese staff.

133. *London Times*, January 17, 1902, 37, quoted in Lund, "Imperial University," 255.

134. "The Educational Outlook," *North China Herald*, April 9, 1902, 673.

135. News item, Peking, *North China Herald,* February 26, 1902, 371.

136. Martin, "The Imperial University," Peking, 144.

137. News item, Peking, *North China Herald,* March 12, 1902, 469.

138. *Ibid.,* April 2, 1902, 628.

139. *Ibid.*

140. Martin, *The Awakening of China* (New York, 1907), 231-32. A writer in the *North China Herald* observed that Chang's offer "removes from the Empire generally, though not from the Capital, a deep and self-imposed stigma." April 2, 1902, 628.

141. These men numbered as many as sixty on certain occasions. Martin, *Awakening,* 237.

142. *Ibid.,* 230.

143. *Ibid.,* 231. See Nathaniel G. Gee, *The Educational Directory for China* (Shanghai, 1905), 135. He said that Martin was Professor of International Law at the Mandarin Institute in Wuch'ang. Of the educational ferment in these central provinces, he observed that sixty schools had been opened in one day in Wuch'ang and that most foreign teachers were Japanese or German. He added, "In this so-called educational reform throughout the Empire the *nominalists* far outnumber the *realists.*"

144. Robert E. Lewis, *The Educational Conquest of the Far East* (New York, 1903), 173.

145. *Ibid.*

CHAPTER EIGHT

The Gospel in Peking — Martin as a Reformer

EVEN THOUGH W. A. P. Martin resigned from the Board of Foreign Missions of the Presbyterian Church in 1869, during his years in Peking previous to the Boxer Rebellion he never completely abandoned specific kinds of missionary work. He often preached on Sundays, led Bible classes, helped in the organization and work of the Peking Presbytery, and gave advice to the Presbyterian Board on a variety of missionary matters. He prepared lectures for the two general conferences of Protestant missionaries, held in Shanghai in 1877 and 1890, participated in the work of various committees organized at these large gatherings, and did literary work for several tract societies. He was not ashamed of his missionary past, and never wavered in his evangelical beliefs or in his zeal to work for the conversion of China.[1]

Even though Martin was no longer formally connected with the institutional missionary movement, he continued to be deeply concerned for its future, and this concern ultimately led him into many reform activities in China, first expressed as a reaction to violent anti-missionary sentiment which broke out only ten years after the treaty provisions which had enabled missionaries to scatter all across China. In the summer of 1870, like a bolt from the blue, over twenty Roman Catholic missionaries in Tientsin, accused of crimes like kidnapping and child mutilation, were cruelly put to death.[2] In the wake of this the Chinese government issued several proposals to restrict the activities of Christian missions.[3]

Martin had several reactions to the Tientsin massacre. He traced the riot largely to an anti-Catholic spirit among the Chinese people, and, like most missionaries in China, he believed that Christians were being opposed not on account of their religion but

> ... solely on account of their connection with foreigners, and charges brought against them of murdering and poisoning constitute a louder call for preaching the Gospel which alone is able to extirpate such abominable superstitions.[4]

Martin was also convinced that Protestants needed to be far more careful to avoid provoking the Chinese. He recommended once again that single men be sent into the interior of China,[5] specifically opposing the policy, inexpedient in the present situation, that urged young missionaries to marry before coming to the field.[6]

Martin believed strongly that something had to be done to eliminate the superstitious naiveté of the common people, whom evil officials could manipulate to believe that Christian workers were guilty of such absurd crimes.

> The cure for these beliefs will not come merely by diffusing religious truth but in the dissemination of such secular knowledge as will give the people juster ideas concerning the people of other countries and the agency of national laws.[7]

Early in 1872, after months of discussing the best way to eliminate superstitious beliefs, Martin and a group of Peking missionaries organized the Society for the Diffusion of Useful Knowledge.[8] The stated purposes of this organization of "secular missionaries" were

1. By the introduction of modern science and liberal thought to endeavor to overthrow those ancient superstitions which constitute the most formidable barriers in the way of material and social improvement;
2. To prepare the way for inevitable innovations by rendering the idea of such changes familiar to the public mind, and leading the Chinese to regard them with desire instead of aversion.[9]

Many missionaries and other Westerners in China responded well to this appeal and subscribed five taels each to support the proposed endeavor.

In July, 1872, the Society began publishing *Chung-hsi wen-chien-lu,* an illustrated monthly, known to the foreign community as *Peking Magazine.* Martin compared it to Silliman's Journal,[10] which was a popular name for the technical periodical *The American Journal of Science,* founded in 1818 by Yale Professor Benjamin Silliman.[11] Silliman utilized his journal and special institutes to give science a rank equal with classical education in America. Martin apparently hoped his magazine and its activities might accomplish the same results in China.

While the periodical was seeking to become self-supporting, most of the one thousand copies issued monthly were distributed without cost. The inability or unwillingness of most readers to pay the nominal cost of one dollar belied Martin's observation that it had "met with unexpected favor in influential quarters," although he was probably right that its "readers number some of the leading minds of the empire."[12]

The Society's hope that native writers would contribute articles did not materialize, and most of the work on the magazine was assumed by the three editors, Martin, Joseph Edkins, and John S. Burdon,[13] all of whom had worked together translating the Peking Mandarin New Testament. When Edkins and Burdon left Peking for work elsewhere, Martin assumed most of the responsibility for the magazine during the last two years of its life.[14] Shortage of articles, failure to attain economic self-sufficiency, and the difficulty of getting news into Peking, which had no telegraphic links to the outside world, during the winter months, forced the magazine to cease publication in June, 1875, at the end of its third year.[15] It was taken over by John Fryer of the Chinese Polytechnic Institution and Reading Rooms, and he incorporated it into his new magazine *Ko-chih hui-pien* (The Chinese Scientific and Industrial Magazine).[16]

The magazine's measurable impact was uncertain, but it was significant in that it was the first journal in China devoted exclusively to reform. Early Protestant missionaries to China such as Robert Morrison, William Milne, Walter Medhurst, and Karl Gutzlaff utilized small Chinese periodicals to promote the Christian faith and to counteract Chinese notions of cultural superiority by acquainting them with basic facts about European civilization.[17] In 1835 Elijah Bridgman, Peter Parker, S. Wells Williams, and others organized a Society for the Diffusion of Useful Knowledge in Canton.[18] The magazine which they produced, really the continuation of an earlier publication by Gutzlaff, included secular information of all types, Chinese classical literature, and a smattering of "natural theology." In general, the material was not very practical, and both the magazine and the society were discontinued in 1839.

Another early missionary interested in reform publications was Young J. Allen, editor of the *Chiao-hui hsin-pao* (The Church News) and its more secular successor, *Wan-kuo kung-pao* (The Globe News). The first was published in Shanghai from 1868 to 1874, and while it included a large number of carefully selected news items,[19] fifteen to twenty percent of its content was religious.[20] Its Christian aim was very explicit; one early issue, for example, included the following topics: Samson overthrowing the Temple of Dagon, Christian morality compared with the moral code of Confucius, and a consideration of the immoralities of gambling.[21]

Up to this point all missionary-sponsored periodicals, whether published outside China or in Canton, Hong Kong, or Shanghai, had included some explicit religious materials and were not completely oriented toward reform — the *Peking Magazine* was the first exception. Described by Martin as "the first periodical besides the official gazette ever published in Peking,"[22] it included articles on practical science, internal improvements, travel, adventure, moral fables, and world news, carefully selected to stimulate China to reform according to what the editors deemed the superior achievements of the Western world.[23]

From 1872 to 1875 this type of material was not available in any other continuing way to Chinese in Peking or in other parts of the Empire. In Peking itself there was *The Peking Gazette,* a type of daily Imperial Chronicle, issued under close government supervision and including news of court affairs, judicial and revenue administration, civil and military administration, religious matters (instruction, worship, and images), external relations, and provincial and colonial affairs.[24]

Many items of local interest for the capital or the Empire were printed in the *Gazette,* but virtually nothing that would expose a Chinese to the wider world was included. Several Chinese periodicals were started by foreigners at Shanghai in the early 1870's, but they had limited circulation. The *Shanghai Hsin-pao,* a daily Chinese edition of the English language *North China*

Herald, was published from 1864 to 1872, but was not in circulation during the same years as the *Peking Magazine.*[25]

Even after the magazine was discontinued in 1875, Martin, desiring to perpetuate its reform influence, published four volumes (thirty-six issues) of *Selections,* comprising about twenty-five percent of the original material.[26] He had had almost sole responsibility for *Chung-hsi wen-chien lu* for over two years of its life, and had prepared many of the articles and most of the news items. In the *Selections,* issued in Peking in 1877, eighty-five percent of the material bore his signature, and the other fifteen percent was included by his choice alone and obviously represented the emphasis which he desired to make.

Each volume of the *Selections* contained a total of seventy to seventy-five leaves, a total of nearly six hundred pages. The material may be roughly divided into four categories: geography, popular science, edited news articles, and miscellaneous items. Many of the edited news items concerned scientific developments and could as well be included under that category. Articles on geography often appeared in the news section, but the only ones listed as "geography" were those including a significant amount of background information about a city or country.[27]

No specifically religious articles or news items were included. The names God and Jesus do not appear more than once or twice and then only in a descriptive, not a dogmatic, sense. Martin and his colleagues apparently believed that this policy would gain greater sympathy for the West and its ways, and thus ultimately achieve a Christian objective.

Scientific articles in the *Peking Magazine* did not include highly technical data with detailed plans for the construction of particular machines or for the use of a specific methodology.[28] This more precise scientific function was later fulfilled by John Fryer's *Ko-chih hui-pien* which absorbed the *Chung-hsi wen-chien lu*, but Martin's purposes were broader and more popular. He intensely desired to convince the Chinese that science, like their classics of old, was "holy" and could be of great value to them.[29] Even this kind of material could lend itself to a moral lesson. England, France, and Italy were reported, for example, to be submitting competing claims for a small volcanic island in the Mediterranean, only to find to their chagrin that it had disappeared.[30] After an explanation of the reason for "salt seas" in various places, Martin commented that such data caused one to "reflect on the wonders of creation."[31]

Many articles provided an overview of a particular subject for the obvious purpose of imparting general information.[32] Although it was hoped that some of these would apply to China, the articles made no particular recommendations or suggestions. Nothing that would discredit anti-scientific views was usually included — for example, in the article about eclipses there was no mention of the popular Chinese view that attributed them to a dog nibbling away at the sun.

In other instances, however, direct aim was taken at superstitious beliefs. Martin noted, for example, that the comet of July, 1874, and Venus passing by the sun in November of that same year, had been viewed by the Chinese as heavenly omens to explain respectively the Sino-Japanese conflict over Formosa and the Emperor's death from smallpox. How, he asked, could these be omens for the Chinese alone and not for the rest of the world, some portions of which had enjoyed great prosperity and military success? Furthermore, he observed, when Venus passed by the sun about one hundred years earlier, Emperor Ch'ien-lung had been at the height of his prosperity and power. These laughable beliefs, he asserted, must be put away, and science must be used to "seek certainty and to pacify the minds of the people."[33] The West, he added, had once believed similar things but had discarded them as without foundation.

Martin specifically advocated that China adopt the metric system and in two articles devoted fourteen pages to a detailed explanation of its history and values, as well as to the terms which would be needed in its implementation. He noted that China's decimal system was simple, concise, and practical, but that greater national uniformity was needed. He found a precedent for seeking uniformity in the classical Chinese concept of the *ta t'ung*, but his main emphasis was practical — such a change would facilitate China's trade with the nations of the world which were on the metric system.[34]

In an English article on the same subject, Martin spoke of the moral value of the metric system, a subject he did not mention as specifically in Chinese.

Show me a people whose micrometer foot-rule will serve to split a hair, whose scales are so sensitive as to mark the 1000th part of a grain, and trembles at a breath of falsehood, whose clocks and watches are truer than the sun, and I will show you a people who have, in no small degree, been educated in honesty and fair dealing.

"On the contrary," he observed, "those whose tape-lines appear to be made of gum elastic . . . are a people among whom commercial morality is, to say the least, somewhat lax."[35]

Martin missed few opportunities to stress the orderly nature of the universe. He began an article on meteorological balloons with the observation that since man was a creature who "wears heaven on his head and treads upon earth as his foot stool,"[36] he had the interest and the ability to investigate and control natural phenomenon. As man made good use of his mind, "heaven and earth" would submit to him. Had not England's wealth, he asked, come from the power of machines? He pointed out that when England was taken by the Romans in the Han period, its people were without culture, clothes, or wealth, and had extremely crude habits. Even their conquerors gave up on them. Now, however, having subdued nature, they were able to meet not only their own needs but those of a kingdom spreading around the world.[37]

He described a Frenchman who had created, in Algeria, an inland lake that had changed the climate of the surrounding area. He commented that there were "no limits in assisting heaven's labor and in helping to change nature."[38] This obviously required scientific expertise, he observed, and "may result in the loss of life — a price often exacted for progress."[39]

Occasionally, the magazine followed a subject of general interest for several issues. The first notice that the planet Venus would soon pass close to the sun was made in September, 1873. He reported that scientists from America, France, England, and Russia would travel to many countries to gain good vantage points from which to view this phenomenon. Their purpose was not to predict future weal or woe, but to measure the distance between the sun and the earth and to learn more about the planet itself.[40]

Other articles appeared, often in the news section concerning the country involved, giving further details of Venus' appearance. He noted, for example, that American scientists would travel to eight different observation points and that all the methods they hoped to use had first been successfully tried out in Washington, D.C.[41]

After the long-anticipated day had passed, Martin reported that visibility in Peking had been very good, adding that at least a year would be required for reports from around the world to be collated and for scientific results to be announced. Eight years would elapse, he wrote, before another such heavenly event, which would not be visible from China. Would China send her scientists around the world to observe it, as progressive nations had done so enthusiastically on the present occasion?[42]

Expeditions to explore the Arctic fascinated Martin, and he reported them to the Chinese people in many news items. The North and South Pole were, in his opinion, the only real geographical frontiers left to man. His pioneer spirit took special delight in recounting the struggles necessary to conquer this difficult type of environment. To the practical Chinese who struggled simply to make a living, he explained that men went to these regions not to hunt, fish, or get salt, but merely to "investigate the world."[43]

Superstition was not the only obstacle to the introduction of modern technology into China. Many Chinese were afraid of the new inventions, particularly the steam engine. To allay their fears, Martin included material which frankly described the dangers involved with these machines and then explained how they could be overcome. He discussed the recent wreck of an English steamer, part of the fleet of the "Black Star Company," which had carried sixty thousand passengers a year in its twelve ships for over twenty-four years without any serious accidents. He concluded that the steamship, not at the mercy of the wind, was far better able to avoid shoals and rocks."[44]

Some problems, he admitted, defied solution even by the Westerner who had been able to control nature so well. One of these was the earthquake. Various methods had been contrived to protect men from its dangers, but, in the final analysis, "heaven has its will."[45] This type of emphasis, probably interpreted by Chinese as according with their own fatalistic philosophy, could have negated all that Martin sought to accomplish if it had appeared too often in the pages of the *Chung-hsi wen-chien lu*. He recommended that the danger from fires, different from that from earthquakes, could be minimized in China, particularly in the crowded southern cities, by fire brigades, special alarm systems, fire trucks, and long extension ladders.[46]

The basic presumption in all of these articles was that China's failure to develop features of modern Western life — the telegraph, steamships, railway, and so on — was caused by ignorance, fear, or superstition. There was undoubtedly some truth to this, and Martin confronted it realistically, but more recent studies have indicated that a complex of rational objections, later labeled "Confucian patriotism," were also present. These included the fear of foreign control, an understanding of the corrupting influence upon the classes of people able to control and manipulate these new inventions, the economic fears of the poor, and the desire that China be economically independent.[47] Articles which directly discussed such problems would possibly have accomplished even more of the goals which Martin and the Society for the Diffusion of Useful Knowledge in China hoped to achieve.

Martin often expressed his amusement and amazement that even high Chinese officials knew so little about geography.[48] Therefore, in common with other contemporary foreign writers and translators, he desired to inform the Chinese about other parts of the world. Many of the articles[49] on New York, Siberia, Australia, Iceland, Denmark, New Zealand, and Formosa were simply intended to give interesting descriptions of far-away, unknown places, and to expand the perspective of Chinese who still tended to think of their country as the "holy land" into which all other nations would flow.

A favorite topic was the building of the Suez Canal. Martin traced the history of the negotiations, the geographic factors that dictated the choice of its site, and the commercial advantages that would be derived from it. He observed that the reduction of a ship's travel distance from 3500 miles to a short span of several hundred was surely a fulfillment of a Chinese proverb, "Enlarge the home by contracting the land."[50]

An obvious moral or clarifying explanation was frequently slipped into the narrative. In the course of describing Naples, Martin digressed long enough to explain that Pompei's destruction came from *t'ien-tao* (heavenly way or doctrine) which blesses the good and destroys the licentious.[51]

More often, the geographical articles aimed to stir the

Chinese to emulate the development and progress that had taken place in a particular country. Chile, recently independent and without extensive outside help, had developed rail and ship transportation systems and greatly increased its trade.[52] Hokkaido, the once desolate northern island of Japan, was using Western techniques to develop its agriculture and fishing and hoped to be able to sell some of its products to China.[53]

Two articles on Algeria explained the values of wells in promoting the people's livelihood, and the use of railroads to bring people into these irrigated areas to develop agricultural commerce. Martin observed that the local people had objected strongly to the construction of railroads, but that soldiers had been deployed to overcome resistance.[54]

To Chinese who thought of all the various places mentioned in the magazine as being a very long distance away, Martin introduced Jules Verne's *Around the World in Eighty Days.* He charted how such a trip would proceed from Shanghai, noting where the stops would be and how long each leg of the journey would take.[55]

The *Peking Magazine* included news items from over thirty countries and every continent.[56] The sources of Martin's information were usually not mentioned explicitly. The *North China Daily News and Herald,* the most prominent foreign newspaper in the Far East,[57] provided him with much that he needed, and the many newspapers available in the T'ung Wen Kuan library supplemented this. The *Peking Gazette* carried such news as the Court deemed proper for the Chinese, but Chinese papers in Hong Kong and Shanghai gave better coverage for south China. During the winter months Peking was virtually cut off from other portions of China, and it was difficult to get information. Most of the news articles, however, were not urgent by nature; material several years old was still new to his audience and served his purposes as well as something "hot off the press."

The news that Martin presented to his Chinese audience fell into a number of broad categories: internal improvements, industrial, commercial and financial, social and cultural, educational, political and diplomatic, moral, scholarly, military, and human interest. Western countries were the examples for desirable reform, and non-Western countries, particularly Japan and India, were held up as Eastern models that had best emulated the West.

Whenever possible Martin utilized Chinese news events to encourage his readers that China was also making progress.

Railroad building was reported for almost every country that Martin mentioned. He presented statistical tables to show that America had built 4710 miles of new railways in 1873.[58] An article from an English newspaper giving instructions on how to lay regular and narrow-guage rail beds was featured prominently.[59]

England's war against the Ashantis along the Gold Coast in Africa served as evidence for the military value of building railways. Any English attempt to push inland by foot against the enemy would be foolhardy, Martin observed, because of the heat and prevalent sickness.[60] He presented rail-building projects as one benefit of Western domination in India and North Africa.[61] On her own initiative Japan had erected a short rail line from Tokyo to Yokohama that had elicited the praise of the Japanese emperor.[62]

Martin also included a news item reporting transportation by steam-powered vessels in American rivers and canals, explaining that steamships, far from merely being useful for ocean travel and commerce, served local needs, such as lowering the price of food.[63] In two or three other articles he commented that one of the greatest services to be rendered by the China Merchants' Steamship Company would be to travel to China's inland ports where Western ships were forbidden to go.[64]

Undersea cable lines and telegraphic communication were also presented as signs of great progress. The benefits were many: greatly improved interchange of news and information among countries linked by cable lines,[65] quick reports of natural tragedies such as floods or tornadoes,[66] identification of criminals apprehended in distant places,[67] efficient administrative control over large territories, more efficient commerce and business, and easier and swifter mobilization of troops for war.[68] Superstitious rumors about telegraph and cable communication circulated widely, and Martin commented that it was untrue that a broken cable line between India and the Red Sea had been caused by an attack by a whale.[69]

In this area, Martin could find only two signs of encouragement in China — a short line between Shanghai and Woosung, and a projected effort, supervised by Danish technicians, that would link Amoy and the capital of Fukien Province.[70] No telegraph line connected Shanghai and Peking, and this was a decisive factor in the demise of the *Chung-hsi wen-chien lu*. China manifested little concern to join with other countries in cooperative planning for expanded international facilities.[71]

Martin mentioned canals as another index of progress, but paid relatively little attention to them, presumably because China's extensive waterways far antedated any other examples that he might give. He did use American canal building, with the exception of the Erie, to present private enterprise — whether for construction of canals, railways, ships, or telegraph lines — as far superior to government financing and control.[72] He explained that the United States was planning to build a canal across Central America and showed how this would facilitate travel between the East coast of America and Japan and China.[73]

Martin printed a news report that there were over one hundred news publication agencies responsible for printing a large number of newspapers and magazines in the city of London.[74] He included an item from India reporting a recent increase in newspapers resulting from an expansion of schools and literary programs. The consequent enlightenment, he suggested, had produced railways and commerce, and brought in a new civilization that eliminated many old evils such as suttee, the practice of a Hindu widow cremating herself on her husband's funeral pyre.[75] Several months later, he reprinted a Shanghai report indicating local fear that a new newspaper would not be supported by the populace; Martin countered editorially that Western experience proved this fear to be groundless.[76]

Many of his edited news articles explained how Western powers were actively seeking to improve Oriental countries. He noted the discussion of plans to build a railway between India and England which would shorten travel time to even less than the one month it had been reduced to by the construction of the Suez Canal.[77] The British Parliament had also proposed a road from India through Burma into Yunnan Province, a direct route between India and China that would greatly facilitate commerce between the two countries.[78]

Reporting German plans to construct a railway into China through Ili, Martin commented that this route was more convenient than through India or Mongolia. He also observed that there was coal along this proposed rail line, and that it could be mined and used in industrial projects.[79]

Expanded trade and commerce were obvious benefits to be derived from improved communication and transportation. Martin referred to America's great growth, to be celebrated in the 1876 centennial, as an encouragement to the rest of the world.[80] He also reminded his readers that England and France's wealth had been derived from commerce.[81] Transportation and communication were also listed as basic ingredients of growth in India, Peru, Chile, Egypt, and Japan.[82] *Chung-hsi wen-chien lu* hammered at the implication that China's path to progress lay along these same lines.

China obviously needed to develop her resources if she were to trade, and Martin's selection of news articles emphasized this as well. He portrayed Western countries busily exploiting their copper, gold, iron, and coal, and creating new products, which they demonstrated for sale at home and abroad at international trade fairs.[83]

Martin used detailed statistics to show that China possessed the greater share of the world's commercial silk industry,[84] and urged that she obtain the capital and machines necessary to develop factories for cotton-cloth production. During America's Civil War, he pointed out, England had been forced to obtain some of her cotton from China, as well as from Egypt and India. Now, with the war over and cotton production expanded to meet England's need, she ought to develop her own cloth industry.[85]

Martin stressed the importance of a country's willingness to learn from others in developing new products. Five years previous, he noted, Japan, anticipating the future opening of Hokkaido, had invited an American agriculturalist to set up experimental farms for seeds and animals. This project was now continuing under local supervision, and Japanese scientists and farmers had shown readiness to use whatever would work.[86] Japanese representatives had even come to learn from China, and the Chinese, hopefully, would learn from them. Such mutual interchange of information, he observed, was the only way to reform a country.[87]

Travel was one method of obtaining information. Relating that Chinese officials, sent to America to observe, had gone on to England, he observed that "to go abroad for learning is much better than seeking foreign treasure."[88] The Prince of Zanzibar visited England for advice on how he could improve his country. "Since a country's prospect depends upon the enlightened policy of those who administer it, what evil," Martin asked, "can possibly cause Zanzibar not to be strong?"[89]

He reported at length about the King of Persia, who traveled throughout Europe and England to learn of modern developments.[90] Amazed when told that the streets of London, put end to end, would reach from England to India, the king determined to build railways, telegraph lines, and factories upon his return to his own country.[91] He tried to carry out this resolution, Martin reported, but railway construction was stopped halfway through because of a disagreement with a German firm with whom he had contracted the project.[92]

Martin applauded the king's intentions but doubted if much would be accomplished after learning that the king's personal diary recorded little about machines, government, and education, but was filled almost entirely with accounts of "banquets, theatres, and beautiful dancing girls." How different, Martin observed, from Peter the Great who had avoided the banquet circuit and learned as much as possible about that which could benefit his country.[93] He later conceded that there had been considerable benefit — the railway was completed, a mint to create a uniform currency was established with Australian help, and a postal system that helped the king redress the grievances of his subjects was developed.[94]

An even better method to obtain information than travel, Martin believed, was to reform the old educational system that taught little besides the ancient Chinese Classics. He reported that America had over ten thousand schools of all types,[95] and that England, still seeking to develop all her human resources, had opened a new school for girls.[96]

The best model for China was Japan, her old pupil, and now a potential teacher. Martin predicted that Japan would soon be the "England of the Eastern Sea" — she had established eight colleges and thirty-two primary schools in eight of her larger cities. Often staffed with American teachers, these institutions offered mathematics, science, foreign languages, and astronomy on the primary level, and the colleges included departments of law and medicine.

Martin included relatively few political items in the *Chung-hsi wen-chien lu,* although he did mention such things as the resignation of an English prime minister and a German premier, the visit of an Hawaiian chief to the United States, civil conflict and political upheaval in Spain, and the interchange of visits by a variety of official dignitaries in different countries.[97] He commented on the coronation of Chulalongkorn of Siam, noting that, although he had spent the usual month of instruction in a Buddhist monastery, he had also traveled abroad and was determined to Westernize many aspects of his country's life.[98]

Foreign diplomacy was accorded only minimal attention. What Martin did report — the Treaty of Washington, for one example — indicated that large, powerful nations found it in their interest to negotiate their disputes.[99] He reported, with very little comment, some continuing results of the Franco-German conflict, the continuing tension between Japan and Russia over Sakhalin, the Cuban civil war, and Sino-Russian border conflicts.[100]

The diplomatic conflict in which he, and presumably his readers, took most interest was that between China and Japan over Formosa. Aborigines in southern Formosa had killed fifty-three Ryukyan sailors shipwrecked there. Japan, which claimed sovereignty over the Ryukyu Islands, demanded redress from China, which controlled Formosa. China, however, also received tribute from the Ryukyu Islands, and rejected Japan's demand, stating that the incident was purely an internal Chinese affair.[101] Japan eventually sent troops into Formosa, and a dangerous confrontation seemed imminent,[102] but the affair was finally resolved through Great Britain's mediation, and peace was restored. Martin's sympathies clearly lay with China. He pointed out that Japan had committed two errors: she had tried to deal directly with the aborigines in Formosa as if they were a political entity separate from China, and she had sought to punish the aborigines herself. He wondered aloud to his readers if Japan were really familiar with international law.[103]

Selections from the *Chung-hsi wen-chien lu* included no mention of the first audience of Western envoys with the Chinese Emperor in 1873. The magazine itself printed a detailed account of this event, drawn up and submitted to Martin by Sir Thomas Wade who wished to scotch the rumor that the Western representatives had yielded to pressure and performed the kowtow.[104]

Martin reported favorably on special missions to investigate the situation of Chinese immigrants in Cuba and Peru and hoped that these would lead to permanent embassies and consuls in foreign lands. He believed that this would help Chinese immigrants orient themselves to new languages and customs and also afford legal protection against evil men ready to take advantage of them.[105]

Several brief news items on military matters were included. Martin gave a breakdown of ironclad war vessels possessed by European countries and pointed out that one of these had stopped in a Chinese port, causing considerable excitement.[106] He reported on a disarmament debate in the English Parliament, noting that if all disputes were settled in the manner of the Washington Conference, not only would peace be realized but a great deal of money to invest in national improvement would be saved.[107] More realistic than to believe war would disappear, however, he applauded the rules and regulations for the conduct of war spelled out at the Belgium conference as a distinct improvement over many inhumane practices in current use.[108]

A few rather short news articles passed moral judgments on a variety of social problems. From the first time he visited Macao in 1851, Martin had despised the Portuguese traffic in Chinese coolies. He reported how nearly 110,000 Chinese, many of them young boys, had been either forced or lured to Cuba from 1848 to 1871. He recommended that Macao and China either enforce existing laws or create new ones to stop this traffic.[110] Statistics reporting the number of Chinese laborers sailing from Macao, and accounts of disease-laden ships, tragic sea fires, and mutinies were reported in succeeding issues of the magazine.[111] Even though the trade decreased and conditions in Cuba and Peru improved somewhat, Martin recommended that Brazil, a productive land, with a good government that had recently banned slave trading, would be a far better haven for Chinese immigrants.[112]

He commented gladly on progress in the fight against slave trading, with special commendation to those "benevolent princes" in Parliament, and to David Livingstone, the missionary, who had fought to wipe it out in Africa.[113] He reported its prohibition in Brazil and Cuba and noted that Egypt and England were seeking to stop trading in slaves at its origin in the Sudan.[114]

Other things which Martin condemned, either directly or

indirectly, in the magazine were the opium trade, concubinage, wine, superstitious falsehood, and religious intolerance. He regretted that all British discussions of whether or not to prohibit opium planting in India considered only the economic aspects and never really raised the moral issue.[115] Nothing was said in any of the thirty-six issues of the magazine to condemn the use of opium by the Chinese, or to indicate the various ways in which its social effects were being combatted.[116]

News about American temperance unions afforded Martin the occasion to detail the impact of alcohol on the individual, family, and society.[117] He noted that a temperance society, modeled after the American pattern, had been organized in Tientsin. A later article quoted the statement of a doctor, working in an insane asylum, that of one hundred people being treated in an American institution, thirty-four were suffering from the excessive use of alcohol.[118]

Recounting the story of a widow who denied that the death of her new husband had occurred because their marriage did not accord with movements of the planets, he commented, "In today's world no ignorance or crime (*tsui*)[119] is greater than this." He quoted Confucius' maxim that the "superior man must exert himself to get rid of falsehood."[120] After reporting that Japan's most recent census revealed significantly more men than women, he concluded that concubinage or polygyny "injured the law of nature."[121]

The magazine's only specific comment referring to the Christian faith accompanied a news brief on religious toleration in Japan. "After over two hundred years of restriction, Japan, *without others using weapons or force,* has removed edicts that proscribed the Christian faith."[122]

Martin reported on the activities of scholarly groups to try to stimulate a similar international academic interest on the part of the Chinese literati. Describing the formation of the Society for the Study of Eastern Literature, he noted the variety of scholarly topics on the society's agenda. Such activities, he believed, promoted world friendship. He expressed the hope that Chinese scholars would establish a Society for the Study of Western Literature.[123] He chided them for often having less academic interest in their own country than did foreign scholars.[124]

Many articles and news stories which Martin reprinted in

the *Chung-hsi wen-chien lu* appealed to human interest.[125] Some of these were of the Horatio Alger variety, and appealed to humanitarian and moral motives to think and do good. For example, he told the story of a young girl, on duty as a telegraph operator on a stormy night, who went out with a red light to warn an oncoming train of a tree fallen on the track. Although fatally injured when the train pushed the tree over her, she died with the satisfaction of having done her duty.[126] A passenger on a late night train to Philadelphia saw a fire break out in a small village and jumped out to warn the people of the pending disaster, breaking his leg in the process. Such response to human need, Martin observed, illustrated how a person might love another as himself.[127] His examples of altruistic heroism contrasted markedly with articles extolling the virtue of celibate widows or loyal officials, then current in the *Peking Gazette*.

True stories and fables were both used to illustrate the moral order of the universe. Martin believed that men everywhere possessed the same moral nature and were subject to the same principles of right and wrong.[128] *T'ien-tao* was responsible for punishing evil, protecting from danger, and rewarding good.[129]

T'ien-tao could not, however, be bent to respond to the whims of capricious man. Martin included a fable about a priest who was unable to pray simultaneously for the requests of his two sons-in-law — one a farmer needing rain for his crops and the second a pottery-maker who required more rainless days in order that his pots might dry.[130]

In conclusion, what may be said of Martin's attempts to interpret Western civilization to the Chinese through the *Chung-hsi wen-chien lu*? First, he utilized many types of materials, told in interesting detail and a refined, semi-classical style, to attract his Chinese readers. The magazine made a reasonable effort to explain where different places were located, to simplify scientific descriptions, and to eliminate extraneous personal and place names that might hinder communication.

Second, the aim of *Chung-hsi wen-chien lu* was, in effect, to challenge the sacral nature of the Chinese world view. Martin appealed to *t'ien-tao*, but suggested that man could work with it to control a nature no longer perceived as mysterious, predetermined, and unmanageable. This attitude was epitomized in one of

Martin's fables relating how several men were stranded on a beautiful island controlled, they learned, by the three fearful gods of water, wind, and fire. These gods were awe-inspiring, but gradually the men learned how to subdue them and harness their power for good. Martin appended a moral: "Whether these three things will harm or help men depends on whether the knowledgeable man will investigate their nature and use their power."[131]

Third, however, since there was no distinctive Christian message in the *Peking Magazine,* the attempt to challenge the sacral content of Chinese thought may have helped instead to inoculate it against the Gospel. The Christian God, in Martin's view, was the God of nature, personally involving himself in the physical world and in the affairs of men. But the magazine did not present this view in such a way that it offered a ready substitute for the "gods" being replaced by Martin's approach. It may have suggested that Western techniques had only functional value and could be separated from the Western religious essence. The message of the *Chung-hsi wen-chien lu* was totally secular and neglected to relate the religious message that Martin and his colleagues felt was the indispensable foundation for the achievements of Western civilization.

There were probably several reasons for this omission: many Chinese would not have read a religious periodical; the magazine was a "wedge" to create a desire for Western culture which Martin hoped would lead to an interest in the Gospel; such an approach was necessary in Peking where there was more than usual opposition to Christianity; the editors believed that the Christian message and European civilization were but two aspects of the one message of salvation and progress.

Fourth, popular science, geography, and news of all kinds were utilized to give the Chinese a model and a stimulus for reform. There were hardly any explicit statements of Western superiority,[132] but the implicit assumption was that China's only future lay in progress patterned after the Western world.

Fifth, Martin's analysis of China's needs was essentially missionary: once ignorance, fear, and superstition were removed, all of China's economic, military, social, and educational problems would disappear. He often applied moral maxims and platitudes idealistically, in fact simplistically, to complex situations and gave little consideration to historical, economic, or sociological realities.

Sixth, *Chung-hsi wen-chien lu,* candid and comprehensive in its portrayal of the techniques, activities, and life of the Western world, may have been counter-productive in its impact. Western nations, far from being a model for China, had problems of their own. Their scientific methods were awesome, and the prospect of extending them into China — roads into Yunnan, railroads into the Northeast, assistance with a telegraph line in Foochow, technical advice in Tientsin — produced as much apprehension as appreciation.

Martin presented new types of morality, free world trade, schools with new aims and different kinds of students, a new attitude toward the world, and many other features of Western life with intensity and with little sensitivity to Chinese feelings. In fact, Chinese needs, *as the Chinese perceived them,* were either unconsidered or casually dismissed. His communication was essentially a monologue which stimulated Chinese to reassert their traditional values rather than open themselves up to the reception of new ideas.[133]

William Martin's efforts to promote reform in China through the *Peking Magazine* and by other literary projects[134] were earlier, more intense, and more comprehensive than those of any other missionary. Despite the lack of any immediate response by Chinese leaders to his attempts to change China, Martin remained determined to promote the secular gospel of reform. His work within a government institution undoubtedly contributed to China's increased interest in Westernization, but it was always shackled by the enervative control of the Tsungli Yamen. The missionaries were limited to methods of persuasion — education, evangelism, and literature — and these were too slow and weak to overcome the staid traditionalism of the Chinese. The impetus toward reform had to come from external events, and from 1870 to 1900 there was no lack of these. British aspirations in Yunnan in 1875; Russian aggression at Ili in Sinkiang, 1871-81; the French conquest of the tributary state of Annam and the war of 1884-85; Japanese militarism in Korea; the tragic Sino-Japanese conflict of 1894-95, and the subsequent efforts by France, Germany, Russia, and Great Britain to carve up China were signs that advances in technology and pursuit of new types of learning were not radical enough solutions for China's ills.

These external pressures intensified the internal disunity —

> . . . the power struggle between the emperor and the dowager, the conflict between the conservative and the progressive, the strife between the moderate reformers and the radicals, and the racial antipathy between the Manchus and the Chinese.[135]

The Ch'ing dynasty was clearly at a point of crisis, faced with either changing or perishing.

New leaders rose up to direct China's destiny at this juncture. Chang Chih-tung, Governor-General of Hunan-Hupei, 1889-1907, made moderate proposals for reform. In his well-known work, *Exhortation to Learning,* he proposed a program to save China by education — decreasing levels of schools from colleges to primary in provinces, prefectures, and districts — and by industrial development. He still embraced Feng Kuei-fen's slogan, "Chinese learning for the fundamental principles, Western learning for practical application,"[136] and also advocated the revival of Confucianism to save the Manchu dynasty.[137]

By comparison with Chang Chih-tung, who often went no further than earlier proponents of "self-strengthening," K'ang Yu-wei was a radical reformer. Although never in a high official position, he used his brilliant literary gifts to influence his contemporaries. He used the Confucian classics, in his view not merely edited, but written by the sage, to promote reform. He argued that Confucius had devised the idea of a past utopia to convince rulers of his day to reform society even as the earlier rulers Yao and Shun had done. The socialistic utopia which he envisioned included a single world government with popular elections at both the central and regional levels, freedom, equality and independence for all, government care for children, and state ownership of property.[138]

K'ang did not wish for dynastic change. He wanted to find in the old classics both China's *essence* and the *functional* attitude necessary to incorporate Western values. He chose Japan's modernization through constitutionalism for his model. With the help of Liang Ch'i-ch'ao, who later took a more liberal path to republicanism, and T'an Szu-t'ung, K'ang founded the "Society for the Study of National Strengthening," and promoted the reform movement in many areas.

In the early formation and later development of his reform ideals, K'ang gave much credit to missionary influence.[139] The

Kuang hsüeh-hui (Society for the Diffusion of Christian and General Knowledge Among the Chinese, or SDK), formed in Shanghai in 1887, claimed such distinguished missionary figures as Young J. Allen, Timothy Richard, and Gilbert Reid as members. They promoted modernization and reform through translations of Western works on science, history, and literature, and through lectures, editorials, and discussions.[140] Despite Martin's interest in and contribution to the reform impetus, the more radical proponents of change — men like K'ang and Liang — did not consult him as much as they did Allen and Richard, who were not part of the "establishment" and who lived outside of Peking.

Martin joined the *Kuang hsüeh-hui* and thoroughly favored its reform program, although residence in Peking meant that he could not get to the annual meetings.[141] His absence in America from 1895 to 1896 caused him to miss the furor created when "reform clubs," organized among the censors and Hanlin scholars in Peking, were summarily dissolved by Imperial edict two months later in January, 1896.[142]

After his return to Peking in January, 1897, and before he accepted his new post with the Imperial University, Martin became associated with Gilbert Reid, one of the advisers of the defunct Peking "reform club" and a man who had long worked for reform in China. Reid had come to China with the American Presbyterian Mission in 1882 but became progressively disenchanted with traditional sorts of mission work. On January 27, 1888, he presented a paper on "The Duty of Christian Missions to The Upper Classes of China" to the Missionary Association of Peking.[143]

Reid was dismayed that missionaries in China were almost totally committed to the policy of spreading the Gospel from "the bottom up" rather than from "the top down." He argued that Biblical principles and the hierarchical nature of Chinese society demanded that they make a major effort to reach the upper classes. He proposed five methods to accomplish this: medical work, use of scientific and religious literature, educational activities, direct involvement with officials in lecture halls, book-depositories, and reading rooms, and through contact with consuls, diplomats, and other government officials.[144]

Martin was already using most of these methods — Reid, in

fact, referred to him as his prime example. Reid resigned from his mission in 1892, and when he returned to China in the fall of 1894, he organized The Mission Among the Higher Classes in China.[145] Two years later he laid plans for an International Institute, to be established in Peking, that would utilize a museum, library, classrooms, a reception hall, and a large auditorium as a means of enlightening the Chinese literati.[146] Broadly motivated by a philanthropic spirit, the Institute would be controlled by no church or creed and would aim to promote progress, break down prejudice, and establish friendships.

The total cost for this project was estimated at $75,000. Reid obtained a formal sanction of approval from the Tsungli Yamen and a striking testimony from Li Hung-chang who wrote, "The society, education and official systems of China have tended to give to the educated classes control of the destinies of the nation." He noted that he was not to judge whether this was good or bad, but that "suspicion, jealousy and self-sufficiency" were marked tendencies of educated Chinese. He concluded with the encouragement that "if you can give to the blind leaders of our people light and learning enjoyed in the West, they, in turn, will lead our people out of their darkness."[147]

Armed with a four-page prospectus printed on large glossy paper and including notices of official sanction, Li's testimony, and elaborate building plans, Reid sought and obtained endorsement and promises of help from the missionary associations in Shanghai and Peking, the diplomatic corps, and foreign merchants. Martin was so impressed that he quickly yielded to Reid's entreaty to join him in the work.

In the summer of 1897 personal matters required Reid to return to America, and during his two-year absence Martin was left to "hold the fort." Part of Martin's task was to edit a new magazine sponsored by the International Institute and designed to reach the "literary and official classes."[148] He also continued his private literary efforts which he was glad to consider a part of his Institute writing.[149] A significant amount of his time was spent conversing with high officials regarding ways to promote China's progress.

When Reid returned to Peking in 1899, he found that the reaction of 1898 had returned the Empress Dowager to power and had changed the hopeful climate for progress to one of despair. Following the Boxer Rebellion, Reid moved to Shanghai and continued the International Institute at a safe distance from the capital. Martin, in the meanwhile, had become involved with the Imperial University, which served as one of the few remaining means for reform before the Boxer tragedy.

Notes

1. For a detailed elaboration of his activities see Ralph R. Covell, "The Life and Thought of W. A. P. Martin, Agent and Interpreter of Sino-American Contact in the Nineteenth and Early Twentieth Century" (unpublished Ph. D. dissertation, University of Denver, 1975), 313-18, 324-26.

2. Kenneth S. Latourette, *A History of Christian Missions in China* (London, 1929), 350.

3. China Letters of the Board of Foreign Missions of the Presbyterian Church in the United States of America, Peking, Martin to Board, #60, March 30, 1871. China Letters are subsequently abbreviated "CL." Some of these restrictions were abolition of asylums and foundling hospitals except for the children of native Christians; prohibition of Chinese women attending public meetings and of foreign women doing mission work; provisions that missionaries in the interior should be subject to native authorities, and that no kind of protection should be extended to native Christians.

4. CL, Peking, Martin to Board, #159, October 21, 1871.

5. *Ibid.*

6. CL, Peking, Martin to Board, #242, April 24, 1872. He referred to McIlwaine who lived alone in the interior because he had no other single male colleague.

7. CL, Peking, Martin to Board, #159, October 21, 1871.

8. See note 18.

9. *First Annual Report* of the Society for the Diffusion of Useful Knowledge in China, *North China Herald,* January 29, 1874, 89.

10. W. A. P. Martin, Letter to Professor Whitney, December 4, 1874, Box 65 of W. D. Whitney Collection, Yale University.

11. "Benjamin Silliman," *Dictionary of American Biography,* IX, 160-63. In the first one hundred years of the magazine there were only four editors — Silliman himself, his son, his son-in-law, and his grandson.

12. *First Annual Report* of the Society for the Diffusion of Useful Knowledge in China, *North China Herald,* January 29, 1874, 89. The language of this unsigned report is similar to CL, XI, Peking, Martin to Board, #19, February 21, 1873.

13. Roswell S. Britton, *The Chinese Periodical Press, 1800-1912* (Shanghai, 1933), 59.

14. Edkins departed for England in the fall of 1873, and Burdon was consecrated as Bishop of Victoria, H.K., on March 18, 1873. News item, *The Chronicle of the London Missionary Society,* January, 1874, 20; "Bishop Burdon of Victoria," *The Church Missionary Gleaner,* II (January, 1875), 2-3. Dr. John Dudgeon of the LMS helped Martin after the departure of Edkins and Burdon. Letter of Martin to Professor Whitney, December 4, 1874. Box 65 of W. D. Whitney Collection, Yale University.

15. *Annual Report* of the Society for the Diffusion of Useful Knowledge in China, *North China Herald,* December 23, 1875. 633.

16. *Ibid.* Also see Britton, *Periodical Press,* 60. The first issue was entitled "A Monthly Journal of Popular Scientific Information with which is incorporated The Peking Magazine." Adrian Bennett, *John Fryer: The Introduction of Western Science and Technology into Nineteenth-Century China* (Cambridge, Mass., 1967), 51.

17. Britton, *Periodical Press,* 17-24.

18. *The Chinese Repository,* IV (December, 1835), 354-61; V (March, 1837), 507-13. This group was probably modeled on A Society for the Diffusion of Useful Knowledge in England, founded in 1832, which educated the masses through a Penny Magazine, a Penny Encyclopedia, and an Almanac. *North China Herald,* February 22, 1872, 138. Also see Britton, *Periodical Press,* 22.

19. These numbered "nearly one hundred." Adrian Bennett, "A Nineteenth-Century View of America and China" (unpublished manuscript of an address to the Mid-West Association of Asian Studies, University of Illinois, October 13-15, 1972).

20. Adrian Bennett, "Missionary Journalism in China: Young J. Allen and the Early Wan-kuo kung-pao, 1868-1883" (unpublished Ph. D. dissertation, University of California at Davis, 1970), 157.

21. Young J. Allen, ed., *Chiao-hui hsin-pao,* II (January 1, 1869), Table of Contents.

22. CL, XI, Peking, Martin to Board, #19, February 21, 1873.

23. *First Annual Report* of the Society for the Diffusion of Useful Knowledge in China, *North China Herald,* January 29, 1874, 89.

24. Translation of *The Peking Gazette* for 1874. Reprinted from the *North China Herald* and *Supreme Court and Consular Gazette* (Shanghai, 1875).

25. Britton, *Periodical Press,* 49-51.

26. This was called *Chung-hsi wen-chien lu hsüan-pien* (Selections from the Chung-hsi wen-chien lu) (Peking, 1877). See the preface written by W. A. P. Martin.

27. The percentage of material to be found in each category is: Geography, 7.8%, 45 pages; Popular Science, 26.2%, 152 pages; Edited News, 54.8%, 318 pages; Miscellaneous, 11.2%, 65 pages. Presumably, these percentages reflect the proportions of the same kind of material in the original issues of the magazine.

28. Some authors have stressed that *Chung-hsi wen-chien lu* began to include more quasi-technical scientific material after the popular reception accorded articles on flood-control by Joseph Edkins. None of these is included in the *Selections*, and presumably, at least in Martin's opinion, they were not all that important. Britton, *Periodical Press*, 59.

29. "Cable Car," *CHWCL*, IV, 34. Citation from *Chung-hsi wen-chien lu*, Volume IV, Issue 34. There is no clear pagination which can be used. Neither is there any indication of date. After this footnote the abbreviation *CHWCL* will only be used after an intervening footnote has cited another work. *Ibid.* will not be used.

30. II, 14.

31. "Salt Sea," III, 27.

32. In this category would be the following topics:

Steam-Driven Car	I, 1.
Grinding of Grain	I, 1.
Value of Glass	I, 1,2.
Iron-Refining Processes	I, 5,6.
Discussion on Whether the Earth or the Sun is at the Center of the Universe	IV, 30.
Permanent or Moving Stars	IV, 30.
The Telegraph	IV, 34.
The Speed of Light	IV, 36.
An Eclipse of the Sun	IV, 32 (Not by W.A.P.M.)

33. "Comet," III, 24, and "Astrology Wrong," XXX, 29.

34. "The Metric System," II, 17, 18.

35. W. A. P. Martin, "The Metric System for China," *The Chinese Recorder*, V (March-April, 1874), 58-59.

36. "Flying Machines Measure the Weather," *CHWCL*, III, 23.

37. "The Means By Which England Became Wealthy," II, 14.

38. III, 27.

39. "Balloonists Killed when Balloon Bursts," IV, 34.

40. "Venus Orbits the Sun," II, 15.

41. "Americans to Observe Venus," III, 24.

42. "Viewing Venus from the Capital," III, 28.

43. "Americans Explore the North Pole," I, 13, and "Three Nations Explore the Ice Sea," II, 17.

44. "Discussion of Safety and Danger Features of the Steamship," II, 15.

45. "A Method to Protect Against Earthquakes," II, 14.

46. "Fire Extension Ladders," IV, 30.

47. David Pong, "Confucian Patriotism and the Destruction of the Woosung Railroad," *Modern Asian Studies*, VII (October, 1973), 647.

48. W. A. P. Martin, *A Cycle of Cathay* (3rd ed.; New York, 1900), 340-41. The examples cited do not really prove that much ignorance. Contemporary American officials might have experienced similar difficulties with the exotic names of places they were not required to learn.

49. *CHWCL*, II, 22; III, 29; III, 22; III, 26; IV, 31; IV, 34; IV, 36.

50. "Account of Newly Opened Suez Canal," I, 6.

51. "The City of Naples," II, 19.

52. "Chile Plans to have a Trade Fair," III, 26, and "Descriptions of Chile," IV, 30.

53. "Profit from Fishing in Japan's Northern Island," IV, 34.

54. "France Drills Artesian Wells," IV, 36, and "Construction of Railroads," IV, 36.

55. "Around the World in Eighty Days," IV, 32.

56. The percentage distribution of news coverage for each country was: England, 18.9; America, 12.8; China (including Macao, Hong Kong and Singapore), 11.5; Japan, 10.5; France, 10.3; Russia, 4.2; India, 4.1; Africa (including Egypt), 4.1; Persia, 2.9; Austria, 2.8; Latin America, 2.7; Spain, 2.6; Italy, 2.2; South Seas (including Australia and various islands), 2.2, Germany, 2.1; Scandinavia, 1.4; Portugal, 1.1; Burma-Siam, 1.1; Holland, 0.9; Belgium, 0.9; Greece-Turkey, 0.9.

57. Britton, *Periodical Press*, 49.

58. "America Adds Rail Mileage," *CHWCL*, II, 20.

59. "A New Form of English Railroad," II, 26.

60. "England Prepares a Railway to Attack the Enemy," II, 17.

61. "Progress in India," II, 17, and "Grass and Insects Obstacle to French Train," III, 24.

62. "Japan Builds Railroad," II, 19.

63. "America Transports Goods by River Steamships," III, 28.

64. II, 16; I, 1; I, 7.

65. Examples were England, Denmark, and Sweden, II, 16; Portugal and Brazil, II, 16; and America and England, I, 13.

66. "Establish Telegraphs to Warn of Tornadoes and Floods," I, 9.

67. II, 17. The example given was a report of the identification by the use of telegram of an American criminal who committed a crime in Shanghai and was fleeing by ship when apprehended.

68. "Foochow Plans to Establish a Telegraph Line," III, 24. He noted that this telegraph line had been useful in giving news of Japan's attack on Taiwan in 1874 and in mobilizing Chinese troops in Fukien and Chekiang Provinces. IV, 33.

69. "Indian Whale Injures Cable Line," II, 16.

70. "Foochow Land Telegraph Line," III, 25.

71. "Meeting in Russia of Telegraph Bureau," IV, 36. Twenty-four countries, including Japan with two delegates, sent representatives to this meeting. No one from China was present.

72. "American Canal Building," IV, 34, and "Canal Opened in Eastern Russia," IV, 33.

73. "America Plans to Construct a Large Canal," II, 14.

74. "English Newspaper Publishers," II, 18.

75. "India Increases New Newspapers," IV, 14.

76. "Newly Established Newspaper Company in Shanghai," III, 24.

77. "England Plans a Railway," I, 12.

78. "A Road to Yunnan," II, 15. Progress on this project was reported two months later in December, 1873. II, 17; IV, 31. It was while traveling to meet a British delegation coming over this road to China that Augustus Margary, British vice-consul, was killed by a guerilla band at Bhamo near the border on February 21, 1875. Immanel Hsü, *The Rise of Modern China* (New York, 1970), 366. Martin did not include a report on this very significant event in later issues of the *Selections* from *Chung-hsi wen-chien lu.*

79. "Germany Plans a Railway into China," *CHWCL,* III, 25.

80. "America Plans for a Fair," II, 17.

81. "Ways in Which England Became Wealthy," II, 14. See also "Volume of French Trade," III, 19. He analyzed trade at two of France's fifteen ports, commenting that he had gone into considerable detail since "trade was an index of prosperity."

82. II, 17; II, 21; III, 26; II, 17; IV, 33; I, 1,2.

83. He included news items on trade fairs or exhibitions in Austria, Japan, America, and Australia. Representatives from many countries who attended these learned about products available for sale. See I, 13; II, 15, 17, 19; IV, 31; III, 17; and IV, 33. He observed that China had displayed

her products at the fair in Austria and received good publicity as a result. II, 15. Museums, such as one recently established in Shanghai with English financial aid, were also means of "making known the wonder of Western machines." III, 27.

84. "Analysis of Each Country's Silk Trade," IV, 33.

85. "India Plants Cotton," IV, 32.

86. "Japan Develops New Agricultural Policy," IV, 34.

87. "Japan Investigates and Inquires About Agricultural Policy," IV, 35.

88. IV, 31.

89. "The Prince of Zanzibar Visits England," IV, 36.

90. The first mention of this trip in I, 11, was accompanied by the comment that Persia is a Muslim country and, although once strong, is "very weak at present."

91. I, 13; II, 14, 15.

92. II, 14.

93. "Diary of a Persian King," III, 28.

94. "Persia Established a Mint and a Postal System," IV, 35.

95. II, 17.

96. "England Establishes a Girls' School," II, 19.

97. Respectively, II, 20; I, 7; IV, 31; II, 14, 15, 20; III, 22, 24, 26; IV, 30; III, 24; IV, 34.

98. "Siam Changes Its Policy," II, 20.

99. "Settlement of America's Claim for Land," I, 8.

100. II, 14; III, 29; IV, 35; I, 12.

101. Hsü, *Rise of Modern China,* 377-81.

102. *CHWCL,* III, 22, 27.

103. III, 23. Apparently the Chinese were indebted to Martin for some of their arguments against the Japanese. Martin, *Cycle,* 402.

104. Martin, *Cycle,* 435-36.

105. "China's Representatives Return to the Capital," *CHWCL,* III, 29.

106. "Armed Vessels," II, 18; "Iron Clad Vessel Visits China," IV, 32.

107. "England Revives Its War for Peace," II, 15.

108. "Congress on Just Wars," III, 25.

109. Martin, *Cycle,* 31-33.

110. *CHWCL,* I, 2. This number does not include those shipped to Peru. Was Martin referring to the *Chung-hsi wen-chien lu* with the follow-

ing comments? "These [verses on the misery of Chinese coolies in Cuba] referred to the 'blundering philanthropy of Las Casas in substituting black slaves for red. The time had now come for yellow to take the place of black at the behest of anti-slavery sentiment not more intelligent than that of a Chinese prince, who, pitying an ox, ordered a sheep to be sacrificed in its stead.' My paper deepened the determination of the Chinese authorities not to permit their people to be made the 'sheep' of the fable. Needless to say, it drew on me the hostility of those interested in the coolie traffic." Martin, *Cycle*, 383.

111. *CHWCL*, I, 8, 11; II, 15, 14, 21; III, 23.

112. "Brazil Frees Black Slaves," I; IV, 33.

113. "Each Country Prohibits Trade in Human Lives," I, 12. Livingstone was mentioned with commendation in two other articles. II, 19, and III, 23.

114. "Egypt Prohibits Trade in Human Lives," II, 14.

115. "England's Parliament Discusses Prohibition of Opium Planting," IV, 35. Also see III, 26.

116. For a good, concise treatment of the types of reform stimulated by missionaries in the battle against opium see Hilary J. Beattie, "Protestant Missionaries and Opium in China," *Papers on China* (Cambridge, 1969), 104-34.

117. "America Prohibits Wine," *CHWCL*, III, 23.

118. II, 14.

119. The word used by the Chinese church for "sin."

120. "New Bride Opposes Family Falsehood," II, 22.

121. "Japanese Census," II, 19.

122. "Japan Removes Prohibitions," I, 12. Italics mine.

123. "Eastern Literary Society in Paris," II, 16, and "Eastern Literary Society in England," III, 28.

124. "Society of Natural History in England," II, 17.

125. Among these would be the following: "The Marriage of Two Elderly People," III, 23; "A Hunting Dog Kills an Otter," IV, 31; "Child Prodigies," IV, 32; "Elephants in India," II, 19; "Killing a Cobra in Singapore," II, 15; "Apprehension of a Left-Handed Thief," I, 10; "Death of Elderly Twins at the Same Time," II, 20; "A Whale Overturns a Fishing Boat," II, 20; "A Crystal Palace in England," I, 13; "Fog in London," II, 21.

126. "Righteous Girl is Killed," I, 12.

127. "Risking Life to Save Others," I, 12.

128. "Bandits Experience Shame," II, 21. He described three separate robberies in Arabia, America, and Germany, and showed how the criminals responded to appeals to their moral sense of right and wrong.

129. "Present Retribution of Rapists," I, 12. Two men who had unsuccessfully seduced young girls met violent deaths. "A Reason for Blessing and Evil," IV, 35. An old Muslim wanderer, refused entrance to a desert village, spent the night in the wilderness experiencing much discomfort. Going again to the same village the next day, he found it totally ravaged by a roving marauder band. He believed that this experience taught him not to "complain against heaven and murmur against man."

130. "The Difficulty of Completely Fulfilling Man's Destiny," IV, 32.

131. "Fable of Three Gods," II, 16.

132. Young J. Allen, later editor of the *Wan-kuo kung-pao,* noted in his diary for May 16, 1867, that when he spoke to a Chinese audience, he asked them "to show one thing comparable to foreign manufacture and skill and asked if everything the foreigner made was so superior to theirs, was not their [the foreigner's] doctrine also. . . ." Bennett, "Missionary Journalism," 54. One advantage of Martin's separation of science and salvation in this volume was that the latter would not be forced on the Chinese by explicit statements of Western superiority in the sciences. Some of his statements in English (see "Western Science as an Auxiliary to the Spread of the Gospel," *Missionary Review of the World*, X, New Series [October, 1897]) would seem to imply this, but he avoided this impression in his Chinese writing.

133. Suzanne W. Barnett, "Protestant Expansion and Chinese Views of the West," *Modern Asian Studies,* VI (April, 1972), 146, wrote, "Rather than encouraging their Chinese readers to be more receptive to Western intrusion, the missionaries inadvertently supported China's continued inhospitality to the West."

134. Among these would be included all of his translation work with the T'ung Wen Kuan, his translation of Wheaton, his work on *Natural Philosophy,* an article for the *Ko-chih hui-pien* describing the typewriter, several articles for the *Wan-kuo kung-pao* and *Chiao-hui hsin-pao,* and sixteen articles on international law which appeared in the 1888 edition of the *Ching-shih-wen* collection. For details on these numerous writings see Ralph Covell, "Life and Thought of W. A. P. Martin," 300-1.

135. Hsü, *Modern China,* 423-24.

136. *Ibid.,* 429.

137. S. Y. Teng and John Fairbank, eds., *China's Response to the West: A Documentary Survey, 1838-1923* (New York: 1966), 165-74.

138. *Ibid.,* 147.

139. Cyrus H. Peake, *Nationalism and Education in Modern China* (New York, 1932), 15. See also Chi-yun Chen, "Liang Ch'i-ch'ao's 'Missionary Education': A Case Study of Missionary Influence on the Reformers," *China Papers*, XVI (Cambridge, 1962), 66-125; Shu-huai Wang, *Wai-jen*

yü wu-hsü pien-fa (Foreigners and the Reform of 1898) (Taipei, 1965).

140. Hsü, *Modern China*, 426.

141. *Tenth Annual Report* of The Society for the Diffusion of Christian and General Knowledge Among the Chinese, 1897. He is listed as one of sixty-seven members. See also Wang, *Wai-jen yü wu-hsü pien-fa*, 14, 33-34, 44.

142. News items in *The Chinese Recorder*, XXVI (November, 1895), 545; XXVII (February, 1896), 101-2; XXVII (July, 1896), 358. Among the members in Peking were K'ang Yu-wei, Liang Ch'i-ch'ao, and Yüan Shih-k'ai. Timothy Richard and Gilbert Reid had advised the group on their organization. See Meribeth Cameron, *The Reform Movement in China, 1898-1912* (New York, 1963), 28. Also see Diplomatic Despatches, China, C, #2347, Charles Denby to Olney, and #2474, Denby to Olney, February 3, 1896.

143. (Shanghai, 1888).

144. *Ibid.,* 13-17.

145. Gilbert Reid, *The International Institute of China*, n.d., 4. Also Gilbert Reid, *A Prospectus of the International Institute of China* (New York, n.d.), 6.

146. Reid, *Prospectus*, 1.

147. *Ibid.,* 3.

148. Gilbert Reid, *Mission Among the Higher Classes in China*, Seventh Report (October 15, 1897), 2. This apparently is the *Scientific Monthly* referred to by Henry Rankin in his unpublished "Notes on W. A. P. M.," 3.

149. *Ibid.* Revision of his *Western Education*, the report he had done for the government after his trip in 1880-82, was specifically mentioned.

CHAPTER NINE

Interpreting China to the West — From Commendation to Condemnation

CONCURRENT WITH his many activities designed to change the Chinese, William Martin felt responsible for reforming American attitudes toward China. He frequently lectured to scholarly groups, and these lectures were later published in scholarly or semi-popular journals, eventually finding their way into one of his several popular books where they served to dispel the public's ignorance about the Middle Kingdom.

> Never have a great people been more misunderstood. They are denounced as stolid, because we are not in possession of a medium sufficiently transparent to convey our ideas to them, or transmit theirs to us; and stigmatized as barbarians because we want the breadth to comprehend a civilization different from our own. They are represented as servile imitators, though they have borrowed less than any other people; as destitute of the inventive faculty, though the world is indebted to them for a long catalogue of the most useful discoveries; and as clinging with unquestionable tenacity to a heritage of traditions, though they have passed through many and profound changes in the course of their history.[1]

Four of Martin's major books — *A Cycle of Cathay, Siege in Peking, The Lore of Cathay,* and *The Awakening of China* — as well as most of his better articles, were written at a time when it was unmistakably apparent that China, whether she liked it or not, was going to be brought "within the compass of the family of Christian States." This would produce a mutually "open door" of commercial, political, and intellectual interaction, much of its success depending, in Martin's view, on Western understanding of the "principles at the basis of Chinese history and life."[2] He felt this could best be accomplished if America became familiar with basic ideas about Chinese history, law, science, and education.

When he discussed Chinese history Martin sought to destroy the myth that China was a "people of eternal standstill" with an unchanging past. Changes in political ideas, religious thought, and intellectual conceptions, Martin insisted, had characterized all of China's past, and these invalidated the assertion that the Chinese "have . . . been content . . . to hand down from the earliest times a small stock of crystallized ideas without increase or modification."[3]

Martin claimed the international law and diplomacy of the ancient Chinese as a field of his own discovery. His translations of Wheaton and other Western books about law stimulated him to search for something from Chinese history that would roughly parallel current relationships among national states and thereby enable the Chinese to better understand the concept of an international code. Moreover, such a discovery would help convince the West that China was not all that different from itself. Surveying the fourth and fifth century B. C., Martin found what he was looking for.

> If we turn to the history of the period . . . we find . . . a family of states, many of them as extensive as the great states of Western Europe, united by the ties of race, literature, and religion, carrying on an active intercourse, commercial and political, which without some regarded *Jus gentium*, would have been impracticable. We find the interchange of embassies . . . treaties solemnly drawn up and deposited for safe keeping in a sacred place called *Meng Fu.* We find a balance of power studied and practised, leading to combinations to check the aggressions of the strong and to protect the rights of the weak. We find the rights of neutrals to a certain extent recognized and respected. Finally, we find a class of men devoted to diplomacy as a profession. . . .[4]

Martin was not the only person to point out the many practical discoveries and inventions for which the West was indebted to the Chinese. In common with most nineteenth-century writers about China, he noted gunpowder, the mariner's compass, printing, porcelain, and the manufacture of silk and paper.[5] One of his more controversial contributions was the perception that a number of the concepts of modern science were anticipated by

Chinese thought, particularly from the creative Sung dynasty between 1020 and 1120 A.D. As he analyzed the Sung thinkers' descriptions of *ch'i* (matter), he concluded that they were describing the "all-pervading ether of our modern science." He equated their concept of the interaction between *li* (force) and *ch'i* with the "dynamical theory of the molecule," and their idea of the process by which *ch'i* was differentiated to form *yin* and *yang* with the vortex motion transforming molecular structure.[6]

At least one of Martin's contemporaries, C. K. Edmonds, dismissed his views as pure speculation. Edmonds asserted that verbal similarities, though seeming to indicate beliefs anticipating modern science, did not do so when placed in historical context.[7] On the other hand, Joseph Needham, the most prolific modern writer about "science and civilization in China," has commended Martin's theories on the history of the concepts of ether and of the "negative and positive" forces within the universe as "prophetic" and worth serious consideration.[8]

Martin reported both the past achievements of, and the contemporary situation in, Chinese education. A self-confessed "worshipper of antiquity," he sketched the history of the ancient *Kuo Tze Chien* (School for the Sons of the Empire) and of the Hanlin Academy, a community of scholars in charge of the Imperial court's literary activities, in glowing terms. Always the pragmatist, he envisaged these two institutions being remodeled to further reform.[9]

His detailed analysis of the Chinese educational examinations — their history, procedures, types of questions, and the advantages gained by degree holders — had a very specific purpose. Proposals to establish an American civil service system were in the air. Martin did not advocate transplanting a Chinese institution to the United States, but felt that a system which had worked so well through hundreds of years in the Celestial Empire should at least be studied seriously. "It would not be the first lesson we have learned from the Chinese, nor the last they are capable of giving us." With characteristic overstatement he explained that in this

> . . . genuine democracy China stands unapproached among the nations of the earth; for, whatever imperfections may attach to her social organization or to her political system, it must be acknowledged that she has devised the most effectual method for

> encouraging effort and rewarding merit. Here at least is one coun-
> try where wealth is not allowed to raise its possessor to the seat of
> power; where the will even of an emperor cannot bestow its of-
> fices on uneducated favorites; and where the caprice of the mul-
> titude is not permitted to confer the honors of the state on incom-
> petent demagogues.[10]

Obviously, his portrayal of this most influential Chinese institution was highly positive. It was so commendatory, in fact, that
Sun Yat-sen, father of the 1911 Revolution, liked to quote Martin on
the merits of Chinese education, to justify his own desire that it
continue in use.[11]

Martin seldom referred specifically to the "missionary question" in his English books.[12] These books were written to educate
the American public, and missionary material was usually included only to allay concern, caused by reports of anti-Christian
riots in China, that missionaries were trying to force their religion
on an unwilling people.

Martin ascribed the chief blame for the riots to the mandarins who cleverly manipulated the ignorant common people with
malicious rumors, by mouth and in print, that the foreigners kid-
napped children, used Chinese blood to make opium, supported
the Japanese (a later accusation), promoted sexual immorality,
and committed many other abuses, none of them actual. He
pointed out that the mandarins' motivation was basically anti-
foreign and that missionaries, more visible than other foreigners in
the interior of China, were their obvious victims. Once a riot was
under way "the mandarins stood aloof and allowed the storm to
take its course."[13]

Martin could only suggest the usual remedies for this knotty
problem: "the most-favored-nation clause," a new toleration edict,
and continued treaty privileges. The latter, he suggested, could
only be revised when China was ready to "revolutionize her judicial system, and show that her entire government is penetrated
with the modern spirit." He was convinced that opposition from
the "literary corporation" would be lessened when, with science
introduced into the civil service examinations, the mandarins
would come to sympathize "with the educational and humane
agencies of the church of Christ."[14]

In both his English and Chinese writings, Martin consistently linked religious liberty with natural human rights,[15] although not in the overbearing manner assumed by many of his colleagues.[16] He did not, however, emphasize that missionaries were privileged to decline to assert their treaty rights.[17] Nor did he share the convictions of Alexander Michie, one-time editor of the *North China Herald,* who analyzed many of the religious, social, and cultural factors involved in the anti-missionary riots more perceptively than did the missionaries themselves, concluding that opposition spread far beyond the official class. Michie accused the missionaries of preoccupation with

> . . . themselves, their doctrines, their organization, their methods, their efforts, their disappointments, their piety, their charity, their humility, and self-effacement; while the condition of the Chinese *mind* and *conscience* is passed over with some thread bare common places, as if no account need to be taken of that great factor in the problem.[18]

Although Martin believed that "there is no necessary conflict between Christ and Confucius, any more than there was between Paul and Plato,"[19] he was not prepared to let this view be tested in the crucible of time — in the passage of decades during which China might be penetrated by much less aggressive means. He and his colleagues insisted to the American public that Christian missionaries and merchants had the *right* to be in China, and implicitly suggested that this right had been obtained and must be maintained by *force.* This attitude was one of the tragic components contributing to the Boxer Rebellion, which temporarily set back reform and turned Martin's commendation of China to condemnation.

The great rebellion of 1900 came when the Boxers, originally an anti-dynastic secret society that later became prodynastic and anti-foreign, allied themselves with the Empress Dowager and her reactionary followers against Emperor Kuang-hsü and the party of progress.[20] The Boxers had their beginning in southern Shantung and had been opposed by the government as early as 1803.[21] When Shantung was penetrated by German missionaries, German troops, and German industry — symbolized by the hated railroads — the Boxers,[22] touting superstitious claims of immunity to bullets, attacked railway engineers, missionary stations, and villages where there were large numbers of Christian converts.[23] They were encouraged by Yü Hsien, a Manchu governor, whose complicity in the murder of Christians caused him to be replaced, but not without Imperial decoration and transfer to Shensi where he continued to support Boxer groups in their increasingly anti-foreign activities.[24]

Missionaries in the northern provinces appealed to their Peking legations for help against this madness, but were rebuffed by their ministers who believed the Court's assurances that the Boxers only

> . . . practice a sort of innocent gymnastics with a view to the protection of their homes . . . they cannot make head against the militia. The Dowager Empress will at once issue orders for them to disperse and return to their homes.[25]

Martin confessed that he had been hoodwinked and ruefully recalled assuring friends that "Peking is the safest place in China."

Finally, the Western ministers woke up and obtained a contingent of 450 marines to guard the legations. The marines arrived in the nick of time, just before Boxer forces tore up railway tracks connecting Peking with the sea.[26] The ministers' fears were not unfounded. By this time, if not indeed much earlier, the Empress Dowager had cast her lot with the Boxers as the best hope of expelling the foreigner from Peking and from China.[27] In Martin's view this was merely the final step in her opposition to the reform program, which had started with the T'ung-chih Restoration and reached its height in the ill-fated "One Hundred Days of Reform" in 1898.[28]

Alarmed by news that communication with Peking had been cut off, an international force sought unsuccessfully to reach Peking from Tientsin; following this, allied naval forces captured the Taku forts on June 17. The Tsungli Yamen reacted quickly to this by declaring war on the Western powers and demanding that all foreigners leave the capital within twenty-four hours.[29] Martin termed this initial period from June 3, when rail lines to Peking were destroyed, until the declaration of war on June 19, the "Boxer Siege" — the insurgents were in control and the government was in the background. The period after the declaration of war, and until the legations were relieved eight weeks later on August 14, he called the "Government Stage."[30] This analysis is the basis of his claim that

> The besiegers [of the Legation] were not, as they have been represented by Chinese diplomacy, a howling mob that had overpowered the imperial government, but an organized army under the orders of the government.[31]

When the situation became acute in the first days of June, Martin moved from his home near the University to the United States Legation. After the declaration of war and the assassination of the German Minister, Baron von Knettler, on June 20, all the refugees in the various legations, including Martin, went to the British Legation, feeling it to be the only place capable of defense.[32]

Several days after the siege had begun, Martin penned a memo and distributed it to "some of the diplomats in the capital," now powerless and imprisoned with him. He recommended four lines of action: exile the Empress Dowager, annul all her recent actions beginning with her *coup d'etat* in 1898, resume Emperor Kuang-hsü's program of reform, and grant each major Western power a well-defined sphere of influence within China and power "to control the action of provincial governments within its own sphere."[33]

This was a time of mental anguish for Martin as he reevaluated a lifetime of service in China. He spoke of his first meeting with Robert Hart at the legation during the siege.

> As we looked each other in the face, we could not help blushing for shame at the thought that our life-long services had been so little valued. The man who had nursed their Customs revenue from three to thirty millions, the Chinese were trying to butcher; while from my thirty years' teaching of international law they had learned that the lives of Ambassadors were not to be held sacred.[34]

As the Allied forces entered Peking, the Court fled to Sian, and "more than half the population abandoned their dwellings and fled from the city."[35] The temptation and opportunity to loot were great. Allied soldiers, Chinese scavengers, and even Chinese officials did not let the occasion pass. Nor did the missionaries; Martin and others, concerned to help needy converts who had lost all their possessions, did a "little looting on their behalf."[36]

In the month following his release Martin cared for personal matters and those of the Imperial University, and then returned to America by way of Shanghai, where on September 28 at Union Chapel he delivered a lecture that was a "strong and unqualified ... impeachment of the Empress Dowager."[37] When the ship on which he was traveling arrived in New York, he dressed in the full regalia of the Siege defenders — pith helmet, long trench coat, rifle slung across the shoulders, and bed-roll. When a young boy asked him what he had been hunting, he answered, "Tigers," but said later that he should have replied, "Hyenas."[38]

In a flurry of activity between his arrival on October 23, and November 14, 1900, he wrote his book *Siege in Peking* and several newspaper articles. One of the principal recommendations made by this "angry" book, still considered one of the best primary sources concerning the siege, was that America ought to take the island of Hainan. Martin argued that, by doing this, the United States, like all the other great powers apart from Austria and Italy, would have a "*tangible ground* for demanding to be heard on all great questions relating to the future of China."[39]

For the United States to seize a piece of China's territory and the authority derived from it was not "imperialism," according to Martin, but only a final step in the *natural growth* that had expanded American territory across the continent to the Pacific Ocean and now thrust her out toward Japan, China, and the Philippines. America had a God-given destiny in the Orient and she must decline

> Her proud pre-eminence to abdicate
> Through craven fear of growing great.[40]

At a meeting on September 7, 1900, the Shanghai Missionary Association, which represented over four hundred American and British missionaries, passed a resolution including some points similar to Martin's suggestions: restore Kuang-hsü to the throne, reaffirm missionary rights and privileges as guaranteed in the treaties, and punish the Manchu officials most guilty for the tragedy.[41] This statement drew heavy criticism in many American circles, and the missionaries issued another to clarify their position. They emphasized again that the Boxer Rebellion was anti-foreign rather than anti-Christian in its thrust and that, far from being animated by a spirit of vindictiveness and revenge, they simply desired "law and order" instead of anarchy and unrighteousness in China.[42]

Martin could not have agreed more. He had consistently argued that all "missionary incidents" were basically anti-foreign in nature, and at this time he pointed out again that "the killing of missionaries was not the cause, but the occasion of the Boxer outbreak."[43]

Martin did not directly attempt to influence United States policy on political matters, but, as he had done at the time of the Burlingame mission, he sought to wield indirect influence by bringing his cause to the American people. Various newspapers and journals had appealed for the American government to act as "good Samaritan" to China. Martin wrote an open letter to the New York newspapers, strongly supporting indemnity, execution of officials responsible for the rebellion, restoration of the Emperor, and a continuing contingent of troops to defend the Legations in Peking.[44] Reminding his readers that his past record of consistently defending China entitled him to attack her now, he particularly condemned her violation of established norms of diplomatic treatment, and her inhumanity. Whatever he demanded was far less than China deserved, he suggested — "we could ask for the Empress Dowager to be drawn and quartered."[45]

Siege in Peking, published at the height of this war of words, was another appeal for the American people to pressure the government to follow a hard line and punish China. Martin epitomized his position with a home-spun tale.

> It is related of a Methodist preacher that a notorious bully swore that the next time he came around he would put a stop to his psalm-singing and his exhortations. He, however, reckoned without his host, for the preacher was himself a boxer, and, when attacked, succeeded in less than no time in flooring his antagonist. Jumping astride him, he pounded away until the bystanders begged him to let the poor devil up.
>
> 'No,' said he, 'I will not let the devil up. My object is to keep the devil down; nor will I cease pounding until this wretched man promises to seek the salvation of his soul.'
>
> This is what I would have the allies do in the case of China. . . .[46]

How different was his advice from that of Robert Hart. Hart also decried murdering ministers and ransacking legations but observed that

> To accord religious liberty or to subordinate such liberty to considerations of state is not denied to independent powers; to feel the pinch of certain treaty stipulations and, when strong enough to do so, to throw off such as were originally imposed by force, is a practice for which even Christian powers have set pagan states more than one example. . . .[47]

Martin was not advocating that Christianity be made the "state church," but he insisted that Allies use force to keep China open to the Gospel. America must insist, he demanded, that missionary rights and privileges not be limited in China, and the United States must bear her "full share in the Christian crusade of the coming age," a crusade that would lead China to a national resurrection.[48]

> The greatest enemy to the orderly and profitable intercourse of nations is heathen darkness. . . . Without these [the light of science and religion] our railway and mining enterprises will be insecure and we can have no assurance that that monster, the dragon, who has now been cast down before the Soldiers of the Cross, will not again raise his head and bring about another catastrophe. . . .[49]

His expectations, and those of the missionaries in China, were not met by the final settlement.[50] Eleven princes and officials were executed, indemnities and permanent legation guards were provided for, and, in 1903, the position of missionaries was reaffirmed with stronger guarantees. However, no territory was granted to the United States, and the Emperor was not restored to power. The Manchu government, headed by the Empress Dowager, continued to rule China,[51] even though some of its leaders had been eliminated, its military capacity restricted, and its erstwhile allies, the Boxers, suppressed. Martin was disappointed, but recognized that the West still possessed sufficient leverage to "guarantee . . . a liberal policy which shall make provision for all legitimate interests and enterprises."[52]

Martin's proposals were obviously contrary to traditional American policy of non-intervention in the affairs of other countries, politically hazardous, and in the final analysis not very significant in determining the shape of the agreement. Like the opinions of the missionaries, whose spirit he shared, they reflected a "misjudgment of the essential basis of American foreign policy and a failure to understand the international and diplomatic implications of the policies . . . advocated."[53] More unfortunately, Martin's communication to the West about China from 1870 to 1900 — ranging as it did from wholehearted commendation to partial condemnation — tends to confirm the thesis that "missionary attitudes toward the Chinese . . . [were] mirror-images of Chinese attitudes toward them."[54]

Notes

1. W. A. P. Martin, *The Lore of Cathay* (New York, 1912), 8. These books were certainly not denominational propaganda in the pattern of W. E. Soothill's *A Typical Mission in China* (New York, 1900), which was intended "to depict our own Mission, as typical of many others." (vii) Neither did he utilize his books to give detailed information about the Christian mission nor as a means for seeking recruits. This was in marked contrast with William Dean's *The China Mission* (New York, 1859), or even with John Nevius' *China and the Chinese* (New York, 1869). The first half of the latter book gives a general description of China, but the last half is a specific missionary presentation. Nor did Martin see his literary endeavor as an apologetic for missionary work in the sense of James Dennis who frankly stated that "Christianity by virtue of its own beneficent energy as a transforming and elevating power in society, has already wrought out a new *apologia* of missions." *Christian Missions and Social Progress* (3 vols.; New York, 1897), I, x.

2. Martin, *Lore,* 2.

3. *Ibid.,* 10-15.

4. *Ibid.,* 431.

5. He first wrote on this subject in an article in *Harper's New Monthly Magazine,* XXXIX (November, 1869), 909-12. The same material, with some revision, appeared in *The Journal of the Peking Oriental Society,* IV (1898), 19-28, and in *The Lore of Cathay,* 23-32.

6. Martin, *Lore,* 39.

7. C. K. Edmonds, "Some Aspects of the Chinese Conception of the Universe as Compared with Modern Scientific Knowledge," *Records of the*

Fifth Triennial Meeting of the Educational Association of China (Shanghai, 1906), 262.

8. Joseph Needham, *Science and Civilization in China* (4 vols.; London, 1954-71), IV, *Physics and Physical Technology* (London, 1962), 33.

9. Martin, *Lore*, 378, 372, 338-39.

10. *Ibid.*, 308-9, 11.

11. John C. H. Wu, *Sun Yat Sen: The Man and His Ideas* (Taipei, 1971), 341; Y. C. Wang, *Chinese Intellectuals and the West* (Durham, N.C., 1966), 336.

12. W. A. P. Martin, *A Cycle of Cathay* (3rd ed.; New York, 1900), 439-57.

13. *Ibid.*, 447-48, 445.

14. *Ibid.*, 442, 451, 455-56.

15. W. A. P. Martin, *The Awakening of China* (New York, 1907), 280.

16. D. Z. Sheffield, "Treaty Protection of Christian Missionaries in China," *The Chinese Recorder*, XXXIX (December, 1908), 657-71.

17. D. E. Hoste, "The Missionary and His Relation to the Treaties," *The Chinese Recorder*, XXXIX (December, 1908), 671-75.

18. Alexander Michie, *Missionaries in China* (London, 1891), 40; Alexander Michie, *China and Christianity* (Boston, 1900). For an excellent analysis of multiple factors present in many of the anti-missionary riots, matters which Martin only hinted at but which Michie made explicit, see J. K. Fairbank, "Patterns Behind the Tientsin Massacre," *Harvard Journal of Asiatic Studies*, XX (December, 1957), 480-511.

19. Martin, *Cycle*, 455.

20. W. A. P. Martin, *Siege in Peking* (New York, 1900), 17.

21. *Ibid.*, 60-61.

22. The name "Boxer" comes from the Chinese name I-ho ch'uan ("Righteous and Harmonious Fists"), which was given to them because they made a fetish of practising the traditional Chinese form of calisthenics. In tracing the origin of the Boxers to the early 1800's Martin was following the theory still held by most scholars today. For a recent alternative hypothesis, not yet widely accepted, that the group originally was the *I-ho t'uan* ("Righteous and Harmonious Militia"), organized in the 1850's to oppose the Taiping rebels, see Immanuel Hsü, *The Rise of Modern China* (New York, 1970), 465-66.

23. Martin, *Siege*, 63-66.

24. *Ibid.*, 64-65.

25. *Ibid.*, 71.

26. *Ibid.*, 72.

27. *Ibid.*, 16.

28. *Ibid.*, 31-44.

29. *Ibid.*, 77.

30. *Ibid.*, 74-77.

31. *Ibid.*, 15.

32. *Ibid.*, 78, 80-81.

33. Martin, "Memo of June 18, 1900," *Siege*, 146-47.

34. Martin, *Siege*, 97.

35. This dramatic rescue was the "work of Christendom aided by Japan which deserved to be admitted into that honored brotherhood." W. A. P. Martin, "Story of the Siege and Fall of Peking," *New York Times*, October 5, 1900, 7:4.

36. Martin, *Siege*, 135-37, 131.

37. News item, *The Chinese Recorder*, XXXI (October, 1900), 526. In the first month following the lifting of the siege, Martin wrote several journal and newspaper articles. See W. A. P. Martin, "The Fall of Peking," *The Independent*, October 11, 1900, 2421. This article was written August 24, 1900, from Peking. His June 18 memo, slightly elaborated, was reprinted after the siege and also published in the Peking and Tientsin *Times* of September 15, 1900. *Siege*, 145.

38. Martin, *Siege*, 7. A picture of Martin in his "siege suit" is in the frontispiece of the book.

39. *Ibid.*, 155. Italics his. In *The Awakening of China* he noted that the Manchus, a foreign race, had governed China for several hundred years and that European powers should surely be able to do as well, 22. He even suggested that it might have been better for Great Britain to have controlled China from 1842, rather than to have let it remain independent.

40. Martin, *Siege*, 156-57. See Albert Weinberg, *Manifest Destiny* (Baltimore, 1935), for the use of the catch-phrase "natural growth" as one symbolic rationale for American expansion.

41. See *The Chinese Recorder*, XXXI (October, 1900), 529-30, and the *North China Herald*, September 12, 1900, 553-54.

42. "Statement by the Protestant Missionaries in China on the Present Crisis," *The Presbyterian Banner*, July 25, 1901, 13.

43. Martin, *Siege*, 160.

44. Martin, "Dr. Martin Defends the Demands on China," *New York Times*, November 19, 1900, 7:3. Also see the earlier article, "Story of the Siege and Fall of Peking," 7:4.

45. Martin, "Dr. Martin Defends the Demands on China," 7:3.

46. Martin, *Siege*, 143.

47. Robert Hart, *The Peking Legations: A National Uprising and International Episode* (Shanghai, 1900), 37.

48. Martin, *Siege*, 143-44.

49. W. A. P. Martin, "The Causes That Led to the Siege of Peking," *National Geographic Magazine*, XII (February, 1901), 63.

50. John Lindbeck, "American Missionaries and Policies of the United States in China, 1898-1901" (unpublished Ph. D. dissertation, Yale University, 1948), 466.

51. Martin, *Siege*, 163-64.

52. *Ibid.*, 165.

53. Lindbeck, "American Missionaries," 467.

54. Harold R. Isaacs, *Images of Asia* (New York, 1872); Sidney Forsythe, *An American Missionary Community in China, 1895-1905* (Cambridge, Mass., 1971), viii.

CHAPTER TEN

Strategy for the Conversion of China

ALL OF WILLIAM MARTIN'S activities in the Orient — whether his specific methods of missionary outreach in Ningpo, his efforts to persuade his government to support the Taiping rebels, his pressure on the Manchu dynasty to grant more religious liberty, his literary ministry, or his long period of cooperation with national and provincial officials in educational projects — were various facets of one aim to win China to the Christian faith. He saw salvation as a coin with two sides — the material and the spiritual — but the spiritual was always the more important.

He expressed this conviction in various ways. For example, he nearly always spoke of science and education in one breath — the former was the content and the latter the method. His final aim was also clear — "science might wing the arrow, but religion should be its point."[1] He conceded that instruction concerning steam and electricity might not be necessary for an illiterate peasant, but in general "the missionary *must* first convince his hearers that he knows more than they do about the structure of the universe and the laws and powers, visible and invisible by which it is governed."[2]

He was careful to explain that he was not arguing that "education must in all cases precede the Gospel, or that Christianity is not in itself the most effective of all instruments for enlightening the human mind."[3] If the Chinese received the Gospel, he insisted, "it alone will do more than anything else to place them on an intellectual level with the people of Europe."

What was the exact relationship between "civilization" and

245

Christianity? Martin was not a mission theorist in the mold of Timothy Richard, the famed English Baptist missionary, and he presented no systematic and consistent theories concerning this subject.[4] He clearly believed that Christianity produced a more "civilized" people, and that efforts to promote reform produced a climate conducive to the spread of the faith. He also frequently emphasized, as the Jesuits had earlier, that secular knowledge earned the missionary the right to speak on spiritual matters. He argued, for example, that Christian missionaries were obligated to create a new secular literature for China. The ability to use the written page to instruct a civilized people like the Chinese in worldly matters "proves our commission to teach . . . spiritual things."[5]

Although many Protestant colleagues shared his viewpoint,[6] Martin was usually more in debt to the Jesuits, whose early efforts in China he admired deeply. His commitment to literature, his emphasis upon science, his readiness to work with a government institution, his desire to influence high officials, his acceptance of the Confucian rites, his work as political confidante to the Chinese government, his recommendation that single men be used to penetrate China's vast interior, his patience when he felt high officials had betrayed him, and his ultimate dogged desire to die in Peking all reflect the examples of Matteo Ricci and Adam Schall.

More important in Martin's missionary strategy than specific methodology, which was subject to change with varying circumstances, was his flexible attitude toward Chinese religions and the ancestral cult. The ancestral cult was *the* sore point between Christianity and the Chinese, and the Christian failure to properly empathize meant that sound doctrine and effective methods had lost their point of contact with the Chinese mind.[7]

In his analysis of the Chinese religious system Martin suggested that the three major religions, although different in their assumptions, beliefs, and practices, were supplementary in the Chinese experience. "In ordering their lives, they are regulated by Confucian forms, in sickness they call in Taoist priests to exorcise evil spirits, and at funerals they have Buddhist priests to say masses for the repose of the soul."[8] Furthermore, he argued, each religion represented an historical advance in religious thinking, and he was optimistic that Christianity would eventually become the "fourth stage" for the Chinese people.[9]

Martin proposed that the Christian faith could be related to the Chinese religious system as either the "successor of Buddhism" or as the fulfillment of the Confucian ethical philosophy. Early in his missionary career Martin had very little good to say about Buddhism, but over a period of time he came to believe that two basic elements in Buddhism, a belief in a divine being, and in the immortality of the soul, contributed "to make it [China] ready for the cultivation of our Christian epoch." The spiritual universe in which Buddhists believed, filled with Buddhas and Boddhisattvas — kind, just, and providential beings — was far different from that of the Chinese who worshipped "natural objects and . . . human heroes . . . not one of [whom took] any strong hold on their affections."[10] The failure to restrict worship to one Buddha and the basic atheistic tendency[11] of the religion did not deter him from stating that praise to the Buddhist divinities was "worthy to be laid as an offering at the feet of Jehovah."[12] Few fellow missionaries took kindly to this suggestion. D. Z. Sheffield exclaimed,

> I have no sympathy with that sort of thing and think that Christian men, and above all missionaries, are in the poorest kind of business when they set out to coquet with heathen religions, magnifying their virtues and belittling their vices.[13]

Martin conceded that the Buddhist doctrine of the future life was "vitiated by mixture with the errors of metempsychosis." This error was offset, he felt, by the strong emphasis on the immaterial essence of the soul and its future existence in a state that accorded with present conduct.[14] These elements in Buddhist teaching constituted a better preparation for the Christian faith, he thought, than the materialism of Taoism or the agnosticism of Confucianism.

He also asserted that "faith, hope and charity," cardinal Christian virtues, were taught by Buddhism. He showed how many Buddhist terms — heaven, hell, devil, soul, life to come, new birth, advent, sin, repentance, retribution —[15] were taken by the earlier Catholic and later Protestant missionaries, "sprinkled . . . with holy water, and consecrated to a new use." He was persuaded that the hand of Divine providence, preparing China to receive the Gospel, even as it had done in the Roman Empire, could be seen in this provision of religious concepts and vocabulary useful for presenting Christianity.[16] He believed that the mission of Buddhism was not completed, but that it served as the trunk of a tree to which the "vine of Christ" could now be grafted.

Martin also viewed Buddhism as an "example of a foreign creed winning its way and holding its ground in spite of opposition." Would not Buddhists themselves, taught by their own leaders to look for a fuller manifestation of their faith, see Christianity, also a non-Chinese religion, as the fulfillment of that hope?[17]

The earlier Martin occasionally reappeared and harshly criticized Buddhism's stoic negativism, its principle of self-annihilation, and its melancholy spirit.[18] He referred to the Buddhists as "religious atheists" whose highest motivation was to "escape from having their souls pounded in a spiritual mortar, or ground between spiritual millstones in Hades."[19]

Martin always related Christianity to China's dominant philosophy as a matter of "Confucius *plus* Christ" and never "Christ *or* Confucius."[20] He believed Confucianism to be an ethical philosophy "consonant with the spirit of Christianity."[21] Its teaching concerning the five basic relationships was rooted in the very nature of man, and lacked only the "last link with Heaven" to complete it.[22] He did not feel that the prevailing Chinese view of the "radical goodness" of human nature, sometimes denied and modified in various ways by others, was an insuperable obstacle to the Christian faith. "The Bible," Martin claimed, presents

> . . . a complete view of a subject which their various theories had only presented in detached fragments. In the state of primitive purity, it gives them a heaven-imparted nature in its original perfection; in the supremacy of conscience it admits a fact on which they rely as the main support of their doctrine; in the corruption of nature, introduced by sin, it gives them a class of facts to which their consciousness abundantly testifies; and in its plan for the restoration of the moral ruin, it excites hope and satisfies reason.[23]

Martin believed that the cardinal virtues of Confucianism — benevolence, justice, order, wisdom, and good faith — were in many ways superior to those advocated by other civilizations. Fortitude, always prominent among martial Europeans, was inferior, he claimed, to justice. He pointed out that benevolence and good faith, extremely important in Chinese thought, were not given such prominence in the "heathen systems of the West."[24] He explained, however, that this moral creed, admirable in its completeness and in the interaction of its related elements, was only practiced by a very few Chinese, and that this revealed the need for a supernatural faith which would supply the "motives and supports of which their own system is wholly destitute."[25]

The idea of the *sheng-jen* (holy men), "teachers providentially raised up ... through which the Will of Heaven is revealed,"[26] provided a link, he thought, by which the Christian message might be given to China. Confucius, Martin claimed,

> ... so far from arrogating definitive completeness for his own system, leads his disciples to expect the appearance of *sheng-jen* in coming ages. Nor is the advent of such Heaven-sent teachers limited to China. There is, therefore, nothing to prevent a sound Confucian accepting Christ as the Light of the World, without abandoning his faith in Confucius as a special teacher for the Chinese people. ... As a matter of fact, native Christians continue to believe in the mission of Confucius, much as converted Jews do in that of Moses.[27]

The Confucian system, acceptable in its origins and concepts, and a stepping-stone for the Christian faith, did not, however, receive Martin's unqualified support. He argued that it had led to skepticism, idolatry, expediency, and a dogmatic, unreasoning attitude of mind.[28] Lacking in spiritual vitality, "its noisiest professors, i.e. the whole body of so called literati ... are steeped in formalism and hypocrisy."[29]

Some of Martin's missionary colleagues accepted, to a greater or lesser degree, his contention that the Christian faith fulfilled the aspirations and beliefs found in Confucianism and Buddhism. Very few, however, were prepared to implement this conviction in a concrete missionary strategy to deal with the ancestor cult and the Confucian rites.

The ancestral rite consists of four activities related to the dead: burial, the ritual in the home, annual sacrifices at the grave, and annual services in the ancestral hall.[30] The most important part of the funeral itself is the selection, by processes of divination and geomancy, of the proper date and place for burial. When this has been determined, the wooden ancestral tablet, inscribed with the name and birth and death dates of the deceased, and thought to be the abode of his spirit, is prepared.

A ritual is then held in the home, and large amounts of money are spent to provide the dead with a symbolic paper outfit — house, clothing, bed, and perhaps slaves and concubines — for his needs in the spiritual world. Other major services follow at prescribed intervals, and a routine daily ceremony is eventually established, conducted morning and evening before a home altar by the father or oldest son, and consisting of prostrations, burning incense, and offerings of food.

Twice a year, at the Autumn and Spring festivals, sacrifices which serve both as religious ceremonies and festive social gatherings for dispersed family members are conducted at the grave. As important as family rituals in the home and at the grave are ceremonies held twice yearly in the ancestral hall, where sacrifice is made to the tablets of all those bearing a common clan name.[31]

Throughout his missionary service Martin possessed an accommodating spirit toward Chinese inquirers who were groping toward Christian truth. Yet even he confessed sadly that he had once insisted "on the surrender of ancestral tablets as a proof of sincerity on the part of an applicant for baptism."[32] His perception of this early incident as a failure motivated him to help others by widely propagating his views on the ancestral rite.

His first prominent opportunity to influence his colleagues was an invitation to deliver a major paper on the theme "The Worship of Ancestors" at the General Missionary Conference in Shanghai in 1890. Far different from the well-prepared but inconclusive technical discussion of the subject presented by Matthew Yates at the first General Missionary Conference in 1877,[33] Martin's paper, presented for him by Gilbert Reid, sounded the Conference's only real controversial note, although Martin said nothing essentially different from what he had written ten years earlier in his book, *The Chinese, Their Education, Philosophy and Letters.*[34]

At the outset of his lecture he stated that there were only two basic approaches to what was admittedly "the most serious impediment to the conversion of the Chinese." One was to remove the obstacle, and the other was to make a temporary accommodation while seeking a more permanent solution.[35] Refusing to get bogged down in technical religious niceties, he concentrated on the historic and social role of the ancestral cult. He noted, for example, the historical function of the rite in announcing dynastic succession, reporting important imperial events, and in promoting morality and courage by appealing to the honor of the departed. He pointed out, moreover, that at the present time the system, although tainted by "a large intermixture of superstition and idolatry," still served a three-fold social purpose:

1) To strengthen the bonds of family union, and stimulate to active charity;

2) to cherish self-respect, and impose moral restraint;

3) to keep alive a sort of faith in the reality of the spirit-world.[36]

Martin rejected outright both the possibility and the wisdom of abolishing a cult with such cohesive power in the society.[37] Although he shared with his colleagues the conviction that the missionary must "avoid giving countenance to anything that can fairly be construed as idolatry," he affirmed that those features to which the church most objected were "its excrescences, not its essence."[38] His approach unconsciously utilized techniques widely adopted by many agents of cultural change confronting adverse institutions. First, he rejected both the form and function of idolatrous elements, that is, invocations and offerings which implied that the deceased were tutelary deities. Second, he sought to modify both the form and function of certain "announcements" so that they would be regarded not as prayers but as mere expressions of "natural affection." Third, he accepted both the form and function of kneeling and bowing, affirming that while these actions were idolatrous in certain contexts, they definitely were not in others. He placed salutations and announcements to the dead in this same category.[39] A fourth proposal, to develop functional substitutes, would have made his views more palatable to his colleagues, but was omitted from this presentation.

Martin claimed that much of the Protestant difficulty with the ancestral rite was related not to fear of idolatry but to repugnance for "any kind of connection with the dead,"[40] an aversion which he traced to an extreme reaction to the dogma of the Roman church. He urged restoring natural expressions of affection for the dead, if not among the tradition-bound churches in the West, then at least among congregations in China where "Protestant missions are still in the morning of their existence." He added that "the venerable usages of a civilized people should be judged by their own merits, and it is to be borne in mind that our aim is not to Europeanize the Chinese, but to make them Christians."[41]

This approach, fraught with obvious dangers and demanding caution, "kept the way open for counteractive teaching" and avoided an "uncompromising conflict" that would "close the ears of the better class to all good influences." Martin argued that taking a rigid position on this issue would cause the "incipient conviction" of the common man to be stifled before it ripened "into practical conversion."[42]

In the heated discussion following the presentation of this paper, Hudson Taylor, whom Martin once said had "erred in leading his followers to make war on ancestral worship, instead of seeking to reform it,"[43] asked all "those who dissented from the conclusions of Dr. Martin's paper to rise."[44] Nearly everyone did. Martin's views were defended largely by Timothy Richard, the noted English Baptist missionary, and Gilbert Reid. Martin stated later, however, that "many missionaries have assured me that they concur in the general sentiment of the paper."[45]

In later writing about the ancestral cult Martin suggested that functional substitutes — bouquets of flowers, or planting flower seeds and shrubs — might be used in place of offerings of meat and drink.[46] But since he had less difficulty with the original form and functions in the first place, he never pushed this option as hard as other liberal spirits did.

Homage to the tablets of Confucius and the Emperor — two closely related issues — became prominent in the late nineteenth and early twentieth century. With Western learning being introduced into schools and the examination system being threatened, early signs of what would later become a concerted drive to make Confucianism the state religion were apparent everywhere.[47] One aspect of this was insistence by school officials that teachers and students bow before the tablet of Confucius. Martin and his fellow-faculty members had voluntarily participated in this rite at the inauguration of the Imperial University in 1899 and had stirred the indignation of the Peking missionary community.[48] Now it became an issue for Christians, both student and faculty, in the proliferating government schools and in the Christian schools over which the government was seeking to exercise more rigid supervision.

Martin's views on this approximated what he had said about ancestral worship in general. He contended that bowing before the tablet of Confucius or the Emperor was an exaggerated Oriental mark of respect intended to secure loyalty.[49] The Christian who performed these rites "renounces nothing, nor is he supposed to accept any anti-Christian doctrine."[50] Christian students, if not burdened by their churches with the weight of this "imaginary offense," would be able, he claimed, to matriculate in government schools, to exercise positions of influence on the faculty and administration, and "to deal with the moral issues that meet them in daily life."[51] Appealing for "cool logic, unbiased by any question of advantage," he urged his colleagues to take the path that would give Christian youth the best opportunity to exert an influence in China.[52]

Martin's Chinese publications, while phrased in a manner calculated not to offend the conservative views of many Chinese Christians, carried the same essential message as his English writings. In *Evidences of Christianity* he urged potential converts not to turn their backs on Confucius.[53]

In another of his Chinese books, *Christianity and Other Creeds,* written in 1909, Martin traced the details of the famed "Rites Controversy" and clearly took a stand with the Jesuits against the Franciscans and the Dominicans. *Shang-ti* was the most acceptable name for God, he felt, and he further claimed that if the ancestral rites had been permitted, even temporarily, the Emperor K'ang-hsi might have become a modern-day Constantine, bringing officials, gentry, and the common people into the Christian fold. In his opinion, this would at least have bought time until Chinese Christians were granted liberty to practice customs which were such an integral part of Chinese life.[54] He regretted the lack of Protestant unity on the "rites" question — almost a replay of the earlier Catholic controversy — but believed the problem would have been settled much earlier if an "open policy," giving all groups liberty to follow the dictates of their own consciences, had been adopted.[55]

As a natural outgrowth of his convictions concerning the ancestral cult and the Confucian rites, Martin developed a new strategy for reaching China for Christ. He had always been concerned with winning the common man, whether through the Taiping "peoples' movement," through simple literature, or through first evangelizing the influential upper classes. In the post-Boxer period, when China was awakening from a deep slumber, Martin saw the possibility of "conversions en masse."[56] Nations, not individuals, should be the goal of the Christian mission.

How did he believe that this vision should be fulfilled? First, baptism should precede inquiry and catechism, rather than following them. Second, "whole families, entire clans, villages or districts" should be admitted to baptism as soon as they "committed themselves to a better doctrine, however imperfectly it might be apprehended." Third, the catalyst for this would be the conversion of the head of the family or clan. Fourth, teaching and training, having gained a much larger audience, would follow rather than precede baptism, and this would eliminate many false motives. Fifth, the rapidly growing number of converts would "exert an irresistible influence on the community to which they belong."[57]

The key to success was to not examine candidates for baptism so rigidly. Speaking of some of his legalistic colleagues, Martin commented,

> If I were to illustrate their attitude by the use of a cartoon I should draw a picture of the blind Polyphemus feeling the fleeces of his sheep one by one, lest his cunning enemy should be crouched on the back of some of them.

He observed that "the devil . . . [often] escapes detection by attaching himself to the *belly* of the sheep rather than on the back."[58] The obvious point, not lost on his readers, was that even extremely careful pre-baptismal screening did not guarantee the elimination of unworthy candidates.[59]

Martin summed up his strategy in a short translation from Chinese entitled "Remarks of Momo, A Native Christian, on the Preaching of Missionaries." This unidentified Chinese convert, possibly Martin's own creation, observed that "if you are not acquainted with the moral relations of men how can you understand the nature of God?" The Chinese church, he claimed, had failed at precisely this point — it had "thrown off the duties of society under the cloak of religion" and thus "rebelled against the teaching of the Gospel." What could correct this state of affairs and implement a deeper Christian impact upon Chinese life? "To teach reverence for the Supreme Ruler let them begin by teaching loyalty to the Emperor and to teach the service of our heavenly Father, let them begin by insisting on the service of earthly parents."[60]

At the core of Martin's strategy for the conversion of China was the idea that the Christian church must relate its theology to the central aspects of Chinese culture. He did not intend to compromise the central Gospel message, but neither did he wish to adopt a policy which, in many of its features, reflected the fears and thought patterns of the culture from which he and other messengers of the Gospel had come. Unfortunately for the development of a truly indigenous Christian community in China, this policy was no more acceptable to most missionaries in Martin's time than it had been to the Franciscans and Dominicans in the time of the great Jesuit, Matteo Ricci.

Notes

1. W. A. P. Martin, "Western Science as Auxiliary to the Spread of the Gospel," *Missionary Review of the World,* New Series X (October, 1897), 773.

2. W. A. P. Martin, "The Intellectual Wants of the Chinese — A Plea for Education in China," *The Church at Home and Abroad,* IX (February, 1891), 144.

3. Martin, "Western Science," 770.

4. Timothy Richard, a very realistic "life-time" missionary, had more detailed, carefully thought out proposals than did Martin for training missionaries in the "science of missions." Timothy Richard, "The Present Crisis and How to Meet It," *The Chinese Recorder,* XXIV (January, 1903); Timothy Richard, "Some of the Greatest Needs of Christian Missions," *The Chinese Recorder,* XXVIII (April, 1907); Rita Johnson, "Timothy Richard's Theory of Christian Missions to the Non-Christian World" (unpublished Ph. D. dissertation, St. John's University, 1965).

5. W. A. P. Martin, "Secular Literature Viewed as a Missionary Agency." This was a message written by Martin but read for him at the

General Conference of Protestant Missionaries in 1877 at Shanghai. It is found in the printed records of that conference.

6. Many of these, such as Calvin Mateer, Hunter Corbett, and others, were from the Presbyterian mission. Gilbert Reid and Timothy Richard shared his perspective. Other men, such as Hudson Taylor and Griffith John, felt that he was too secular. For a debate on the question of "secular literature" see *Records of the General Conference of Protestant Missionaries in China.* Shanghai, May 10-24, 1877 (Shanghai, 1878), 235-40.

7. It was at this point that Martin tried hardest to influence his missionary colleagues, through both his Chinese and English writings. *Evidences of Christianity* was required reading for many new missionaries after they had reached a certain stage of proficiency in the Chinese language, to which some of them at least had been partially introduced by his language manual, *The Analytical Reader*. China Letters of the Board of Foreign Missions of the Presbyterian Church in the United States of America, Reel 255, Peking Annual Minutes, 1910, 5. China Letters are subsequently abbreviated "CL." *The Lore of Cathay,* the *Hanlin Papers*, and *A Cycle of Cathay* were also used in language school programs. CL, Reel 255, Peking Annual Minutes, 1910, 5. Another means through which his views influenced fellow-missionaries were his articles, memoranda, and book reviews in *The Chinese Recorder,* an interdenominational Protestant monthly (occasionally a bi-monthly) which commenced in Foochow in 1868 and was transferred to Shanghai in 1874.

8. W. A. P. Martin, *A Cycle of Cathay* (3rd ed.; New York, 1900), 289, and *The Lore of Cathay* (2nd ed.; New York, 1912), 193.

9. Martin, *Hanlin Papers,* Second Series (Shanghai, 1894), 274.

10. These views were described in an evening lecture, "Buddhism, a Preparation for Christianity," delivered to the Peking Missionary Association in 1889. It was reprinted in *The Chinese Recorder* (May, 1889) and included in the *Hanlin Papers,* 278-303, and *Lore,* 249-63.

11. In a discussion held after the meeting, Martin emphasized again that he was not talking about classical Buddhism which had no deities, saviours, or doctrine of salvation. *Hanlin Papers,* 303.

12. Martin, *Lore,* 256. The *Hanlin Papers* contain a further statement: "It matters little by what name God may be called, provided that which is predicated of him be agreeable to truth." 291.

13. D. Z. Sheffield to Judson Smith, ABCFM Records, North China Mission, A. B. C.: 16.3.12. XII, #201, 3. May 29, 1889. Criticism of this type may explain why some of the material found in the earlier *Hanlin Papers* was deleted when the same lectures were incorporated in his later work *The Lore of Cathay.*

14. Martin, *Lore,* 257.

15. Martin, *Hanlin Papers,* 301.

16. Martin, *Lore,* 259-62.

17. *Ibid.*, 262. Martin, ever sensitive to the sympathies of his audience, never spoke this highly of Buddhism in any of his Chinese writings. Timothy Richard, English Baptist missionary who translated *The Awakening of Faith, Essence of the Lotus Scripture, A Mission to Heaven,* and *A Guide to Buddhahood* into English, believed that certain schools of reformed Buddhism were but a "Chinese manifestation of the Christian message of hope and redemption." See Rita Johnson, "Timothy Richard's Theory of Christian Missions to the Non-Christian World," 88-89, 126. See also Timothy Richard, *Forty-Five Years in China: Reminiscences* (London, 1916), 334-38; William Soothill, *Timothy Richard of China* (London, 1924), 199. The last source mentioned the prophecy in the Diamond Sutra about the coming Buddha. Martin's views on Buddhism were formed a bit earlier, and, though similar to Richard's, were not as radical.

18. Martin, *Lore,* 195, 185-86.

19. *Ibid.*, 185, 188.

20. *Ibid.*, 247-48.

21. *Ibid.*, 221.

22. *Ibid.*, 212.

23. *Ibid.*, 218.

24. *Ibid.*, 221-22.

25. *Ibid.*, 225.

26. Martin called attention to an early theory of revelation through tortoises and dragons presented in the *I Ching* and then showed how the more common view of the Confucian canon exalted man as the medium of Heaven. *Lore,* 242-43. This chapter, entitled "Chinese Ideas of Inspiration," was a lecture given before the American Oriental Society at Princeton, October 23, 1890.

27. Martin, *Lore,* 247-48.

28. *Ibid.*, 176-77.

29. Martin, *Cycle,* 209.

30. Karl Reichelt, *Religion in Chinese Garment* (New York, 1951), 62.

31. *Ibid.*, Summary of Chapter 3, "The Cult of Ancestors," 61-71. See also C. K. Yang, *Religion in Chinese Society* (Berkeley, 1967), 28-57, and David K. Jordan, *Gods, Ghosts and Ancestors* (Berkeley, 1972), 87-133.

32. Martin, *Lore,* 277.

33. Matthew Yates, "Ancestral Worship," *Records of the General Conference of the Protestant Missionary in China, Shanghai, May 10-24, 1877* (Shanghai, 1878), 367-86.

34. W. A. P. Martin, *The Chinese, Their Education, Philosophy and Letters* (New York, 1881), 257-70.

35. W. A. P. Martin, *Hanlin Papers,* Second Series (Shanghai, 1894),

328. He compared the first alternative to a man trying to remove a hill in front of his home rather than shifting his habitation. The latter option was to build a railroad track over the mountain while construction proceeds on a tunnel to go through it.

36. *Ibid.,* 341.

37. *Ibid.* "Let us ask ourselves whether, if we had the power by a pen-stroke to sweep it all away, we should dare to incur the responsibility of doing so?"

38. *Ibid.,* 342.

39. *Ibid.,* 343-46.

40. *Ibid.,* 348.

41. *Ibid.,* 350.

42. *Ibid.,* 350-51, 354.

43. Martin, *Cycle,* 214.

44. *Records of the General Conference of Protestant Missionaries in China, 1890* (Shanghai, 1891), 59.

45. Martin, *Hanlin Papers,* Second Series, 355.

46. Martin, *Lore,* 277.

47. Wing-tsit Chan, *Religious Trends in Modern China* (New York, 1953), 4-11.

48. "Peking University," *North China Herald,* February 6, 1899, 211.

49. W. A. P. Martin, "The Worship of Confucius — Is It Idolatry?" *The Chinese Recorder,* XXXIV (February, 1903), 92-93.

50. W. A. P. Martin, "The Worship of Ancestors, How Shall We Deal With It?" *The Chinese Recorder,* XXXV (June, 1904), 308.

51. W. A. P. Martin, "How May Christian Schools Bring Their Influence to Bear Most Effectively on the Educational System of the Chinese Government?" *Records of the Sixth Triennial Meeting of the Educational Association of China* (Shanghai, 1909), 45-46.

52. Martin, "The Worship of Confucius," 93. The editor of *The Chinese Recorder* disassociated himself from Martin's position, asking, "How ... can a Christian who holds this view of Confucianism [that it blocks morality and true progress] bow in reverence to the tablet of him who is honored as the representative of a system which is the chief hindrance to the spread of Christianity in China?" He conceded that Martin's respect for Confucius, unlike his own, might be profound enough to enable him to bow without it being idolatry, 94. Martin certainly would agree that "to him who thinks it is a sin, to him it is sinful." Martin, "How May Christian Schools ... Influence ... China?" 45.

53. W. A. P. Martin, *Evidences of Christianity* (Ningpo, 1854), 73a, 9. "a" refers to the first side of the double leaf and "9" to the line.

54. W. A. P. Martin, *Christianity and Other Creeds* (Tungchow, 1909), 80-81.

55. *Ibid.,* 81.

56. W. A. P. Martin, "Conversions En Masse," *The Chinese Recorder,* XL (November, 1909), 625-27.

57. *Ibid.,* 626-27.

58. *Ibid.*

59. Martin's proposal, unique for the day in which he lived, was apparently ignored as an old man's dream. A noted Chinese Christian, Lin Shao-yang, described it as a "peculiar policy." Lin Shao-yang, *A Chinese Appeal to Christendom Concerning Christian Missions* (New York, 1911), 12.

60. *The Chinese Recorder,* XXXIV (May, 1903), 240-41.

CHAPTER ELEVEN

Return to Missionary Life — Martin's Last Years in Peking, 1905-16

FOLLOWING APPROVAL by the Board of Foreign Missions of the Presbyterian Church, Martin returned to China early in 1906.[1] He was given the status of an "honorary missionary" with no salary and with freedom to work out his schedule in cooperation with his colleagues in China.[2]

As he came back to his adopted land he observed that "China is the theater of the greatest movement now taking place on the face of the globe."[3] This "awakening," he and others felt, had come with the fall of Peking in 1900.[4] The conservative Empress Dowager, fighting for her political life, was "converted to a policy of progress,"[5] and had instituted a wide variety of social, educational, and military reforms that provided the climate for many changes.

Japan's amazing victory over Russia in 1905 stimulated the Chinese government to investigate the constitutionalism which had worked so effectively in her rise to power. Martin, his memory of past tirades against old Jezebel weakened by age, praised the reign of the Empress Dowager, particularly its last six years, as "the most brilliant in the history of the Empire."[6] He specifically lauded the new freedom for women, wayside reading rooms for reform, changes in the penal code, freedom of newspapers to criticize the government, and educational reforms that had abolished the old civil service examinations and made it possible even for students who had studied abroad to receive the conventional degrees. He commended the government for sending abroad a commission to investigate foreign political systems.[7]

He also noted the many signs of physical improvement in both the new and the old city: new buildings, paved roads, electric lights on the streets, post boxes, and telephone wires, as well as railway and telegraph lines to many parts of the Empire.[8]

He was alarmed, however, that the government had instituted a policy seeking to revive Confucianism. In 1905 when the civil service examinations had been abolished to make way for a modern educational system, ceremonies had been introduced into all government schools and into the performance of civil duties in order to inculcate loyalty to Confucius, thus preserving the spirit of traditionalism within the new institutions. Martin viewed this deification of Confucius as a challenge to Christ, for, in his opinion, it debarred Christians from schools and from civil office.[9] He believed that until Chinese Christians were exempted from such disabilities, "the government of China must be branded as illiberal and oppressive."[10]

With characteristic zeal, Martin commenced a busy round of activities as "a self-supporting professor of things-in-general."[11] Preaching and lecturing stood high on his list of priorities.[12] He still held firmly to his Presbyterian convictions, but participated in cooperative endeavors whenever possible. In 1907 he observed that at Chinese New Year there had been a

> . . . sort of love feast between Protestants, Greek Catholics, and Roman Catholics — a Protestant pastor being in the Chair. The Apostles' Creed was recited as a basis of belief; the Lord's Prayer repeated by each in his own tongue and a doxology to the Holy Trinity sung in unison.[13]

He predicted that such cooperative efforts would lead to a "fuller manifestation of the Holy Spirit."[14]

Opportunities to lecture in other cities, usually on the subject of change in China, came frequently. The presence of friendly officials at these gatherings encouraged him to believe, probably erroneously, that they

> . . . would welcome the adoption of something better than the worn-out tenets of Buddhism or the negations of Confucius. They are in fact *coming to think of Jesus as the light of the World.* Their own great Sage can never be more than a local luminary.[15]

He stated that these potential believers from the official class "take their cue from the Court. Many secretly believe in Christ, but until some Constantine hoists the banner of the Cross they dare not make an open confession."[16]

During the twilight years of Martin's service in China literary work was as important to him as public speaking. Traveling back to China by ship, he had commenced work on his last major book, *The Awakening of China.*[17] Completed several months after his arrival, it was published in 1907 and received only a lukewarm welcome. Most reviewers made fun of his optimism, noting that he was still a "firm believer" but that in electing to support the Manchu government, a distinct change from what he had recommended in *Siege in Peking*, he was putting "his money on the wrong horse."[18] Another debunked his naive moral idealism and observed that the "regeneration of China is ultimately a question of whether she will ever be a first rate military power."[19]

These years, also filled with revising and reworking of previous works published both in English and Chinese, saw Martin's first publishing failure.[20] In 1912 he wrote *A History of the Revolution*, a manuscript intended to bring American readers up to date on the political revolution in China. Unlike anything he had written previously, it never saw the light of day.

The concept of a constitutional monarchy had ultimately been used to reinforce Manchu domination over the Chinese, and thus produced greater sympathy for revolutionary proposals that would replace the monarchy with a republic.[21] Sun Yat-sen, father of the Chinese Revolution, had been advocating this course of action since 1895. In 1905 he organized the *Chung-kuo t'ung-meng hui* (The Chinese United League), allying various Chinese revolutionary groups in a concerted effort that produced the Wuch'ang revolution of October 10, 1911, and led to the fall of the Manchu dynasty.[22] Sun Yat-sen was made the provisional president of the new republic, but yielded to Yüan Shih-k'ai, who was inaugurated to succeed him on March 10, 1912.[23]

Martin viewed these events as evidence that "God overrules the rise and fall of nations. . . ." Observing that the new government "favors the Holy Faith," he may have felt that Yüan Shih-k'ai was the Constantine for a Christian China.[24] He hurried, as he did when he wrote *Siege in Peking*, to rush something into print. E. L. Johnson, the Presbyterian missionary with whom Martin had been living since 1909, typed the manuscript while Martin dictated. When *A History of the Revolution* was completed, it was mailed to his son, Newell Martin, who was to arrange for its publication in New York. Martin's tremendous haste apparently resulted in an inferior work, and, much to his sorrow, it was rejected.[25]

This unpublished manuscript, now lost, undoubtedly shed much light on Martin's personal relationship with Yüan K'e-ting, the oldest son of President Yüan. Beginning in 1909, about the time when his father had been summarily dismissed from the Manchu government,[26] Yüan K'e-ting came to Martin's home three times a week for private instruction in political economy, international law, and the Bible.[27]

For Martin, a highlight of these years was his opportunity to attend the Centenary Missionary Conference at Shanghai in 1907. He had sent papers to be read at the two previous nation-wide conferences in 1877 and 1890 but had been unable to attend personally. This great gathering, which marked the anniversary of one hundred years of Protestant missionary work since the arrival of Robert Morrison in 1807, afforded him the opportunity to meet old friends, to reminisce on God's providence during the fifty-seven years he had been in China, and to bathe in the glory of being recognized as one of the "senior members" of the missionary family. He was appointed to serve on two committees: the Committee on Education and the Committee on the Translation of Memorials.[28]

Whenever possible he vigorously debated the issues presented to the various sub-committees. His views usually represented a controversial position. For example, he moved unsuccessfully to delete a statement in a resolution that "the influence of Christian [girls'] schools should be against the adoption of foreign dress and customs." He asked if the "ladies here are to put themselves in line with the eunuchs [who disliked a Parisian dress worn by the Empress Dowager] and object to Chinese women wearing *civilized* dress."[29] He supported a resolution made by Timothy Richard to ask churches in China to observe the Sunday before Christmas as Peace Sunday, but, still conscious of power politics, added as a reservation, "I am in favor of Christian nations having heavy armaments . . . [for] without such armaments, we as Christians would not be here to attend the conference."[30]

He saw three significant aspects to the conference. First, it was an expression of the essential unity among Christians. Second, it was a "moral force which the Chinese government cannot afford to neglect." Third, it was a "tremendous morale booster to missionaries and Christians throughout China."[31] A series of Memorials for presentation to the Throne were drawn up in the hope that Christians in China might be able to enjoy more than "qualified toleration." He commented that, "until freedom of conscience is secured, China ought to be made to feel that she is regarded by the civilized nations of the world as rather more than semi-barbarian."[32]

A new tendency of which Martin thoroughly approved was the spirit of independence among Chinese churches. Connected to the concept that nationalism should replace the old sense of cultural identity in China, he believed the movement to be salutary, for it would deliver the church from foreign control and remove it from suspicion of the anti-foreign rulers.[33]

Martin still worked actively for reform during his last years in China. In 1909 the International Reform Bureau, an organization formed in 1905 to promote moral reforms throughout the world, began its work in China. Martin and four others were selected to serve on the Council for North China.[34] The organization's heaviest guns were aimed at opium, but it also opposed liquor, cigarettes, and gambling.[35]

The International Reform Bureau issued tracts, printed articles in Chinese newspapers, and organized Anti-Opium societies in order to help China in her new "Opium War."[36] Members lectured on the evils of opium, and Martin, on at least one occasion, lectured on Commissioner Lin Tse-hsü, who had issued the famous memorandum on opium to Queen Victoria, from the scholarly platform of the Peking Oriental Society, as various efforts were undertaken to eliminate opium from Chinese society.[37] The Chino-American Society, organized in Peking late in 1912, also took a strong stand against its use.[38]

Even though Martin found it increasingly difficult to lecture or teach large groups, he prized many close, personal relationships with Chinese students. Each summer he lived at the "Pearl Grotto" and taught several small classes in both English and Chinese for an hour or two each day.

He often reflected on the great progress that the Presbyterian

Church in Peking had made since that day in 1863 when he had opened the first street chapel there. The Second Street Compound had grown to include six residences, a church building, the Douw hospital for women, a kindergarten, a girls' boarding school, and Truth Hall Academy, the boys' boarding school, whose facilities he had contributed to generously till their completion in 1916. The dormitories housed 150 students, and the buildings were equipped with steam heat, electric lights, and running water. There was another church and the Union Bible Institute, a cooperative enterprise staffed largely by Presbyterians, at the Drum Tower compound. Two other preaching centers with dispensaries and reading rooms also served as social centers.[39]

Political events still interested him, but no longer dominated his thinking as they once had. The rejection of his book on the Revolution had disappointed him, and, although he noted various watershed events such as Yüan's election as President of the Republic on October 11, 1913, in his private letters, he no longer published his political views.[40] Paul Reinsch, United States Minister to China from 1913 to 1919, observed that Martin, somewhat infirm with age, "did not closely follow the course of current events."[41]

Honors were heaped upon him during these last years. In a poll conducted by the Christian Literature Society previous to the China Centenary Conference, *Evidences of Christianity* received the most votes as "the best single book" published in Chinese.[42] On his eightieth birthday over sixty American friends — among them Woodrow Wilson, university presidents and professors, a major-general, and an admiral — presented him a scroll which read in part,

> We regard the influence of your strong personality, your relations with the Chinese people, your official services in positions of responsibility, your advice and counsel to men of high station in the Government, and your stalwart exemplification of the Christian spirit through long years of daily contact with students, officials, and the general community, as counting much toward the promotion of friendly international ties, and adding its full quota of stimulus to the unprecedented advance of the awakened, alert and progressive China of today.[43]

Martin remained physically strong and mentally alert till the time of his death. On his eightieth birthday he made a four-hour round trip to the Western hills by donkey, climbing one thousand feet to his favorite retreat, and did not seem to be tired.[44] A friend, Mrs. Ogilvie, commented that he was "a great believer in daily physical exercise and performed out on our lawn his exercise called 'Indian Dance' clothed in several pairs of pants during the cold weather."[45]

In 1916 Martin spent a busy summer at the "Pearl Grotto" and returned to Peking when the weather started to turn cool at the beginning of October. In early December he contracted bronchial pneumonia, and, although he rallied for a period, he slipped into a coma on December 15 and died on Sunday morning, December 17.[46]

The funeral service was conducted in Chinese, on December 18 at 10:30 A.M. in the Peking Presbyterian Church. Large numbers of his Chinese and foreign friends attended. General Chang, who had been Martin's student fifty-four years earlier, and Mr. Kiu, a government official, spoke of his unique contribution to the Chinese people.[47] Li Yüan-hung, the President of the Republic, sent his secretary to read a eulogy, which said in part,

> He enjoyed an exceptional popularity as well as the respect of the scholars and officials both in the government and elsewhere in the country. The passing away of a figure which has been regarded by scholars of this country as the T'ai Mountain, and the North Pole star, fills me with particular sorrow and grief. . . .[48]

For the graveside service, which was conducted in English, "the American Legation sent a mounted guard of eight soldiers who rode in front of the Army wagon covered with the American and Chinese flags belonging to Truth Hall, the school which Dr. Martin had founded."[49] He was buried beside the grave of his wife in the foreign cemetery outside the West gate of Peking.[50]

At his death W. A. P. Martin was "the senior in age and continuous service of all foreigners resident in China."[51] The length of his stay in the Celestial Empire — sixty-six years — was remarkable, but no less so than the quality and breadth of his influence. A notice in the Chinese *Peking Gazette* stated briefly, "Dr. Martin is dead, but he still lives, and may we not truly say that by his words, his writings and the lives which he has touched, he will live on in China forever and ever."[52]

Notes

1. When he was dismissed from his post at the Imperial University in March, 1902, many friends urged him to return to missionary work. News item, *North China Herald*, March 12, 1902, 470. Similar offers were extended to him when he completed his three years at Wuch'ang. China Letters of the Board of Foreign Missions of the Presbyterian Church in the United States of America, XI, Peking, Martin to Board, #47, November 25, 1905, and #33, August 27, 1906. China Letters are subsequently abbreviated "CL."

2. CL, XI, Peking, Martin to Board, #47, November 25, 1905. Nothing would indicate that in returning to Peking in his original role as a missionary, Martin was rejecting the validity of or need for the type of ministry he had carried on for the previous thirty-five years.

3. W. A. P. Martin, *The Awakening of China* (New York, 1907), preface. He was amazed at signs of modernization, he rejoiced at evidences of cooperation among Christian groups, and he was encouraged by signs of the progress of Christianity. The number of Protestant converts in China increased from 85,000 to 178,251 in the period from 1900 to 1906, a growth rate of over one hundred percent. By 1914 the number was placed at 235,303. Roman Catholics increased from 720,540 to 1,431,258 during the time from 1901 to 1914. Kenneth S. Latourette, *A History of Christian Missions in China* (London, 1929), 567.

4. Mary Clabaugh Wright, *China in Revolution: The First Phase, 1900-13* (New Haven, 1968), 2. She observed that "rarely in history has a single year marked as dramatic a watershed as did 1900 in China."

5. W. A. P. Martin, "Revolutionary Changes in China," *The World's Work*, XII (October, 1906), 8115.

6. Martin, *Awakening*, 199.

7. *Ibid.*, 213-16, 197.

8. CL, XI, Peking, Martin to Board, #18, April 18, 1906. Of new roads in the native city he commented, "Are they not unconsciously preparing a highway for the Lord?" Isaac Headland, *China's New Day* (West Medford, Mass., 1912), 7-13, commented that Emperor Kuang-hsü's personal curiosity symbolized modern improvements in Peking. The palace eunuchs bought him toys, Swiss watches, cuckoo clocks, and phonographs. A telegraph and telephone were installed in the Imperial Palace. A small railway was set up around the Lotus lake in the Palace grounds and small steamships operated in the Lotus lake and in the lake at the summer palace. Martin noted that the emperor had been taken with a "progressive fit." W. A. P. Martin, "China Transformed," *The World's Work*, XII (August, 1906), 7845.

9. CL, XI, Peking, Martin to Board, #55, November 17, 1907.

10. *Ibid.*

11. Arthur Smith, "The Nestor of Protestant Missionaries in China," *The Chinese Recorder,* XLI (April, 1910), 289.

12. He preached at the three Presbyterian chapels. His lectures in Comparative Religion, later published in Chinese as *Christianity and Other Creeds* (T'ien-tao ho-chiao), were given at the new Union Seminary in Peking. He was very happy to have even a small part in the North China Educational Union, which comprised six schools with responsibility shared by four mission societies. The College of Liberal Arts at Tungchow and The College for Women at Peking were run by the ABCFM. Lockhart Medical College in Peking was under the control of the LMS. The Methodists ran the Women's Medical College in Peking, and American Presbyterians were responsible for the Union Theological College in Peking and the Girls' School at Paotingfu. *A Brief Record of the Work of the North China Mission of the Presbyterian Church in the U.S.A., 1909-1910,* 6.

13. CL, Peking, Martin to Board, #14, March 4, 1908.

14. *Ibid.*

15. CL, XI, Peking, Martin to Board, #55, November 17, 1907.

16. W. A. P. Martin, "A Trip to Manchuria," *The Chinese Recorder,* XXXIX (January, 1908), 56.

17. CL, XI, Peking, Personal Reports, 1907; Martin to Board, #2, January 9, 1907.

18. Review of *The Awakening of China* in *Athenaeum,* October 12, 1907, 440.

19. Review of *The Awakening of China* in *The Nation,* July 18, 1907, 60.

20. He revised *Evidences of Christianity* in 1907 and again in 1913. CL, XI, Peking, Martin to Board, #2, January 9, 1907, and Martin, Annual Personal Report, 1913, 1. RG 82-5-12. In 1910 he revised *Chinese Legends and Other Poems,* which, in the enlarged version, was republished as *Chinese Legends and Lyrics.* In 1910 he wrote "a new book in English, *Reminiscences of a Long Life in Two Hemispheres,* to commemorate his sixtieth anniversary in China. This may well have been an expansion of his earlier *A Cycle of Cathay.* This work was never published and was apparently claimed by his son, Newell Martin, after his father's death in 1916. *A Brief Report of the Work of the North China Mission of the Presbyterian Church in the U.S.A., 1909-1910,* 15. Also in 1910, at the request of the Christian Literature Society, he prepared a Chinese work, *Hua-chia i-chi* (Retrospect of Sixty Years in the Far East), which was probably a translation of his English *Reminiscences. A Brief Report of the North China Mission . . . 1909-1910.* 15.

21. Immanuel C. Y. Hsü, *The Rise of Modern China* (New York, 1970), 493-501.

22. *Ibid.*, 540-58.

23. *Ibid.*, 558-63.

24. W. A. P. Martin, Annual Personal Report, 1913, 6. RG 82-5-12. He later observed that "whatever may have been his motive in assisting the progress of the churches, the president indicates thereby his desire to range himself on the side of Christendom." See CL, Miscellaneous, Martin to Board, #21, May 16, 1913. He was not so happy about Yüan's later efforts to "get Confucianism made a state religion." CL, Miscellaneous, Martin to Board, #22, October 17, 1913.

25. Norma Farquhar, "W. A. P. Martin and the Westernization of China" (unpublished M. A. Thesis, Indiana University, 1954), 209-10. She received this information by personal correspondence in 1953 with E. L. Johnson and Charles Corbett.

26. Hsü, *Modern China*, 500.

27. Arthur Brown, "The Death of the Rev. W. A. P. Martin," Minutes of the Board of Foreign Missions of the Presbyterian Church in the U.S.A., XXXIV, 321. Also see CL, Reel 256, Annual Personal Reports of Members of the North China Mission, 1909, Martin's Report, 1.

28. *Records of China Centenary Missionary Conference* (Shanghai, 1907), xxxv-vi.

29. *Ibid.*, 583. Italics mine.

30. *Ibid.*, 753.

31. CL, XI, Peking, Martin to Board, #11, March 1, 1907.

32. CL, XI, Peking, Martin to Board, #15, April 6, 1907.

33. *Ibid.*, and CL, XI, Peking, Martin to Board, #14, March 4, 1908.

34. Donald MacGillivray, *China Mission Year Book* (Shanghai, 1911), 444.

35. The International Reform Bureau organized general reform societies among the Chinese as well as more specific societies to deal with each vice. MacGillivray, *Year Book*, 444-45. It will be recalled that the opium trade was legalized by an agreement between Great Britain and China at the Shanghai Trade Conference in 1859. In subsequent years many attempts were made to reduce either the importation or the use of the drug but with little permanent effect. In August, 1906, a memorial of an earlier Anti-Opium League urging the government to restrict the use of opium was signed by 1200 missionaries of different nationalities and denominations and sent to the Throne. Possibly in response to this petition, the Chinese government issued an imperial edict on September 20, 1906, commanding that "within a limit of ten years this harmful muck be fully and entirely wiped out." Martin, *Awakening*, Appendix III, "A New Opium War," 302-6. Great Britain cooperated with China's desire and passed a Parliamentary action agreeing to reduce by ten percent each year

the amount of opium shipped into China from India. Hosea B. Morse, *The International Relations of the Chinese Empire* (3 vols.; New York, 1910), III, 437-39.

36. MacGillivray, *Year Book,* 443.

37. W. A. P. Martin, "The Opium War in China," *The Independent,* April 10, 1913, 815.

38. CL, Miscellaneous, Martin to Board, #20, January 8, 1913. RG 82-5-14.

39. *Report: Peking Presbyterian Mission* (Peking, 1917), 1-13. Protestant results in China did not seem much compared with the task to be done, but they gave some reason for limited hope. There were now 5,338 foreign missionaries, 20,460 Chinese ministers, teachers and evangelists, 3,880 churches with 330,926 members (a total Christian community of 750,000), 6,716 stations and outstations, 4,748 primary schools, 902 academies, colleges and industrial, medical, nurses' and naval schools, 330 hospitals and seventy-six special institutions such as orphanages, leper asylums, schools for the blind and deaf, and rescue homes for all types of needy people. Brown, "Death of Martin," 319.

40. CL, Miscellaneous, Martin to Board, #21, May 16, 1913, and #22, October 17, 1913.

41. Paul Reinsch, *An American Diplomat in China* (New York, 1922), 50.

42. Brown, "Death of Martin," 321-22.

43. Arthur Smith, "The Life and Work of the Late Dr. W. A. P. Martin," *The Chinese Recorder*, XLVIII (February, 1917), 122-23.

44. Smith, "The Nestor of Protestant Missionaries," 290.

45. Letter from Mrs. Charles Ogilvie to Norma Farquhar, November 12, 1953. Farquhar, "W. A. P. Martin," 212.

46. CL, Miscellaneous, A. M. Cunningham to Board, #11, December 28, 1916.

47. *The Finished Task.* Foreign Missionaries of the Presbyterian Church in the U.S.A. Who Entered Into Life During the Year April 1, 1916-March 31, 1917, 5-6.

48. Smith, "Life and Work of Martin," 123.

49. *The Finished Task*, 6.

50. "In Memoriam — The Rev. W. A. P. Martin, D.D., LL.D., of China," in North China Minutes, 1917. Appendix D.

51. *The Finished Task*, 3.

52. Quoted in John W. Foster, "An Appreciation of Dr. W. A. P. Martin," *Indiana University Alumni Quarterly*, January, 1917, 135.

Concluding Remarks

W. A. P. MARTIN was a "loner" with all the ambivalent characteristics of the pioneer. A man with boundless energy, a creative spirit, an iron will, and brilliant abilities as a teacher and writer, he was compulsive in his desire to find new frontiers — physical, religious, scientific, and educational — to cross. Unfortunately, when some of his innovations were resisted, he revealed a caustic intolerance of "conservative" opinions, took positions designed to accentuate differences with his colleagues, and sometimes deliberately provoked them. Impatient of those with minds less brilliant than his, he frequently showed an impetuous spirit given to hasty decisions and the articulation of only partly-developed ideas. He thought in broad, synthetic concepts that startled people with his imagination and creativity, but he sometimes found these concepts difficult to implement in any detailed, practical way.

From the mid-1860's, his whole life and ministry were directed toward reform in China, and his impact, whatever it was, was cumulative, not merely the result of a few isolated activities between 1895 and 1898. The abounding optimism he brought to all his efforts was both ideological and pragmatic. God's control of history and the power of the Christian faith, he insisted, left no room for a defeatist spirit. The rise of God's Zion on the Indiana frontier as well as in the islands of the far Pacific convinced him that the Church improved the lot of mankind. Millennial expectations apparently did not contribute to his bright hopes for China. He believed in demonic forces of evil but not in a personal Satan — a tenet which he felt "deepens the gloom of a world which is

271

already dark enough."[1] His spirit was naturally exuberant and he exuded optimism, almost to the point of naiveté, in every venture he undertook.

In interpreting Chinese and Americans to each other, Martin trod new intellectual paths. Presenting his Christian convictions to the Chinese, he combined traditional dogma, derived both from the Bible and the Presbyterian Confession of Faith, with the philosophic assumptions of Stewart, Reid, Paley, and other apologists. He believed that God had revealed himself to all mankind in a general way, and this conviction enabled him to relate effectively to Chinese beliefs, particularly those expressed in Confucianism. Although this approach appealed to many Chinese intellectuals, the historian Joseph Levenson has wondered if it was really all that effective. Speaking of the earlier Jesuit efforts to do the same thing, he commented that

> This tactic . . . was self-defeating; in effect, it authorized the potential convert to see in the foreign church organization, and in its foreign-composed Scriptures, at best vessels of the truth which must also exist in his own historical inheritance.[2]

Martin's unique contribution was that the strands of his thought were clearly identifiable, that he systematized in written form what others were only talking about, and that he projected to the Chinese the image of a tolerant scholar ready to build his faith within the context of their "heavenly doctrine."[3] The *message* of his *Evidences of Christianity* was that civilization, no matter how highly developed, did not necessarily lead to true morality or to salvation. The *paramessage* for the nineteenth century, particularly when communicated in a confused China by an American missionary who embodied and taught the virtues of an alien culture, could only be that the Christian faith and Western civilization were inextricably linked. One could not be had without the other. In one respect, this was a beneficial concept. The Christian faith was not presented in a vacuum but was integrally related to all of life. But in another respect, it was tragic. The power of Western civilization was implicitly used to coerce faith. Chinese achievements, no matter how deeply rooted in antiquity, were seen as inferior to those of the West. What the missionary meant to preach about — the equality of all people before one God — was not what the Chinese heard.

As he elaborated on various facets of Western civilization in his more specialized books and in the *Peking Magazine,* Martin proclaimed a more explicitly fragmented message. Western science, law, and technical "know-how" were presented as inherently valuable, but hardly anything was said about the need for a religious foundation. Many sorts of facts — moral, scientific, economic, and political — were linked to the *t'ien-tao* ("heavenly doctrine"), but this, unaccompanied by other information, was hardly sufficient to lead a Chinese reader to an integrated view of life. At best it left him with his Chinese essence and Western techniques. The messages, then, of Martin's Chinese publications were not completely consistent, nor were they harmonious, at least in paramessage, with his own aim to produce salvation and modernity in the context of the Chinese world view. He claimed that he desired Chinese Christianity, but both his activities and interpretation tended to project Western Christianity.

One writer has commented that Martin "gave the Chinese officials, scholars, as well as the common people, what he knew to be best for them at the time, *whether they desired it or not.*"[4] The assumption of superior knowledge accompanied by a patronizing posture toward the Chinese, determining even what they ought to desire, was characteristic of Martin's age, when "agents of change," even the most enlightened pioneers, did not yet realize the necessity of meeting the "felt needs" of people.

In interpreting China to his missionary colleagues, Martin broke new ground to the extent that he urged accommodation to the ancestral cult and to the Confucian rites. His greatest contribution, at best only tolerated by most of his friends, was his open, liberal spirit.[5] His colleagues recognized that his faith, basically unchanged through the years, was evangelical, although, at one time or another, he was accused of heretical views on the doctrine of the Trinity. His denial of a personal devil and his drift toward a concept of theistic evolution under the impact of Darwinism[6] never seem to have elicited unfavorable reaction. In this respect, he was different from Young J. Allen or Timothy Richard whose readiness to accommodate to Chinese views or to participate in what some perceived as non-religious activities was more rooted in expanding theological views. His faith was as evangelical in content as that of most other missionaries of his day, and in private letters he frequently appeared even bigoted and narrow, but he was more sensitive in the way he communicated it publicly.

A critical comparison of Martin's Chinese works with those directed toward American audiences reveals several things. First, only a portion of the material was similar in nature, since it was directed to different audiences and with different aims. For example, when writing for Chinese consumption he encouraged the development of industry and commerce, but seldom emphasized this in his English works. Second, where the content was substantially the same, as in his discussion of the ancestral cult, his English writings, possibly intended to rile his colleagues, often seemed to be more tolerant than what he wrote in Chinese. This appearance may be related to the fact that, writing in Chinese, he used a very polite style that would be as inoffensive as possible, while what he said in English tended to wave red religious flags. Third, his Chinese apologetic works clearly showed his readiness to accept some of the conclusions of the Darwinian hypothesis, an emphasis not at all present in his English books or articles. Fourth, his emphasis upon progress — spiritual salvation and material reform — occurred in all his work, although there was less implied or explicit criticism of Chinese customs in his Chinese writings.

Fifth, his Chinese work, from the present perspective, was "overloaded" with information. His English material, although couched in the rhetoric of the nineteenth century, did much better in this respect. He probably overestimated his Chinese audience's ability to digest the rich diet he was feeding it. He sought to avoid this by organizing his basic Chinese books in catechetical formats, but even then there was probably less communication going on than he realized. Sixth, he projected the image of a scholar, familiar with the background and needs of his respective audiences, in both sets of writing, self-consciously emphasizing titles, degrees, and authorship.

W. A. P. Martin lived and thought in a day when complex and probably irresistible internal and external forces were taking China down the path of reform, nationalism, and revolution. A product of an age with a unified world view, he saw the "hand of God" in all of these changes and sought to be God's agent to bring about what was best for China. In the process he became more the agent and interpreter of an alien culture than of the Biblical faith. In his failure to consistently perceive any distinction between the two he symbolizes the ambiguities of any agent of change and the continued complexity of cross-cultural communication.

Notes

1. W. A. P. Martin, *The Chinese, Their Education, Philosophy and Letters* (New York, 1881), 165.

2. Joseph R. Levenson, *Confucian China and Its Modern Fate: A Trilogy* (Berkeley, 1968), I, 119. One of Levenson's arguments is that both accommodation and non-accommodation had advantages and disadvantages. He claimed that Chinese intellectuals first rejected Christianity because it was untraditional and then because it was unscientific. In other words, Christianity and the missionary were caught up in historical processes and forces beyond their ability to control. Whether they did or did not accommodate was ultimately of little significance to the total fate of their work and message.

3. He did not seek "common ground" with Confucianism or Buddhism but a "point of contact" that utilized terms and concepts as a framework that made communication possible.

4. "In Memoriam — The Rev. W. A. P. Martin, D.D., LL.D., of China," in North China Minutes, 1917. Appendix D, 2.

5. The historian Paul Cohen has asked, "Can a missionary be genuinely tolerant of a society which, to a greater or lesser extent, he wishes to change?" *China and Christianity: The Missionary Movement and the Growth of Chinese Anti-Foreignism* (Cambridge, Mass., 1963), 81. The same question can be directed to a diplomat or a Peace Corps volunteer.

6. Albert Porter, "A Prophet of Progress," *The World's Work*, XII (May, 1906), 7577. "He lived through and was influenced by the doctrinal cataclysms of the Darwinian theories, but at all times he has held to the almost primitive zeal of the fathers of the church." Porter made this observation on the basis of a personal conversation with Martin. Tendencies toward theistic evolution have been noted in both *Evidences of Christianity* and *Christianity and Other Creeds*, Martin's two most notable Christian Chinese books.

Bibliography

Addresses at the China Centenary Missionary Conference. Shanghai: Methodist Publishing House, 1907.

Annual Reports of the Board of Foreign Missions of the Presbyterian Church in the United States of America. These commenced with the First Annual Report in 1837 and continued through the Seventy-Ninth Report in 1916.

Annual Reports of the Chinese Religious Tract Society. Shanghai: American Presbyterian Press, 1878-1916.

Annual Reports of the North China Tract Society for 1884, 1897, 1908 and 1910.

Annual Reports of the Peking Presbytery from 1901-1910. Some of these have been collected with incoming letters on microfilm. Others, largely after 1907, are included with files of incoming letters, and some have been printed in separate booklets.

Annual Reports of the Society for the Diffusion of Christian and General Knowledge Among the Chinese. From the Tenth Report in 1897 to the Twenty-Fifth Report in 1919. Shanghai.

Anson Burlingame Papers. Manuscript Division. Library of Congress, Washington, D. C.

Barnett, Suzanne W. "Protestant Expansion and Chinese Views of the West." *Modern Asian Studies,* VI (April, 1972), 129-49.

_____. "Silent Evangelism: Presbyterians and the Mission Press in China, 1807-1860." *Journal of the Presbyterian Historical Society,* XLIX (Winter, 1971), 287-302.

Beaver, R. Pierce. "Eschatology in American Missions." *Basileia. Walter Freytag zum 60 Geburtstag.* Edited by Von Jan Hermelink and Hans J. Margull. Stuttgart: Evang. Missionsverlag GMBH, 1959. 60-75.

Bennett, Adrian A. *John Fryer: The Introduction of Western Science and Technology into Nineteenth-Century China.* Cambridge, Mass.: Harvard University Press, 1967.

_____. "Missionary Journalism in 19th Century China: Young J. Allen and the Early Wan-kuo kung-pao, 1868-1883." Unpublished Ph. D. dissertation, University of California at Davis, 1970.

Bible Society Record of the American Bible Society.

Biggerstaff, Knight. *The Earliest Modern Government Schools in China.* Ithaca: Cornell University Press, 1961.

_____. "Shanghai Polytechnic Institute and Reading Room: An Attempt to Introduce Western Science and Technology to the Chinese." *Pacific Historical Review,* XXV (May, 1956), 127-49.

_____. "The T'ung-wen Kuan." *The Chinese Social and Political Science Review,* XVIII (October, 1934), 307-40.

Boardman, Eugene, *Christian Influence Upon the Ideology of the Taiping Rebellion, 1851-1864.* Madison: University of Wisconsin Press, 1952.

Boggs, Mary. "William Alexander Parsons Martin. Missionary to China, 1850-1916." Unpublished M. A. thesis, McCormick Theological Seminary, 1948.

British Parliamentary Papers. LXIX (1860), China: State Paper 2685, 1.

Britton, Roswell S. *The Chinese Periodical Press, 1800-1912.* Shanghai: Kelly and Walsh, 1933.

Brown, Arthur J. *One Hundred Years. A History of the Foreign Mission Work of the Presbyterian Church in the U.S.A.* New York: Revell, 1936.

_____. "Rev. W. A. P. Martin, D.D. of China." *The Missionary Review of the World,* New Series XL (March, 1917), 195-202.

Calendar of the Tungwen College. First Issue. Peking: Published by Authority, 1879.

Cameron, Meribeth. *The Reform Movement in China, 1898-1912.* New York: Octagon Books, 1963.

Catalogue of the Presbyterian Mission Library, Ningpo. Ningpo: Presbyterian Mission Press, 1851.

Chinese Recorder, 1886-1916.

Chinese Repository, 1832-1851.

Ch'ou-pan i-wu-shih-mu. Management of Barbarian Affairs. Material concerning W. A. P. Martin may be found in Hsien-feng, XL, 23b2 and in T'ung-chih, XXVII, 25b5,b9;26a,7; XXXI, 4a,4b8,4b9 and 5a1; LXXV, 14a10,14b7; LXXXVIII, 18b5,19a.

The Chronicle of the London Missionary Society.

The Church Missionary Intelligencer, The Church Missionary Record and *The Church Missionary Gleaner* of the Church Missionary Society for the 1850-1860 period at Ningpo.

Clark, Minnie B. "The Old Log College at Livonia." *Indiana Magazine of History,* XXIII (March, 1927), 73-81.

Cohen, Paul. *China and Christianity: The Missionary Movement and the Growth of Chinese Anti-Foreignism.* Cambridge, Mass.: Harvard University Press, 1963.

_____. "Missionary Approaches: Hudson Taylor and Timothy Richard." *China Papers,* XI (1957), 29-62.

Cranston, Earl. "The American Missionary's Outlook on China, 1830-1860." Unpublished Ph. D. dissertation, Harvard University, 1930.

Curtis, Ray Canning. "Samuel Wells Williams: A Party to Impacts." Unpublished B. A. Honors thesis, Harvard University, 1968.

Davidson, Robert. *History of the Presbyterian Church in the State of Kentucky.* New York: Robert Carter, 1847.

Dean, William. *The China Mission.* New York: Shedon and Company, 1859.

De Bary, William T., Wing-tsit Chan, and Burton Watson, eds., *Sources of Chinese Tradition.* Two Volumes. New York: Columbia University Press, 1960.

De Francis, John. *Nationalism and Language Reform in China.* Princeton: Princeton University Press, 1950.

Despatches from the State Department. Legation Archives. China.

Deveria, G. "Histoire du Collège des Interprètes de Peking." In *Mélanges Charles De Harlez.* Leyden: E. J. Brill, 1896.

Diplomatic Despatches. China. This is Record Group 57, M 92 Series.

Diplomatic Despatches from the U.S. Consuls in Ningpo, 1853-1896. Volume I, October 1, 1853-July 15, 1864.

Diplomatic Despatches from the U.S. Consuls in Tientsin, No. 220, May 7, 1897.

Duus, Peter. "Science and Salvation in China: The Life and Work of W. A. P. Martin." In Liu, Kwang-ching (ed.), *American Missionaries in China.* Cambridge: Harvard University Press, 1966. 11-41.

_____. "Science and Salvation in China: The Life and Mission of William Alexander P. Martin, 1827-1917." Unpublished A. B. Honors thesis, Harvard University, 1955.

Ekirch, Arthur A. *The Idea of Progress in America, 1815-1860.* New York: Peter Smith, 1951.

Ellsbree, Oliver Wendell. *The Rise of the Missionary Spirit in America,*

1790-1815. Williamsport, Pa.: The Williamsport Printing and Binding Company, 1928.

Fairbank, John K. *Trade and Diplomacy on the China Coast: The Opening of the Treaty Ports, 1842-1854.* Cambridge: Harvard University Press, 1953.

_____. "Patterns Behind the Tientsin Massacre." *Harvard Journal of Asiatic Studies,* XX (December, 1957), 480-511.

Farquhar, Norma. "A Bibliography of the Writings of W. A. P. Martin." *China Papers,* X (Cambridge, 1956), 128-41.

_____. "W. A. P. Martin and the Westernization of China." Unpublished M. A. thesis, Indiana University, 1954.

The Finished Task. Foreign Missionaries of the Presbyterian Church in the United States of America Who Entered Into Life During the Year April 1, 1916-March 31, 1917.

Fisher, Daniel W. *Calvin Wilson Mateer: Forty-Five Years a Missionary in Shantung, China.* Philadelphia: The Westminster Press, 1911.

_____. *The Story of the Seminary* in *McCormick Theological Seminary — Historical Celebration.* Chicago, 1910.

Fitch, G. F. "Note on Dismissal of Faculty at Imperial University." *The Chinese Recorder,* XXXIII (March, 1902), 140.

_____. "Notes on 'The Worship of Confucius.' " *The Chinese Recorder,* XXXIV (February, 1903), 93-94.

The Foreign Missionary Chronicle of the Presbyterian Church in the U.S.A. for the late 1840's.

The Foreign Missionary of the Presbyterian Church in the U.S.A. for the 1850's and 1860's.

Forsythe, Sidney. *An American Missionary Community in China, 1895-1905.* Cambridge, Mass.: Harvard University Press, 1971.

Foster, John W. "An Appreciation of Dr. W. A. P. Martin." *Indiana University Alumni Quarterly,* January, 1917, 129-35.

Franke, Wolfgang. *China and the West.* New York: Harper, 1967.

John Fryer Collection in Bancroft Library, University of California, Berkeley, California.

Garritt, J. C. "Protest of Martin's Views on Ancestor Worship." *The Chinese Recorder,* XXXIII (April, 1902), 201.

Goodykoontz, Colin B. *Home Missions on the American Frontier.* Caldwell, Idaho: The Caxton Printers, 1939.

Gregg, Alice. *China and Educational Autonomy. The Changing Role of the Protestant Educational Missionary in China, 1807-1937.* New York: Syracuse University Press, 1946.

Halsey, LeRoy J. *A History of McCormick Theological Seminary of the Presbyterian Church.* Chicago: The Seminary, 1893.

Harris Collection in Archives of Indiana University Library in Bloomington, Indiana. This consists of miscellaneous letters from Mrs. Samuel Martin, sister-in-law to W. A. P. Martin, to her father, Andrew Wylie, her mother, and other relatives.

Hart, Robert. *The Peking Legations: A National Uprising and International Episode.* Shanghai: Kelly and Walsh, 1900.

Hills, Margaret T. "Text and Translation: Languages of China, 1861-1900." Available at the American Bible Society, New York, New York.

The Home and Foreign Record of the Presbyterian Church in the U.S.A. for the 1850's and 1860's.

House Executive Documents, 33rd Congress, 1st Session (1853-54), XVI, No. 123.

Hsü, Immanuel C. Y. *The Rise of Modern China.* New York: Oxford University Press, 1970.

_____. *China's Entrance into the Family of Nations.* Cambridge, Mass.: Harvard University Press, 1960.

Instructions and Despatches of U.S. Government, 1843-76. Record Group 84.

Johnson, James. *A Historical Discourse presenting Facts Respecting the Progress of Presbyterianism in the State During That Period.* Indianapolis: Holloway, Douglas and Company, 1865.

Journal of the Peking Oriental Society, IV (1898), 143-44.

Kellen, William V. *Henry Wheaton: An Appreciation.* Boston: Merrymount Press, 1902.

Kensinger, Keith A. *Pilgrims Under God.* Salem, Indiana: Boling Press, 1966.

Kidder, D. P. *Notices of Fu-chau and the Other Open Ports of China.* New York: Jane and Tippett, 1848.

Latourette, Kenneth S. *A History of Christian Missions in China.* London: Society for Promoting Christian Knowledge, 1929.

Letters by W. A. P. Martin to the Corresponding Secretary of the Foreign Mission Board of the Presbyterian Church in the United States of America, and from him to Martin. They include the following periods: Ningpo, 1849-1860; Shanghai, 1860-1863; Peking, 1863-1869; 1905-1916.

Letters by Martin's colleagues to the Board and letters from the Board to them during those periods when Martin was associated with the Presbyterian Board.

Letters by W. A. P. Martin to Young J. Allen.

Letters by W. A. P. Martin to the American Bible Society and kept on file at their headquarters in New York, New York.

Letters from W. A. P. Martin in the Henry Francis du Pont Winterthur Collection of Manuscripts at Eleutherian Mills Historical Library.

Letters by W. A. P. Martin to John Fryer in the Fryer Collection at Bancroft Library, University of California, Berkeley, California.

Letters by W. A. P. Martin to W. D. Whitney in the W. D. Whitney Collection at Sterling Memorial Library, Yale University.

Letters by W. A. P. Martin to Samuel Wells Williams in the Williams Family Collection at Sterling Memorial Library, Yale University.

Letters from missionaries with the American Board of Commissioners for Foreign Missions (ABCFM) to the Foreign Mission Board concerning Martin or some aspect of his work. These are in Houghton Library, Harvard University, and filed under ABCFM Records, North China Mission, A.B.C.:16.3.12.

Levenson, Joseph R. *Confucian China and Its Modern Fate: A Trilogy.* Berkeley: University of California Press, 1968.

Lindbeck, John. "American Missionaries and Policies of the United States in China, 1898-1901." Unpublished Ph. D. dissertation, Yale University, 1948.

Littell, John B. "Missionaries and Politics in China — The Taiping Rebellion." *Political Science Quarterly,* XLIII (December, 1928), 566-99.

Liu, Kwang-ching. "Early Christian Colleges in China." *The Journal of Asian Studies,* XX (November, 1960), 71-78.

_____. *Americans and Chinese: A Historical Essay and a Bibliography.* Cambridge: Harvard University Press, 1963.

_____ , ed., *American Missionaries in China.* Cambridge: Harvard University Press, 1966.

Lü, Shih-ch'iang. *Chung-kuo kuan-shen fan-chiuo ti yüan-yin* (The Origin and Cause of the Anti-Christian Movement Among the Chinese Officials and Gentry, 1860-74). Taipei, Taiwan, 1966.

Lund, Renville C. "The Imperial University of Peking." Unpublished Ph.D. dissertation, University of Washington, 1957.

Lutz, Jessie G. *China and the Christian Colleges 1850-1950.* Ithaca: Cornell University Press, 1971.

_____ , ed., *Christian Missions in China: Evangelists of What?* Boston: D. C. Heath and Company, 1965.

Martin, Jane. "Tartar Women Hearing the Gospel in Peking." *The Foreign Missionary,* XXV (April, 1866), 276-78.

Martin, W. A. P.

    1. Books by W. A. P. Martin.

Hanlin Papers or *Essays on the Intellectual Life of the Chinese.* First Series. Shanghai: Kelly and Walsh, 1880. Also published by London: Trubner and Company, 1880. This work was republished in a revised edition as *The Chinese, Their Education, Philosophy and Letters.* New York: Harper and Brothers, 1881.

Hanlin Papers. Second Series. Shanghai: Kelly and Walsh, 1894. This is a revision and expansion of some of the material in the first series with a few new essays.

Chinese Legends and Other Poems. Shanghai: Kelly and Walsh, 1894. A second edition with thirty-six more pages was published by Kelly and Walsh in 1912 as *Chinese Legends and Lyrics.*

A Cycle of Cathay or *China South and North with Personal Reminiscences.* Third Edition. New York: Fleming H. Revell, 1900.

The Lore of Cathay or *The Intellect of China.* Second Edition. New York: Fleming H. Revell, 1912. This book is a revised and expanded version of the *Hanlin Papers,* first and second series.

Siege in Peking. New York: Fleming H. Revell, 1900.

The Analytical Reader: A Short Method for Learning to Read and Write Chinese. Shanghai: Presbyterian Mission Press, 1863.

The Awakening of China. New York: Doubleday, Page and Company, 1907.

2. Articles by Martin, arranged alphabetically according to title of publication, and chronologically under each publication.

"Notes on China." *American Journal of Science,* XLVII (1869), 98-103.

"The Speculative Philosophy of the Chinese." *American Journal of Theology,* I (April, 1872), 234-48.

"Chinese Versions of the Bible." *Bible Society Record,* VIII (July, 1863), 108-9.

"The Late Rev. W. T. Morrison." *The Chinese Recorder,* II (April, 1870), 305.

"The Metric System for China." *CR,* V (March-April, 1874), 56-66, 112.

"Traces of International Law in Ancient China." *CR,* XIV (Sept.-Oct., 1883), 380-93.

"Dr. Mateer's Geography — A Review." *CR,* XVII (August, 1886), 314-15.

"The Northern Barbarians in Ancient China." *CR*, XVII (April, 1886), 125-37.

"The Native Tract Literature of China." *CR*, XVIII (Sept., 1887), 329-34, and (Oct., 1887), 369-74.

"Hodge on the Epistle to the Romans — A Review." *CR*, XIX (July, 1888), 322-23.

"Is Buddhism a Preparation for Christianity?" *CR*, XX (May, 1889), 193-203.

"The Archimandrite Palladius." *CR*, XX (Oct., 1889), 449-54.

"The Late Mrs. Dr. Martin." *CR*, XXIV (June, 1893), 286-87.

"Curriculum of Chinese Studies for the Use of Young Missionaries." *CR*, XXV (August, 1894), 365-67.

"Li Hung-chang As a Patron of Education." *CR*, XXVII (Dec., 1896), 576-78.

"A Plea for the Romanizing of Local Dialects." *CR*, XXXIII (Jan., 1902), 18-19.

"The Imperial University, Peking." *CR*, XXXIII (March, 1902), 143-44.

"How Shall We Deal With the Worship of Ancestors?" *CR*, XXXIII (March, 1902), 117-19.

"The Worship of Confucius — Is It Idolatry?" *CR*, XXXIV (Feb., 1903), 92-94.

"Notes on Schereschewsky's Bible in Chinese." *CR*, XXXIV (March, 1903), 148-49.

"Remarks of Momo, a Native Christian, on the Preaching of Missionaries." *CR*, XXXIV (May, 1903), 240-41. Translated.

"The Other Wise Men." *CR*, XXXIV (Nov., 1903), 564-65.

"A Brother's Tribute." *CR*, XXXV (March, 1904), 134-35.

"The Worship of Ancestors, How Shall We Deal With It?" *CR*, XXXV (June, 1904), 301-8.

"On the Use of English in Mission Schools." *CR*, XXXV (Nov., 1904), 576.

"A Term for 'Protestant'." *CR*, XXXV (Nov., 1904), 575.

"A Term for 'Protestant'. Dr. Martin's Rejoinder." *CR*, XXXVI (Feb., 1905), 86.

"Reform in Etiquette Called For." *CR*, XXXVI (March, 1905), 141-43.

"To the Memory of the Rev. J. L. Whiting, D.D." *CR*, XXXVII (Oct., 1906), 556-57.

"A Plea for Romanization." *CR*, XXXVIII (Sept., 1907), 501-2.

"A Trip to Manchuria." *CR*, XXXIX (Jan., 1908), 55-56.

"A Review of *China's Treaty Relations* by Gilbert Reid." *CR*, XXXIX (Sept., 1908), 515-16.

"A Tribute to Dr. Mateer." *CR*, XXXIX (Dec., 1908), 694.

"A Review of *Peru: Its Story, People and Religion* by Geraldine Guinness." *CR*, XL (April, 1909), 228.

"Conversions En Masse." *CR*, XL (Nov., 1909), 625-27.

"Mrs. J. L. Nevius — A Tribute." *CR*, XLI (Aug., 1910), 694.

"A Review of *Confucian Classics* by Dr. Woods." *CR*, XLI (Aug., 1910), 564-65.

"Song of the Tea Kettle." *CR*, XLII (Sept., 1911), 541.

"A Review of *Life of Dr. F. F. Ellinwood* by his Daughter." *CR*, XLIII (April, 1912), 247-48.

"A Review of *Shantung: The Sacred Province of China*." *CR*, XLIII (Oct., 1912), 612-13.

"The Intellectual Wants of the Chinese — A Plea for Education in China." *The Church at Home and Abroad*, IX (Feb., 1891), 143-46.

"Does China Menace the World?" *The Forum*, IX (Dec., 1890), 433-41.

"As the Chinese See Us." *The Forum*, X (Feb., 1891), 678-88.

"The Boy's Legacy." *The Foreign Missionary*, XX (Sept., 1861), 113-14.

"Return to China." *FM*, XXI (Dec., 1862), 210-11.

"Encouragement at Shanghai." *FM*, XXII (Sept., 1863), 103-4.

"Journal of a Trip to Peking." *FM*, XXIII (Jan., 1864), 201-4.

"Missionaries in the Capital of China." *FM*, XXIII (May, 1864), 300-3.

"Missionary Matters at Peking, China." *FM*, XXIII (July, 1864), 52-53.

"Progress at Peking." *FM*, XXIII (Oct., 1864), 122-25.

"Something About the Little Emperor." *FM*, XXIII (Dec., 1864), 175.

"Scenes in Peking." *FM*, XXIV (Jan., 1865), 196-97.

"The Temples of Peking." *FM*, XXIV (Dec., 1865), 176-77.

"Notes of an Inland Journey from Peking to Shanghai — Including a Visit to the Jews in Honan." *FM*, XXV (Oct., 1866), 140-42; XXV (Dec., 1866), 184-87; XXVI (Feb., 1867), 239-42; XXVI (March, 1867), 266-68; and XXVI (April, 1867), 290-92.

"A Chinese Prayer Meeting at Peking." *FM*, XXVII (July, 1868), 46.

"Shanghai." *FM,* XXVII (Dec., 1868), 165-68.

"Thoughts Suggested by the Map of China." *FM,* XXVIII (Feb., 1869), 210-13.

"The Prince of Kung." *Harper's New Monthly Magazine,* XXXII (April, 1866), 584-86.

"Early Chinese Inventions." *Harper's New Monthly Magazine,* XXXIX (November, 1869), 909-12.

"A Missionary Geography Needed." *The Home and Foreign Record,* II (March, 1851), 51-52.

"Journal of W. A. P. Martin." *Record,* IV (July, 1853), 209-10.

"Narrative of a Visit to the District of Funghwa." *Record,* V (February, 1854), 48-49.

"Extracts from the Journal of Rev. W. A. P. Martin." *Record,* VI (August, 1855), 244-45, and VI (December, 1855), 372-73.

"Taiping Rebellion." *Record,* VII (December, 1856); VIII (January, 1857), 20-22, and VIII (February, 1857), 51-55.

"Recent Treaty." *Record,* IX (November, 1858), 338-40.

"Notes of a Visit to the Capital of Chekiang." *Record,* IX (April, 1859), 114-18.

"Interesting Examination of Two Young Men With Reference to Licensure to Teach." *Record,* XI (May, 1860), 148-49.

"Visit of the Rev. W. A. P. Martin to Nagasaki." *Record,* XI (March, 1860), 78-81, and XI (April, 1860), 110-17.

"Journal of the Rev. William A. P. Martin, D.D., at Peking." *Record,* XV (March, 1864), 59-60.

"Rebellion in North China." *The Record of the Presbyterian Church in the United States of America,* September, 1868, 211-12.

"The Fall of Peking." *The Independent* (October 11, 1900), 2419-21.

"Life at the Hills Near Peking." *The Independent* (September 19, 1901), 2216-17.

"Reforms in China — A New Council of State." *The Independent* (October 31, 1901), 2566-67.

"A Tribute to Li Hung Chang." *The Independent* (December 26, 1901), 3065.

"The Opium War in China." *The Independent* (April 10, 1913), 815.

"The Ethical Philosophy of the Chinese." *Journal of the American Oriental Society,* VII Proceedings (October, 1861), xlv. Other remarks by Martin are found in xlviii-xlix.

"Miscellaneous Comments on Reform." *JAOS,* Proceedings (October 14-15, 1868).

"The Early Inventions of the Chinese." *JAOS*, IX Proceedings (May, 1869), liv-v. Condensed version.

"On the Competitive Examination System in China." *JAOS*, IX Proceedings (May, 1869). Condensed version.

"On Chinese Ideas of Inspiration." *JAOS*, XV Proceedings (October, 1890), lxxvi-lxxviii. Condensed version.

"On Reformed Buddhism in China and Japan." *JAOS*, XV Proceedings (October, 1890), lxxv. Condensed version. Reprinted in *The Indian Antiquary: A Journal of Oriental Research*, XI (October, 1882), 294-95.

"On Chinese Anticipations of Certain Ideas of Modern Science." *JAOS*, XVI Proceedings (April, 1895), ccx-ccxiii.

"Translation of the Devotional Portion." *Journal of the North China Branch of the Royal Asiatic Society*, XXIII (January, 1888), 34-38.

"The Jewish Monument at Kaifungfu." *JNCBRAS*, XXXVII (1906), 1-12.

"Presidential Address." *Journal of the Peking Oriental Society*, I (May, 1886), 190-93.

"The Study of Chinese History." *JPOS*, I (1886), 121-38.

"On Two Inscriptions Obtained in Japan." *JPOS*, III (1893), 259-64.

"Chinese Discoveries in the Arts and Sciences." *JPOS*, IV (1898), 19-28, 147-48.

"The Religious Attitude of the Chinese Mind." *The Missionary Review of the World*, New Series IV (April, 1891), 296-301.

"The Empress Dowager of China." *MRW*, New Series IX (January, 1896), 101-6.

"An African Pioneer." *MRW*, New Series IX (June, 1896), 449-51.

"Relation of the Chinese Government to Missions." *MRW*, New Series IX (August, 1896), 608-9.

"Attitude of the Chinese Government Toward Christian Missions." *MRW*, New Series IX (November, 1896), 842-46.

"Western Science as Auxiliary to the Spread of the Gospel." *MRW*, New Series X (October, 1897), 769-73.

"Remarks on 'Letters from a Chinese Official'." *MRW*, New Series XVIII (February, 1905), 104-8.

"The Causes That Led to the Siege of Peking." *National Geographic Magazine*, XII (February, 1901), 53-63.

"Remarks on the Style of Chinese Prose." *New Englander* (April, 1872), 234-48.

"News on Treaties in North China." *New York Times*, September 23, October 12, October 20, 1858, and November 23, 1859.

"China News." *NYT*, June 15, 1863.

"Peking News." *NYT*, January 8, 1864.

"Lay-Osborn Flotilla." *NYT*, January 30, 1864. Signed "Q."

"The Cooperative Policy." *NYT*, April 23, 1864. Signed "Q."

"Fall of Nanking." *NYT*, December 18, 1864.

"Downfall of Prince Kung." *NYT*, April 18, 1865.

"The Chinese Embassy," *NYT*, August 27, 1866. Signed "Q."

"Inland Journey from Peking to Shanghai." *NYT*, August 29, 1866.

"A Colony of Jews." *NYT*, October 22, 1866.

"The Rivers of China." *NYT*, May 23, 1867.

"A University in Peking." *NYT*, September 4, 1867.

"The University of Peking." *NYT*, September 6, 1867.

"Rebellion in the North." *NYT*, October 1, 1867.

"The Chinese Embassy," *NYT*, February 18, 1868.

"Court and Camp." *NYT*, June 8, 1868.

"The Chinese Rebellion." *NYT*, June 17, 1868.

"The Chinese Embassy." *NYT*. A series of six long letters under this title written from New Haven under the pseudonym of "Perry Plus." October 24 (4:1), 26 (2:1), 28 (2:1); November 3 (2:1), 9 (2:1), and 20 (2:1), 1868.

"Sights in Japan." *NYT*, September 14, 1869.

"Chinese Embassy." *NYT*, December 1, 1869.

"The Peking College." *NYT*, December 2, 1869.

"French-Chinese Troubles." *NYT*, October 28, 1870. Signed "Q."

"The Franco-Chinese Affair." *NYT*, November 29, 1870. Signed "Q."

"Mr. Seward in China." *NYT*, January 26, 1071. Signed "Q."

"An Imperial Wedding." *NYT*, December 26, 1872.

"Story of the Siege and Fall of Peking." *NYT*, October 5, 1900.

"Dr. Martin Defends the Demands on China." *NYT*, November 19, 1900.

"Competitive Exams in China." *North American Review*, CXV (1870), 111-62.

"The Hanlin Yüan." *North American Review*, CXIX (July, 1874), 1-32.

"Letters to the Honorable Caleb Cushing on the Taiping Rebellion." *North China Herald and Supreme Court and Consular Gazette*, May 3, 1856, 158-59, and June 7, 1856, 179-80.

"Dominion of the Taiping Dynasty in Nganhui and Keangse." *NCH*, September 12, 1856.

"The Fate of the Manchus Foreshadowed in the Expulsion of the Mongols from China in the Revolution of 1388." *NCH*, December 27, 1856.

"Letter to the Editor on the Anti-Christian Movement." *NCH*, February 21, 1857.

"A Narrative of the Manchu Conquest Abridged from the Latin of Martini." *NCH*, March 10, 1857.

"Letter to Editor on Events in Ningpo." *NCH*, March 21, 1857.

"Imperialist Testimony to the Christianity of the Insurgents." *NCH*, April 14, 1857.

"The Recognition of the Nanking Government." *NCH*, May 13, 1857.

"The Recognition of the Nanking Government." *NCH*, June 20, 1857.

"Tribute to Quarterman." *NCH*, October 31, 1857.

"The American Treaty Violated." *NCH*, February 11, 1860.

"Japanese Christians in Peking." *The Presbyterian* (May 25, 1910), 14.

"Une Université En Chine — Le Présent et L'Avenir De L'Enseignment Supérieur International A Peking." *Revue de Droit Internationale et de Législation Comparée*, V (January, 1873), 8-10.

"Les Vestiges D'un Droit Internationale Dans L'Ancienne Chine." *Revue de Droit Internationale et de Législation Comparée*, XIV (July, 1882), 227-42.

"The Awakening of China." *The World's Work* (January, 1906), 7124-28.

"China Transformed." *The World's Work* (August, 1906), 7844-48.

"Revolutionary Changes in China." *The World's Work* (October, 1906), 8115-25.

"Great Changes Impending in China — Events Which Show the Increasing Strength of the Imperial Government and the Advance of Western Progress." *The World's Work* (March, 1908), 9986-90.

3. Other miscellaneous English works by W. A. P. Martin.

"The Agency of Missionaries in the Diffusion of Secular Knowledge in China." Written originally for Dennis, James. *The Secular Benefits of Christian Missions* and found in *The Awakening of China*.

"How May Christian Schools Bring Their Influence to Bear Most

Effectively on the Educational System of the Chinese Government?" *Sixth Triennial Meeting of the Educational Association of China,* May, 1909, 43-46.

"Li Hung Chang. The Far East." In Lord, John. *Beacon Lights of History.* XIV. New York: Fords, Howard and Hulbert, 1915.

"Report on the System of Public Instruction in China." Circulars of Information of the Bureau of Education. No. 1. Washington, D.C.: Government Printing Office, 1877.

"Terms Used in Diplomatic and Official Intercourse." In Doolittle, Justus. *Vocabulary and Handbook of the Chinese Language.* 2 Volumes. Volume II, 194-201. Foochow: Rozario, Marcal and Company, 1872.

"Terms Used in Natural Philosophy." *Vocabulary and Handbook,* II, 308-15.

"The Tung Wen College." Appendix F in Morse, H. B. *The International Relationships of the Chinese Empire.* Three Volumes. III, 471-78. New York: Longmans, Green and Company, 1918.

"The Peiho and Peking or Two American Embassies to China Together With the Wrongs of Man — A Tale of the Opium War." This is an unpublished book held at the Presbyterian Historical Society in Philadelphia. It is in the handwriting of Jane Martin with frequent corrections by W. A. P. M. Unfortunately, the last section dealing with the Opium War is missing. Some of this material has been included in its exact wording in *A Cycle of Cathay.* This is particularly true of the journal entries of Chapters 10-12. The information on Chinese education, religion, literature, philosophy, etc. was reworked and expanded for later inclusion in the *Hanlin Papers* and *The Lore of Cathay.* Some portions of this manuscript were never published. Apparently written in 1860 or 1861, but not published because of the Civil War, this work is valuable in determining some of Martin's views before they were modified by later experience.

"Narrative of the State of Religion Within the Bounds of the Peking Presbytery, North China." December, 1887.

"Historical Sketch of the Presbytery of Peking." 1888.

4. Chinese works — books and articles — written by W. A. P. Martin that are presently available in American or foreign libraries and which have been used in the research for this book.

Chung-hsi wen-chien lu. Peking, 1872-75. Burdon, Edkins, and later Dudgeon served with Martin as editors of this magazine. Much of the material of this reform magazine has been preserved in *Chung-hsi wen-chien lu hsüan-pien,* a four-volume block-print edition published in 1877 with a foreword by Kuo Sung-t'ao.

T'ien-tao su-yüan (Evidences of Christianity). The volume used for this book was a 1966 reprinting by the Wen Ch'üan Publishing Company in Taipei, Taiwan, of the revised edition of 1912.

T'ien-tao he-chiao (Christianity and Other Creeds). Assisted by Chao, Shou-ling. Tungchow: North China Tract Society, 1909.

Ko-wu ju-men (Natural Philosophy). Seven Volumes. Peking: T'ung Wen Press, 1868.

Jen-tzu hsin-fa (Analytical Reader). Appended is *Ch'ang-tzu shuang-ch'ien.* (Vocabulary of 2000 Frequent Characters). Shanghai: Presbyterian Mission Press, 1863.

Wan-kuo kung-fa (Elements of International Law). Translated by Martin. Peking: Ch'ung-shih kuan, 1864.

"New Writing Machine." In Fryer, John, ed., *Ko-chih hui-pien* (The Chinese Scientific and Industrial Magazine), II (March, 1877), 14-15.

"The Suez Canal" and "San Francisco" in Wang, Hsi-ch'i, ed., *Hsiao-fang-hu-chai yü-ti ts'ung ch'ao* (A Compendium of Geographical Works in Chinese). LXIII. No date or pagination.

Numerous articles in the *Chiao-hui hsin-pao* (Church News). Edited by Allen, Young J.

Volume II, 796-98. "An Obedient Son Finds His Father."

Volume II, 816-18. "The Prodigal Returns."

Volume II, 919-20. "Mercy and Kindness Covers All."

Volume II, 946-47. "Grace and Righteousness Fulfilled."

Volume III, 1217-19. "A T'ung Wen Kuan Examination."

Volume III, 1223. "Be Careful in the Use of Time."

Volume III, 1260-61. "A Clear Mirror Reveals All."

Volume IV, 1559-60. "Reminiscing About Past Mistakes."

Volume V, 2504-7. "Latest News About Science."

Volume V, 2533-35. "Latest News About Science."

"Argument Against Errors of Astrology" in Allen, Young J., ed., *Wan-kuo kung-pao* (Globe Magazine), VII, 687-90.

Fifteen miscellaneous articles on various aspects of international law in a Ching-shih wen collection issued in 1888. These are indexed in a three-volume work known as the *Ching-shih wen pien-tsung mu-lu.* The record of Martin's contributions may be found in Volume I, 135.

"Tribute to Li Shan-lan." *Ko-chih hui-pien,* II (May, 1877), 1.

"Tribute to Li Jen-shu." *Ko-chih hui-pien,* II (July, 1877), 1.

McCollough, John. "Notes from a Class by Andrew Wylie at Indiana University on Sacred History." 1851.

Michie, Alexander. *Missionaries in China.* London: Edward Stanford, 1891.

_____. *China and Christianity.* Boston: Knight and Millet, 1900.

Miller, Stuart Creighton. *The Unwelcome Immigrant.* Berkeley: University of California Press, 1969.

Minutes of the Board of Foreign Missions of the Presbyterian Church in the U.S.A.

Minutes of the Executive Committee of the Board of Foreign Missions of the Presbyterian Church in the U.S.A.

Minutes of the New Albany Presbytery, 1824-1870. This was the Salem Presbytery, Old School, 1824-49, and New Albany Presbytery, 1849-1870.

Minutes of the Ningpo and Peking Presbyteries to be found with incoming letters sent from Ningpo and Peking to the Corresponding Secretary of the Foreign Mission Board of the Presbyterian Church in the U.S.A.

Minutes of the North China Field of the Foreign Mission Board of the Presbyterian Church in the U.S.A.

Minutes of the Session of the Presbyterian Church, Livonia, Indiana, 1820-1850.

Miscellaneous China Correspondence, 1858-68, Volume 39, China. U.S. Government Archives.

The Missionary Herald of the American Board of Commissioners for Foreign Missions.

The Missionary Magazine of the American Baptist Missionary Union for the 1850-60 period at Ningpo.

The Missionary Review of the World.

Needham, Joseph. *Science and Civilization in China.* Four Volumes. London: Cambridge University Press, 1954-71.

Nevius, John L. *San-Poh, or North of the Hills.* Philadelphia: Presbyterian Board of Publications, 1869.

New York Times. Articles and news items about W. A. P. Martin, February 19, 1869; May 16, 1896; and December 24, 1916.

New York Tribune, September 23, 1898; February 27, 1902; March 28, 1902; April 13, 1902.

The North China Herald, December 23, 1916, and many other news items from 1860-1916.

Peking Presbyterian Mission. Peking, 1917.

Personal Diaries of William B. Reed. There are two volumes and a Type-written Sketch of the Voyage to China by his son. Manuscript Division. Library of Congress, Washington, D. C.

Plan of a Theological Seminary for the Presbyterian Church in the Western States Located at New Albany, Indiana. As Revised, Amended, and Adopted October 1840. Louisville: Prentice and Weissings, 1847.

Porter, Albert. "An American Mandarin." *Outlook,* August 24, 1907, 884-888.

_____. "A Prophet of Progress." *The World's Work*, XII (May, 1906). 7577-78.

The Presbyterian Banner.

The Presbyterian Monthly.

Price, Allen T. "American Missionaries and American Diplomacy in China, 1830-1900." Unpublished Ph. D. dissertation, Harvard University, 1932.

Rankin, Henry W. "Notes on W. A. P. Martin." These brief notes also include letters from Helen Nevius and Chauncey Goodrich to Rankin about Martin.

Records: China Centenary Missionary Conference. Shanghai: Centenary Conference Committee, 1907.

Records of General Conference of Protestant Missionaries of China. Shanghai, May 10-24, 1877. Shanghai: American Presbyterian Press, 1878.

Records of the General Conference of Protestant Missionaries in China, 1890. Shanghai: American Presbyterian Press, 1891.

Records of the Synod of Indiana. Volume I (North and South), 1826-1850.

Records of the Triennial Meetings of the Educational Association of China. Shanghai: American Presbyterian Press, 1893, 1896, 1900, 1902, 1905, and 1909.

Reid, Gilbert. *A Prospectus of the International Institute of China.* New York: Press of Eaton and Mains, n.d.

_____. *The International Institute of China,* n.d.

_____. *The International Institute.* Seventh Report of the Mission Among the Higher Classes in China. New York: Revell, 1897.

_____. "The Duty of Christian Missions to the Upper Classes of China." Shanghai: American Presbyterian Press, 1888.

Report of the Central China Religious Tract Society. Hankow, China, 1893.

Reports of the Society for the Diffusion of Useful Knowledge (Canton). *The Chinese Repository,* III (December, 1834), 378-80; IV (December, 1835), 354-61, and VI (March, 1837), 507-13.

Revue de Droit Internationale et de Législation Comparée, XIV (1882), 583.

"The Rev. W. A. P. Martin, D.D." *Outlook,* August 4, 1900, 783.

Richard, Timothy. *Forty-five Years in China: Reminiscences.* London: T. Fisher Unwin Ltd., 1916.

Robbins, Roy. "Crusade in the Wilderness, 1750-1830." *Indiana Magazine of History,* XLVI (June, 1950), 121-32.

Rudolph, L. C. *Hoosier Zion.* New Haven: Yale University Press, 1963.

Sanders, Robert S. *Presbyterianism in Paris and Bourbon County, Kentucky 1786-1961.* Louisville: Dunne Press, 1961.

Senate Executive Documents. 36th Congress, 1st Session (1859-60), X, No. 30.

Senate Executive Documents. 52nd Congress, 1st Session (1891-5), VI, No. 98.

Sherrill, Lewis Joseph. *Presbyterian Parochial Schools.* New York: Arno Press, 1969.

Smith, Arthur. "The Life and Work of the Late Dr. W. A. P. Martin." *The Chinese Recorder,* XLVIII (February, 1917), 116-23.

_____. "The Nestor of Protestant Missions in China." *The Chinese Recorder,* XLI (April, 1910), 288-91.

Smith, Elwyn Allen. *The Presbyterian Ministry in American Culture. A Study in Changing Concepts, 1700-1900.* Philadelphia: The Westminster Press, 1962.

Speer, Robert E. *Presbyterian Foreign Missions. An Account of the Foreign Missions of the Presbyterian Church in the U.S.A.* Philadelphia: Presbyterian Board of Publications, 1901.

_____. *Report on the China Missions of the Presbyterian Board of Foreign Missions.* New York: The Board of Foreign Missions of the Presbyterian Church in the U.S.A., 1897.

Spelman, Douglas G. "Christianity in Chinese: The Protestant Term Question." *Papers on China,* XXIIA, Cambridge, Mass., 1969, 25-52.

The Spirit of Missions of the Foreign Mission Board of the Protestant Episcopal Church in America.

Stewart, Dugald. *Outlines of Moral Philosophy.* Edinburgh, 1793.

Stuart, George H. Autographs Collected, 1850-1862.

Sweet, William Warren. *Religion on the American Frontier, 1783-1840. A Collection of Source Materials.* Four Volumes. *The Presbyterians.* Volume II. Chicago: University of Chicago Press, 1936.

Ta-ch'ing li-ch'ao shih-lu (Records of the Ch'ing Dynasty).

Teng, S. Y. *The Taiping Rebellion and the Western Powers.* Oxford: Clarendon Press, 1971.

Teng, S. Y. and Fairbank, John, eds., *China's Response to the West: A Documentary Survey, 1839-1923*. New York: Athenaeum, 1966.

T'oung Pao, XVII (1916), 624-25.

Triennial Calendar of the Tungwen College. Fourth Issue. Peking: Published by Authority, 1888.

Trinterud, Leonard J. *The Forming of an American Tradition. A Re-Examination of Colonial Presbyterianism*. Philadelphia: The Westminster Press, 1949.

Varg, Paul. *Missionaries, Chinese and Diplomats*. Princeton: Princeton University Press, 1958.

Von Gumpach, Johannes. *The Burlingame Mission*. Shanghai, 1872.

Wang, Shu-huai. *Wai-jen yü wu-hsü pien-fa* (Foreigners and the Reform of 1898). Taipei: Commercial Press, 1965.

Williams, Frederick Wells. *The Life and Letters of Samuel Wells Williams*. New York: G. P. Putnam's Sons, 1889.

_____. *Anson Burlingame and the First China Mission to Foreign Powers*. New York: Charles Scribner's Sons, 1912.

Williams, Samuel Wells. "The Chinese and the Treaties." *The Foreign Missionary*, XVIII (July, 1859), 51-52.

Wright, Stanley. *Hart and the Chinese Customs*. Belfast: William Mullan and Son, 1950.

Wylie, Alexander. *Memorials of Protestant Missionaries to the Chinese*. Shanghai: American Presbyterian Mission Press, 1867.

Wylie, Andrew. *Sectarianism is Heresy*. Bloomington, Indiana: A. E. Drapier, 1841.

Yang, C. K. *Religion in Chinese Society*. Berkeley: University of California Press, 1967.

Index